TRIAL BY FIRE

TRIAL BY FIRE

The Struggle to Get the Bible into English

Harold Rawlings, Ph. D.

The Rawlings Foundation
Wellington, Florida 33414

Published by The Rawlings Foundation
A division of The Rawlings Company
Wellington, Florida 33414

Copyright 2004 by The Rawlings Foundation

First Published 2004
Revised edition 2014

For information about purchasing books from the Rawlings Foundation, please contact: The Rawlings Foundation, P. O. Box 49, LaGrange, KY 40031-0049.

E-mail address: bac@rawlingscompany.com.

Phone number: 502-814-2103. Toll free number: 1-866-365-1051.

Cover design: Tischbein Design

ISBN 978-0-9755006-0-6

Printed in the United States of America

CONTENTS

DEDICATION

To George and Beverly Rawlings

LIST OF ILLUSTRATIONS

FOREWORD

Harold Rawlings has expertly distilled the gripping history of the struggle to "English" the Bible. He provides colorful descriptions of the distinctive contributions of various translators, particularly John Wycliffe in the 14th century and William Tyndale in the 16th century. Tyndale, he points out, is perhaps the most widely quoted writer in the English language ("eat, drink, and be merry," is Tyndale's phrase; so is "the spirit is willing but the flesh is weak").

Rawlings chronicles the ongoing struggles the early translators faced in their attempt to provide a Bible in the vernacular of English-speaking people. Rendering the Scriptures into English in the time of Wycliffe and Tyndale was an act fraught with peril. Simply possessing a Wycliffe Bible was enough to get a layperson tried for heresy. William Tyndale, whose renderings of the New Testament and portions of the Old Testament greatly influenced the King James translators, saw his work confiscated and burned by English ecclesiastical authorities; he was burned at the stake in 1536. Other "Bible men" met the same fate.

Anyone who reads TRIAL BY FIRE will acquire a renewed appreciation of the Bible, the most important Book in the world. Packed with fascinating anecdotes and facts, the book will appeal to laypeople as well as scholars. Having known Harold Rawlings for more than 50 years, beginning when we were college classmates, I am honored to unreservedly endorse and recommend this book to all who love God's Word.

—Jerry Falwell

ACKNOWLEDGMENTS

To paraphrase the familiar words of John Donne, "No book is an island, entire of itself." Every book has co-authors, whether acknowledged or not. A book owes its existence to many people, some living, some long since dead. This book is no exception. Many whom I have never met deserve recognition, but they are legion, far too many to list. Their lucid ideas have stimulated my imagination and fueled a desire to learn more about the most important Book in the world and to share that knowledge with others. A few of their names are listed in the Bibliography. I owe a huge debt of gratitude to Pastor Tom Wells, Professor Jeffrey Hillard, and my brother George Rawlings, all of whom spent hours poring over the manuscript. Their helpful suggestions provided new avenues of inquiry, which, I believe, have rendered the book more readable and more factual. Through the generosity of my brother George and the Rawlings Foundation which he initiated, we have been able to amass a superb collection of ancient Bibles and manuscripts that has been invaluable in providing research material for the book. My father, Dr. John Rawlings, is deserving of thanks, for he was the first to suggest that I write the book. He kept my feet to the fire by both his encouragement and his sound advice.

INTRODUCTION

When Elizabeth Alexandra Mary Windsor was crowned the new Queen of England on June 2, 1953, a time-honored tradition occurred that underscored the importance of the Bible in the long history of England. In a brief but poignant moment, the Moderator of the General Assembly of the Church of Scotland approached the Queen with a Bible in his hands. As the Moderator presented the Bible to the Queen, seated in her chair, the Archbishop of Canterbury of the Church of England solemnly voiced these words:

> Our gracious Queen: to keep your Majesty ever mindful of the Law and Gospel as the Rule for the whole life and government of Christian Princes, we present you with this Book, the most valuable thing that this world affords.

The Moderator then added:

> Here is wisdom; this is the royal law; these are the lively Oracles of God.[1]

Millions throughout the world from every level of intelligence and social status echo the assessment of the Archbishop and Moderator. They are convinced that "the most valuable thing that this world affords" is the Bible, and their hope of eternal life hinges on its promises. They believe the Bible speaks to them as no other book has spoken, and that what it says comes with an authority derived from God Himself. To them, it is much more than a book among books. It is the Book of Books. God's presence permeates its pages, and in it are revealed all those features of His mysterious being that we are permitted to glimpse. In it God speaks and He acts. We humans can also see ourselves in it, in all our weaknesses,

13

potentialities, and grandeur. Our highest aspirations are given voice in this Book. Even more, it embodies all the doctrine of revealed truth. Here one discovers satisfactory answers to the three greatest questions of life: Where did I come from? Why am I here? Where am I going after death? Human minds and hearts find in the Bible rich and never-failing nourishment. It is vain to claim to understand the principles of law, sociology, economics, history, and politics, not to mention the true purpose of life, if one is unaware of the message contained in this Book.

What would art and literature be without this Book? But for the Bible, Michelangelo, da Vinci, Rembrandt, and Rubens would not be the artists we admire. It is the same with literature. The Bible has done more than provide innumerable subjects for dramatists. From its pages flow streams of living water that feed the roots of masterpieces. But for the Bible, would there ever have been a Dante, a Chaucer, an Erasmus, a Milton, a Pascal, a Bunyan, or a Dostoyevsky?

Western civilization is said to rest on three foundations: Greek intellectual curiosity, Roman order, and the Bible.[2] Of these three foundations, the third is the most vital because it endows the whole substructure with its true meaning. Without the Bible the Western world would not be what it is today. President Andrew Jackson, upon hearing a man denigrating the Bible, rebuked him with these well-chosen words: "The Bible is the rock upon which our Republic rests."[3]

But to link this Book with the existence and development of western civilization alone is to misrepresent its meaning and limit its range. As efforts are made by the Wycliffe Translators, various Bible Societies, and other organizations to translate its message into the languages of people-groups throughout the world, it becomes ever more apparent that the Bible is perfectly suited to all cultures and nationalities. If the Western world must to a large extent thank the Bible for the role it has played in elevating our civilization, so must the other nations and peoples who have experienced the stimulus of its transforming message.

14

THE BOOK

The very name we give the Bible sums up and implies all its distinctive qualities. The Greek word which gives us the name Bible—*biblos* or *biblion* (book)—goes back to those distant days in the second millennium before Christ when the Phoenicians of Byblos had made their port the greatest papyrus market of the time and imposed the name of their town on the product they sold. Jerome in the fourth century popularized the expression "the Holy Books" or simply *"the Book."*[4] Thereafter the collection of 66 books came to be known by a singular word, *Bible,* which implies its underlying unity, its supernatural harmony. The synonym that has often been used to describe it, *Scripture,* expresses in a different word the same idea, namely that all the different books with their diversified elements combine to make up a unified whole.

THE MOST WIDELY READ BOOK IN THE WORLD

The Bible is by far the most widely read book in the world. It is only possible to guess at the total number of copies in circulation. The early Christians diligently endeavored to spread the Scriptures, first by word of mouth, then with letters and historical accounts written by the apostles themselves. Joining the New Testament writings with the Old, the complete Bible was then meticulously reproduced by competent scribes in monasteries and institutions to meet the pressing need for more copies. When Gutenberg introduced the moveable type process in the fifteenth century, he turned to Scripture for the first text to which he applied the new technology.

Today the Bible can be read in almost every major language in the world. According to the American Bible Society, at the beginning of the nineteenth century Scriptures were available in just 68 languages. By the middle of 2011, the Bible—in full or partial form—was available in 2,727 languages. The complete Bible has now been published in 457 languages worldwide, compared with 392 at the end of 2002. In addition, portions of the Bible have been made available in some 883 languages.[5] Although this figure represents less than half of the languages and dialects presently in use in the world, it nonetheless includes the primary vehicles of communication of well over 90% of the world's population.[6] This yearning for the Bible never diminishes, and in an age of rampant materialism this success is remarkable. This confirms the power and relevance of the Word—a Word that will never pass away (Isaiah 40:8; Mark 13:31).

THE MOST HATED BOOK

While the Bible can lay claim to being the most widely read book in the world, it also has the unwarranted distinction of being the most hated book in the world. Under fire from enemy attacks almost since the day it was first written down, it has ever since elicited the ire of detractors. The Bible, however, will triumph over those who are intent on discrediting it. The Bible is indeed an anvil that has worn out many a critic's hammer, and no one need fear its final vindication. It has a marvelous capacity to come out of the fires of attack unscathed and to turn the counsel of its foes into confusion. The Book upon which modern civilization is erected, which lies at the basis of our legislation, and which softens rude manners and transforms the most wretched condition, is not in danger.

THE PURPOSE OF *TRIAL BY FIRE*

How did the Bible—the most widely read and influential book in history—come to us in our own English tongue? This little-known story is a drama of indomitable courage, of kings and queens, intrigue, fugitives, bounty hunters, spies, trials, accusations of heresy, excommunication, imprisonment, torture, and burning at the stake, and drops of martyrs' blood. It is a story of momentous struggle that warrants retelling in this twenty-first century when the Bible is so readily accessible and its precepts so lightly regarded.

Although knowledge of how we got our English Bible is an important and valuable study, I will hasten to add that it does not deal with the most important function of Scripture. The Word of God accomplishes something no other book can claim. It endows one with the necessary wisdom to obtain eternal life through faith in Jesus Christ (2 Tim. 3:15). No knowledge transcends in importance the truths found between the covers of the Bible. With the instruction and encouragement gleaned from its pages, we are blessed with the gift of hope—a hope that diminishes all the difficulties and misfortunes of this life (Rom. 15:4). Nevertheless, knowledge of how we got our English Bible will give us a renewed estimation of the value of this extraordinary book.

In examining its history, we will concentrate exclusively on the early English Bibles, beginning with Wycliffe's in 1382, and ending with the King James Version in 1611, a span of 229 years. These early English Bibles laid the foundation for all major English versions through the twentieth century. Much of our attention will be occupied with the enormous struggle, the intense opposition these early translators endured to give to the English-speaking world a Bible in their own language. The story of this struggle should have a special interest for all those who care for the contents of this sacred Book. The knowledge that many have endured unspeakable torture to give us a Bible in our own language should give us a greater appreciation for its accessibility and a more earnest desire to conform to its timeless message.

The pattern God set from the beginning was that we have a Bible in the language of ordinary people. Indeed the Hebrew of the Old Testament exhibited those qualities. Most of the New Testament books, if not all, were written in what is called "Koine" Greek. The word "Koine" means "common." It was much like the simple, popular form of Greek spoken in cities throughout the Greek-speaking world. The most revolutionary concept the early English translators affirmed was that the Bible, if translated into the everyday language of the people, could be readily understood. This was a direct contradiction of the prevailing ecclesiastical notion of the time that only priests

17

were able to grasp the intended meaning of Scripture, and only they had the authority to explain it to the people.

The story of the great struggle to get the Bible to us in our own language should have a special interest for all those who care for its contents. No English-speaking believer should be ignorant of the history of the English Bible and how that history is impacting Christians in the twenty-first century.

TIMELINE: FROM THE FIRST CENTURY TO THE PUBLICATION OF THE KING JAMES VERSION IN 1611

A.D. 43   The Roman Army under Emperor Claudius defeats the Celts in Britain. Latin is introduced to the Celts.

c. 150   Christianity is introduced into Britain.

c. 220   Tertullian speaks of places in Britain subject to Christ.

325   British delegates attend the Council of Nicea.

395   The Roman Empire splits. The capital of Western Europe is Rome (Latin). The capital of Eastern Europe is Constantinople (Greek).

400–1100   Old English (Anglo-Saxon) begins to develop as Angles, Saxons, and Jutes from Germany invade Britain. The name, "Angle land," eventually becomes "England."

400–1300   Europe is conquered by two medieval Catholic Churches—West (Roman) and East (Orthodox).

405   Jerome finishes translating the Latin Vulgate from Hebrew and Greek.

476   The Roman Empire collapses causing the Roman military to leave Britain. Celtic missionaries led by Columba spread the Gospel in Britain.

663/664   Christian Celts in Britain accept union with Roman Christianity.

800–1066   Old Norse and Old French are added to the developing English language as Vikings, originally from Scandinavia who had invaded France, invade England.

1054 Known as "The Great Schism," the term describes the final breach between Eastern (Greek) and Western (Latin) churches, which later became known as the Eastern Orthodox Church and the Roman Catholic Church.

1066 William the Conqueror and his Norman French Army defeats England. French becomes the official language.

1100–1500 Middle English develops as many foreign languages influence England.

1231 The Pope begins the Inquisition. Heretics are to be burned at the stake.

1300–1650 The Renaissance: Northern Christian Humanists stress Bible Study and the ability of laypeople to read and understand.

c.1330 John Wycliffe is born in England.

1337 Hundred Years' War begins between France and England.

1348 The Black Death (Bubonic Plague) kills a third of the population of Europe.

1376 Wycliffe's *Civil Dominion* states, "England belongs to no pope; Christ is Lord."

1377 Wycliffe is banished to his parish in Lutterworth where he begins to translate the Latin Bible into English.

1378 Wycliffe sends Lollards throughout England to preach the Gospel and distribute handwritten English Bible verses and tracts. He writes the tract, "On the Truth of Holy Scripture, the Basis of all Truth."

1382 Wycliffe and helpers finish translating the Bible from the Latin Vulgate into English.

1384 Wycliffe dies peacefully as his writings spread far beyond the borders of England. John Huss and Martin Luther are influenced by Wycliffe's writings.

1400–1415 John Huss preaches in Prague.

1401 Henry IV and Parliament pass a law mandating that heretics are to be burned.

1408 Laws are passed at Oxford condemning translating or reading an English Bible.

1415 The Council of Constance posthumously condemns Wycliffe as a heretic and demands that his remains be exhumed and burned. John Huss is also condemned at the same council and burned at the stake.

1422 Henry V defeats France. English is now the language of business and government.

1428 Wycliffe's body is exhumed and burned at Lutterworth.

1453 Muslim Turks defeat Constantinople marking the end of the Byzantine Empire. Scholars flee west with Greek Bible manuscripts.

1454 Gutenberg prints the Latin Vulgate in Germany; first major book printed by movable type.

1466 Erasmus is born in Holland.

1476 William Caxton introduces the printing press into England.

1483 Martin Luther is born in Germany.

1485 The War of Roses ends. Henry VII is crowned the first Tudor King of England. Tudors reign through 1603 (118 years).

1492 Christopher Columbus sails to the New World.

c.1494   William Tyndale is born in Gloucestershire, England.

1500   Modern English develops by incorporating words from all over the world. Erasmus visits England, and decides to edit the Greek and Latin New Testaments.

c.1506   Tyndale begins studying at Oxford University.

1509   Henry VIII is crowned King of England.

1510–1514   Erasmus teaches at Cambridge University.

c.1512–1515   Tyndale receives his BA and MA degrees from Oxford University.

1516   Erasmus' Greek/Latin New Testament is printed in Basel.

1517   Luther nails his 95 Theses on the church door at Wittenberg, Germany. The Reformation begins.

c.1517   Tyndale moves to Cambridge University.

1519   Seven (one a mother) are burned for teaching English Bible verses to children.

1521   Tyndale becomes chaplain of the Walsh family in Little Sodbury where he witnesses clergy ignorance of the Bible.

1522   Luther's German New Testament is published in Wittenberg, Germany.

1523   England is the only European country without a printed vernacular translation of the Bible. Tyndale moves to London to ask the Bishop's permission to translate. He sees the corruption of the clergy as Luther had seen while visiting Rome.

1524   Tyndale is forced to move from England to Germany to translate the Greek New Testament into English.

1525 Tyndale goes to Cologne, but his attempt to have his New Testament printed there is foiled.

1526 Tyndale's English New Testament is printed in Worms, Germany, smuggled into England, and burned at Oxford and St. Paul's in London.

1530 Tyndale's Pentateuch and Jonah are printed in Antwerp and shipped to England.

1532 Henry VIII (Roman Catholic) and Anne Boleyn (strong Protestant) marry.

1533 Henry VIII is excommunicated by Pope Clement on July 11. Queen Anne Boleyn gives birth to future Queen Elizabeth I on September 7.

1534 Luther's German Bible is printed in Germany. Tyndale's revised edition of the New Testament is printed in Antwerp. Henry VIII declares himself head of the Church of England. Anne Boleyn's initials and the date, 1534, are stamped on a Tyndale New Testament now in the British Library.

1535 Coverdale's Bible is printed, the first complete English Bible. Tyndale is arrested and imprisoned in Vilvorde Castle north of Brussels.

1536 In April, Anne Boleyn is unjustly condemned by a civil trial and beheaded. On July 10, Erasmus dies in Basel. In August, Tyndale is condemned to be burned for believing in "justification by faith." On October 6, Tyndale is strangled and burned in Vilvorde by secular authorities.

1537 Henry VIII grants licenses to Coverdale's Second Edition and Matthew's Bible.

1538 Cromwell has Coverdale revise Matthew's Bible with no marginal notes.

1539 Henry VIII authorizes the printing of the Great Bible and commands one to be placed in every parish church. Taverner's Bible is the first complete English Bible to be printed in England.

1540 Thomas Cromwell is beheaded through the influence of ecclesiastical churchmen.

1546 Martin Luther dies on November 10.

1547 Henry VIII dies on January 28. His son, Edward VI, becomes king and supports Protestantism and the printing of English Bibles.

1553 Edward VI dies on July 6. His sister, Roman Catholic Mary Tudor, is the new queen.

1555 John Rogers (Matthew's Bible) is the first of almost 300 Protestant leaders to be condemned by Queen Mary Tudor and burned at the stake at Smithfield. Bishop Hugh Latimer and Nicholas Ridley are burned side by side in Oxford on October 16. Latimer is quoted as having said to Ridley: "Be of good comfort, Master Ridley, and play the man; we shall this day light such a candle, by God's grace, in England, as I trust shall never be put out."

1556 Archbishop Thomas Cranmer is burned at the stake on March 21.

1558 Mary Tudor dies on November 17. Her half-sister, Elizabeth I, becomes queen and supports Protestantism.

1559 Elizabeth I repeals the Inquisition in England. She institutes The Act of Supremacy and The Act of Uniformity.

1560 The Geneva Bible is published in Geneva, Switzerland, by English exiles.

1569 The Bishops' Bible is published in England.

1571 The Bishops' Bible is to be placed in every English Church.

1582 Roman Catholics print their first English New Testament at Rheims, France.

1588 The English defeat the Spanish Armada sent to re-establish Roman Catholicism in England.

1603 The last Tudor, Elizabeth, dies on March 24 after protecting English Protestantism for 45 years. King James VI of Scotland, a Stuart, is declared King James I of England and Scotland.

1604 King James hosts the three-day Hampton Court Conference beginning on January 14, and responds to the Puritan call for a new translation of the English Bible which he helps plan.

1610 The Roman Catholic English Old Testament is finished at Douay, France.

1611 The King James Bible is published.

Chapter One

THE RISE OF ENGLISH

The story of the development of the English Bible cannot be told without some knowledge of how the English language came into existence, as well as the manner in which Christianity first penetrated the British Isles, finally coming to dominate the English character and culture by the thirteenth century.

The rise of English is a remarkable success story. When Julius Caesar landed in Britain over two thousand years ago, English did not exist. "Five hundred years later, a form of English, incomprehensible to us today, was spoken by about as few people as currently speak Cherokee."[1] At the end of the sixteenth century, about the time the King James translators began their work, English was the native speech of between five and seven million Englishmen. Between 1600 and the present, the armies, navies, missionaries, companies, media, entertainers, tourists, and expeditions of English-speaking countries carried their language and culture with them into every corner of the world. Some estimate that English is spoken today by as many as one billion people.[2] Whatever the total, English at the beginning of the twenty-first century is more widely scattered, more widely spoken and written, than any other language has ever been. It has become the *de facto* language of the planet, the first truly global language. Studied by schools around the world, it is the universal language of pilots; the acknowledged language of global finance, trade, science and technology.

OLD ENGLISH

The English language has passed through three stages: Old English, Middle English, and Modern English. A small island,

England is only about 800 miles long, and no place in the island is more than 100 miles from the sea. Foreign invaders repeatedly swept in and took over different parts of the country, bringing their language and culture with them. Old English began with the Germanic tribes (mainly the Angles, Saxons, and Jutes) who invaded England from the early fifth century onwards. At the time, Britain was a Celtic-speaking land already colonized by Latin-speaking Romans. These Germanic, sea going tribes of northern Germany and southern Denmark eventually achieved a conquest of the land in the middle of the fifth century and drove back the Celtic inhabitants to the western borders of the island where they settled in what is now Wales.[3]

Britain had already been subdued by Caesar's Roman legions in the first century, but the collapse of the Roman Empire in A.D. 476 and the gradual withdrawal of the Roman military presence from Britain made the success of the Germanic tribes possible. These victorious invasions had the effect of developing Old English as a separate language. As is common with conquerors, the Angles, Saxons, and Jutes brought their language and culture to their new home. The Jutes settled in Kent, in the southeast of England; the Saxons in the south and southwest; and the Angles in the middle of Britain, from the Scottish border to the river Thames. These three groups spoke three dialects of Old English. The most important of these groups, the Angles, spoke Mercian or the Midland dialect, which was the language spoken in London and in the university towns of Cambridge and Oxford. In due course the Midland dialect would prevail over the other two and become the favored language of England, forming the foundation of Modern English.

Four centuries after the Germanic invasions, the devastating expeditions of the Danes and Norwegians (collectively, these people are referred to as Vikings) terrorized and destabilized the country. For a time, the Vikings seemed unstoppable. It appeared as if England might be wiped out altogether, effecting the possible eclipse of the English language. The turning point came in the year 878, with a young military commander by the name of Alfred (849–899), King of Wessex, later called "The Great." He is credited with preserving the language by his military exploits against the invading Danes. With a fresh number of recruits, Alfred surprised and overwhelmed the Danes at the Battle of Ethandune, causing their withdrawal to the north.[4] Nevertheless the Danes left their imprint on the English language as well. They spoke Old Norse (ancestor of today's Scandinavian languages). To the Danes we owe such staples as *both, same, again, get, give, are, skirt, sky, skin, bank, knife, window, happy,* and *crawled.*[5]

As Roman Christianity began to spread, gradually becoming the dominant religious force in the country, Latin, the official language of the Church, spread along with it, thus contributing to the developing English vocabulary. Words of Latin origin such as *client, legal, scene, intellect, recipe, pulpit, exclude, necessary, tolerance,* and *interest,*[6] plus numerous ecclesiastical terms entered and embellished the language.

MIDDLE ENGLISH

The invasion and conquest of England in 1066 by William the Conqueror and his Norman French army brought about a new phase in the development of the English language. Originally of Viking ancestry (that is why these French were called Normans—that is Norsemen), the Normans by the middle of the eleventh century had become "Frenchified" in language and culture (their language is designated as Norman French—a dialect of Old French).[7] The effects of the Norman Conquest were profound on the culture and language of England. So immense were the changes that we give a special name to this period of English language development: we call the language from about 1100 to about 1500, Middle English.

Norman French became the language of law and government for the next four centuries. Only French and Latin (the language of the Church) were taught in the schools, not English. This led to the disappearance of the standard Old English language.

English largely became a language of peasants and laborers, indeed a "gutter language" as the aristocracy derisively labeled it. This elitist attitude of the religious literati became the rationale for the Church's opposition to Wycliffe's translation of the Bible into English in the fourteenth century, insisting English was an unworthy language for the Holy Bible.

William the Conqueror and his successors ruled not only England but also Normandy, across the English Channel, until 1204. When France won back Normandy, the Anglo-Normans, no longer politically attached to the continent, began to regard England as their permanent homeland. They ceased to feel like Frenchmen, and gradually adopted English as their ordinary form of speech, rather than Norman French.[8] The Normans introduced no less than seventy-five hundred common terms such as *air, debt, face, joy, people, river, sign, blue, clear, easy, large, mean, nice, poor, carry, change, cry, move, push, save, trip, wait, chair, lamp, pain, stomach, fool, music, park, beef, stew, toast, spy, faith, bar, jail, tax,* and *fry.*[9] Not only did French words come into the English vocabulary in large numbers; English speech and literary style began to be more receptive to borrowings from other languages. Hence, Middle English is a hybrid of German, Latin, Scandinavian (Old Norse), and Norman French. Of all the words in the *Oxford English Dictionary*, no less than ninety-nine percent were taken from other languages; however, the few that trace back to Old English are sixty-two percent of the words most often used: *and, but, father, love, fight, to, will, should, not,* and *from.*[10] These words are central to speaking English. The numerous invasions and intermingling of cultures and languages served only to ripen and enrich the tongue of the English.

In the latter part of the Middle English period (in the years following 1350) there was a movement towards a standardized literary language. Roughly speaking, this movement began with the prose of John Wycliffe (especially his sermons, tracts, and Bible), and the poetry of William Langland *(The Vision of William Concerning Piers the Plowman)* and Geoffrey Chaucer

(Canterbury Tales). Writing in the Mercian or Midland dialect (sometimes called London English), Wycliffe, Langland and Chaucer established that dialect as the dominant language of the country. After a lapse of almost 400 years, England again had a standard language. The mingling of the dialects of the conquerors produced Anglo-Saxon, virtually a new language. It was from the Angles that the name of the country was derived: "Angle-land" eventually became "Eng-land."

The exploits of Henry V, who reigned from 1413 to 1422, also marked a turning point in securing new respectability for the English language. Henry became the first English king since 1066 to use English in his official documents. In the summer of 1415, Henry crossed the Channel to fight the French. In the first letter he dictated on French soil, he chose, symbolically, not to write in the language of his enemies. This national statement indicates a decisive turning point with reference to the use of English. "Henry's predecessor, Edward III, could only swear in English; now it was the official language of English kings."[11] Henry V defeated the French at Agincourt, causing a new nationalistic fervor among Englishmen. In 1422, a ruling was made that henceforth all business and governmental affairs would be conducted in English, not French. Parliament was opened in English for the first time in almost 400 years. No longer was English dismissed as the language of the lower classes. It was now the language of choice in a nation with an increasing sense of national identity and shared purpose.

MODERN ENGLISH

With the English prose works of Sir Thomas More and William Tyndale in the first third of the sixteenth century, early Modern English may be considered to have established itself.[12] The sixteenth century translations of the Bible that followed Tyndale's (and primarily based on his), plus the writings of Shakespeare and other great Elizabethans continued the process of normalizing English. The wide circulation of these writings by means of the printing press helped to stabilize the language and to slow its rate of change in respect to spelling and grammar. Unlike Latin, a fixed language, English is a living language, and as long as it is living, changes will occur. Some words will be dropped, new ones will be made or borrowed, and new meanings will be given to old words. In this modern era, the global economy, the increasing importance of the Internet, and the development of science and technology have brought about the introduction of thousands of new words.

Today, English is not only the most important and recognized language in the world, it is also the most rapidly developing language. The making of English dictionaries presents a vivid picture of the growth of the language in the last 300 years. Samuel Johnson's dictionary of 1755 contained about 15,000 words. The latest unabridged dictionaries record more than 400,000. Once a decade, Merriam-Webster updates its best-selling dictionary, the *Merriam-Webster Collegiate Dictionary.* The 11th edition, unveiled in bookstores on July 1, 2003, includes 10,000 new words and more than 100,000 new meanings and revisions, reflecting the explosion of the new vocabulary.[13]

One Bible sentence, perhaps the most familiar to all English-speaking people, illustrates how much the English language changes over time. The wording of the first sentence of the Lord's Prayer, in the Anglo-Saxon Version (c.1000) reads: "Faeder ure thu the eart on heofonum, si thin nama gehalgod." This is so unfamiliar as not to be readily intelligible except to a student of Anglo-Saxon. Going forward almost four centuries, we read in Wycliffe (second edition, 1389) the same words, but his spelling points to considerable changes of pronunciation having taken place: "Oure fadir that art in hevenes, halwid be thi name." Moving forward about 137 years (1526), Tyndale "modernizes" the translation of the same verse: "Oure father which arte in heven, halowed be thy name." The King James Version (1611), except for spelling, replicates Tyndale word for word: "Our father which art in heauen, hallowed be thy name."

CHRISTIANITY INTRODUCED INTO ENGLAND

It is generally believed that Christianity was introduced into Britain before the end of the second century.[14] Tertullian in about A.D. 220 speaks of places in Britain not reached by the Romans, but yet subject to Christ.[15] Indeed, Eusebius declares that some of the apostles preached in Britain. One widespread tradition claims that Joseph of Arimathea brought the Gospel to Britain in A.D. 35, or about the twenty-first year of Tiberius, and died in England.[16] Among delegates who attended the Council of Nicea (A.D. 325) were several from Britain.[17]

After the Roman Empire collapsed in 476, causing the withdrawal of the Roman military from Britain, the Gospel was spread through the efforts of Celtic missionaries sent out from the theological school founded by Columba on the little island of Iona near the coast of Scotland. Adam Bede (c.673–735), sometimes called "the father of English history," in his *Historia Ecclesiastica Gentis Anglorum* ("Church History of the English People") pictures these Celtic missionaries as:

> going forth far and wide over the heaths and among the hills to preach the Gospel, to visit the sick, to baptize. Neither wolves nor weather hindered them. Sometimes they rode, more often they went on foot; and as they drew near some thorn-fenced village or homestead, the people hurried out to meet them, and bowed joyfully for their blessing. There they would remain for days, for weeks, and sometimes for a month at a time, instructing old and young and gathering them together for prayer at the foot of a rude stone cross which was their first sanctuary. These rugged English folk had learned to love these sincere, unsophisticated teachers whose zeal was sweetened with the exuberance and tenderness of their founder, Columba. They took no thought of houses and land, bestowed on the poor the money they received from the rich, and were content that even their bishop's church should be of hewn oaks thatched with reed.[18]

When the Roman domination of Britain came to an end, the Britons had for the most part been converted to Christianity. But when the Saxons, Angles, and Jutes, as well as the Danes, established themselves in the country, they brought with them their old incipient paganism and an attitude of antipathy towards the original settlers and their Christian faith. The British population and Christianity along with it were driven back into Wales, and the new faith suffered a temporary eclipse.

In the late sixth and early seventh centuries, a Roman mission under Augustine of Canterbury began the conversion of England to Catholicism. Although resisting the Roman brand of Christianity for many years, especially the date Easter should be observed, the Celts finally succumbed at the Synod of Whitby (663/664) and accepted the Roman customs. The way was thereby opened for the organization of the whole Church in England under one head.[19] By the thirteenth century, Roman Catholicism had become firmly entrenched in England. This was clearly seen in King John's recognition of the kingdom as a papal fief in 1213, and the King resigning his crown to the Pope.[20]

Chapter Two

THE BIBLE OF A THOUSAND YEARS

for almost a thousand years the only Bible of the Western Christian world was a Latin Bible. Old Latin translations circulated in the early centuries; then the Vulgate supplanted these older versions and remained the authorized text until the modern era. Translated by Eusebius Hieronymus (c.345–419), better known to us as Jerome, the Latin Vulgate is a significantly relevant translation for our consideration, inasmuch as it forms the basis for the first complete English translation of the Bible (1382). A brilliant linguist and scholar, Jerome lived at a time when Latin was the universal language of the Roman Empire. For centuries Greek had been the universal language; but as the Roman Empire began to expand, the Greek language gradually waned in influence, and by the fourth century Latin became the dominant language. It was deemed necessary by ecclesiastical authorities that Christians in the Empire have a reliable translation in their native tongue, and Jerome emerged as the most qualified scholar to accomplish the task.

Born in Dalmatia in about A.D. 345 to wealthy Christian parents, Jerome received the best education of the day in grammar, rhetoric, law, philosophy, and Latin poetry.[1] He was baptized as a young man, but his interest in Christianity was lukewarm at best. He disliked reading the Scriptures. In his day, these had been translated from Greek into a crude Latin which offended the ear of a scholar like Jerome accustomed to the majestic cadences of the Latin poets. The Old Latin versions of the Bible suffered in comparison to Virgil, Horace, and Cicero.[2] They were also defective in translation accuracy.

One night in Antioch while Jerome lay sick of a fever, he dreamed he was called before the judgment bar of God (up to this time he had given much of his time to the study of classical writers). Christ stood beside his bed and rebuked him, saying: "You care more about being a follower of Cicero than of me." Stung by this reprimand, Jerome cried: "O Lord, you know that when I read secular books I deny you!" When Jerome recovered from his illness, he determined to turn from the Odes of Pindar to the Psalms of David and to devote his life to the Holy Scriptures instead of Greek and Latin classics. A marked spiritual change resulted from this experience.

With his new desire to break completely with the world, Jerome retired to the Syrian desert near Chalcis in 374 to live as a hermit. In this vast and menacing desert, Jerome, now in his early forties, would spend two to three years studying Hebrew and perfecting his Greek, in addition to carrying on a voluminous correspondence.

After brief stints in Antioch and Constantinople, Jerome set off for Rome. Here he was introduced to Pope Damasus, who soon recognized Jerome's extraordinary talent and hired him as his personal secretary. Concerned about the inferior Latin translations of the Bible in circulation, Damasus urged Jerome to undertake the work of revising them.

Jerome's early classical training—his years of travel in the East, his time spent in the desert of Chalcis in self-discipline, and his thorough study of the Hebrew language under a rabbi who had been converted to Christianity—prepared him for this immense undertaking. Jerome agreed to attempt it and Pope Damasus commissioned him in 382. This momentous project would occupy Jerome off and on for the next twenty-two years.[4]

Although Jerome accepted the commission, he did so with a hint of reluctance, knowing it would be a lengthy and costly endeavor. Moreover, he recognized that replacing an old version with a new one was bound to incite the disfavor of many, even if the new one was better. There were those who were inclined to condemn every deviation from the traditional text, however necessary or beneficial the change might be. Furthermore, his decision to translate from the original Hebrew rather than the Septuagint (considered by many to be more inspired than the Hebrew) would incite additional scorn. Jerome did not relish the thought of inviting censure and alienating some of his long-time friends. Nevertheless, "his intensive Biblical studies over the past decade had finally convinced him that, however revolutionary it might seem and whatever hostility it might provoke, the only ultimately satisfying Bible for Christians was one which reproduced the Hebrew [and Greek] original."[5] Believing that "ignorance of Scripture is ignorance of Christ,"[6] Jerome wisely employed his exceptional linguistic ability to make the Scriptures accessible to the people of his time.

Jerome's method of translation has substantially influenced future translators of Scripture. Although in 395 he informed a friend that Scripture ought to be translated word for word, his guiding principle in practice was that a good translation should express the meaning, not necessarily the actual words, of the original. Since the idioms of one language could not be reproduced in another, he felt justified in preserving the characteristic elegance of Latin so long as he did not alter the sense.[7] He did not strive for literary excellence. What mattered most was the content, not the literary form; and because it was intended for "simple, uneducated folk who form the majority in church congregations," it was appropriate that it should be expressed in the simple, even crude language which most of them appreciated.[8]

Completed around A.D. 405, and although on the whole, excellent, Jerome's Latin translation was applauded only by a limited circle of friends. Not unexpectedly, it was greeted with skepticism by fellow scholars and in some cases outright hostility by the rank and file. Respected figures such as Augustine were appalled by his irreverent tampering, as it seemed to them, with the traditional version hallowed by its use in the Church's life and worship and accepted as inspired by the Holy Spirit.[9] People hated to see their favorite verses changed. In fact, according to one story, when the local bishop at Oea (Tripoli, in Libya) read Jerome's version of Jonah to his congregation, a riot just about broke out because disgruntled traditionalists didn't like the way he translated a familiar Old Testament passage. "In the Old Latin version the word for the vine under which Jonah sat had been translated 'gourd' or 'pumpkin.' Jerome translated this 'ivy.' When the bishop read the new word 'ivy,' his congregation rose in a body and indignantly left the church vowing never again to listen to the reading of such heresy!"[10]

In time the suspicion that almost always greets any new version began to die down as people learned to appreciate the superior quality of Jerome's work. Until the seventh century, the Roman church used both the Old Latin version *and* Jerome's. But by a gradual process Jerome's version emerged as the standard text. Jerome called his work *Translatio Nova,* the New Translation, but by the thirteenth century it became known as the "Vulgate." The Latin word "vulgate" means *common* or *accepted.* The Vulgate became the official or "accepted" Bible of the Roman Catholic Church until the modern era. In its long history it has exerted an incalculable influence not only on the piety but the languages, literature, and art of Western Europe. It inspired Dante, Leonardo da Vinci, Raphael, Michelangelo, and the sculptors of Chartres.[11] When printing was invented, the first book to come from the press of Johannes Gutenberg of Mainz, Germany, in 1454/1455 was Jerome's Latin Vulgate.

The influence of Jerome's Latin Bible on future English translations is noteworthy. Some of the words that Jerome either coined or gave new significance, words that eventually found their way into English Bibles are: "salvation," "regeneration," "justification," "sanctification," "propitiation," "reconciliation," "inspiration," and "scripture."

But paradoxically, the Vulgate turned out to be the very instrument that blocked the road to any other translation. It became so highly esteemed that succeeding generations decided to forbid anyone to make any other translation. Many church authorities insisted that Latin was the "sacred tongue," the language spoken in Heaven—"the angelic language," as it was also called. The Latin Vulgate was considered the only perfectly preserved, divinely inspired, inerrant Word of God, superior even to the Hebrew and Greek originals. In fact, the Council of Trent in the sixteenth century decreed that not only was the Latin Vulgate "better than all Latin translations, but [better] than the Greek text itself, in those places where they disagree."[12] At least sixteen popes pronounced the Vulgate "infallible." Pope Sixtus V released an "official" edition of the Vulgate in 1590, attaching severe penalties for anyone daring to alter it. Yet within two years his successor, Clement VIII, did that very thing, revising and correcting obvious errors.[13]

The fall of the Roman Empire in A.D. 476 sent Europe plunging into the darkness of the Middle Ages, a darkness made all the deeper by the absence of a Bible that was understandable to most of the clergy and laymen. Latin eventually became a dead language to almost everyone, the result being that the Bible became a closed book. Few laymen knew enough Latin to understand the Scripture passages the priests would read at Mass. Many of the priests knew just enough Latin to mumble through their liturgies. The Bible remained a venerated book but a closed book, and would remain so for almost a thousand years.

The Gospel of Luke Chapter One from Jerome's Latin Vulgate, c. 1230

Chapter Three

THE MORNING STAR OF THE REFORMATION

No complete translation of the Bible existed in English when John Wycliffe began his ministry in the fourteenth century. Fragments of the Bible had been translated into English by scholars such as Caedmon in the seventh century, the Venerable Bede in the eighth century, and King Alfred in the ninth century, but no complete English Bible appeared until Wycliffe's in 1382.

The first of a noble band of English reformers, Wycliffe began and ended his career as a Roman Catholic priest. However, his study of Scripture convinced him that much of the doctrine and practice of the Catholic Church, the state Church of England, had become corrupt, and he openly ridiculed these deviations from the faith. A devout student of Scripture, Wycliffe embraced the Bible as his absolute standard of appeal, demonstrating in his many pamphlets and sermons an intimate acquaintance with its contents. In one single volume he had 700 quotations from Scripture.[1] His reverence for Scripture earned him the title, "the Evangelical Doctor."[2] The harbinger of a new day in England and the Western world, Wycliffe would later be labeled, "The Morning Star of the Reformation."

Born into an aristocratic family about A.D. 1330 near Richmond, Yorkshire, Wycliffe was granted educational opportunities many of his young contemporaries did not enjoy. His father, Roger de Wycliffe, a Yorkshire squire, was the owner of a small manor. When the time came for Wycliffe to go to college, the way was open to him for two reasons: first, he was the son of a squire;[3] in addition, his neighbors, the Balliols of Barnard Castle, had founded at Oxford a college bearing their name, and had created a number of scholarships for worthy applicants. It was natural that the precocious young Wycliffe should go to Balliol, and "entirely possible that he received one of the scholarships."[4]

At Oxford University Wycliffe spent most of his life, first as a student of arts and philosophy, then as a professor of theology, and finally as the most influential political and religious reformer of his time. He was a man of superior intelligence, fortitude, and charisma. In a university where the art of debate was all-important, he could dispute with a panel of the greatest academics and reduce them to silence. Scores of young men and women enlisted in his cause and gave their lives to be burned at the stake because they believed so strongly that he was right. To appreciate the stature of Wycliffe and to better comprehend what motivated him to accomplish what he did, it is necessary to know something of the background of the times in which he lived. The fourteenth century was a period of great turbulence—politically, socially, and religiously.

THE BLACK DEATH

The most dangerous epoch in history may well have occurred in the fourteenth century when the Black Death killed almost half the population of Europe, not to mention the devastation it caused in Asia.[5] The toll of life was greater than any other epidemic or war in human history. Rats and fleas brought into Europe by Eastern traders are believed to have been the culprits. So virulent was the disease that it could kill in a matter of hours. The Italian writer Boccaccio said its victims often "ate lunch with their friends and dinner with their ancestors in paradise."[6] So rapidly did it spread from one to another that to French physician, Simon de Covine, it seemed as if one sick person "could infect the whole world."[7] Cases were known of persons going to bed well and dying before they woke, of doctors catching the illness at a bedside and dying before the patient. The malignity of the pestilence appeared more terrible because its victims knew no prevention and no remedy.[8] Almost half of London's inhabitants succumbed. Before the plague subsided, between thirty to forty percent of the entire country had been stricken. "Given that the pre-plague population of England was in the range of five to six million people, fatalities may have reached as high as two million dead."[9] People died without last rites and were buried without prayers, a prospect that terrified the last hours of the stricken, considering they had been educated in their Roman Catholic tradition to believe those rites were necessary to assure a person's prospects for bliss in the next life. "No bells tolled," wrote a chronicler of Siena, "and nobody wept no matter what his loss because almost everyone expected death . . . And people said and believed, 'This is the end of the world.'"[10]

As a young theological student during this terrifying time, Wycliffe was deeply impressed and frightened by the horrible effects of it. He experienced a profound spiritual awakening at the time that reached the core of his being.[11] After his conversion experience, Wycliffe rearranged his priorities and became more earnest in his theological studies. The transformation proved to be permanent. By age thirty-six Wycliffe was Master of Balliol College, and by the time he earned his doctorate in divinity at the age of forty-two, he was considered the outstanding philosopher and theologian at Oxford University, and perhaps in all of Europe. He was a man of remarkable erudition and his masterful eloquence always assured a crowded classroom when he lectured.

THE CORRUPTION OF THE MEDIEVAL
CATHOLIC CHURCH

Wycliffe lived in an era when the Catholic Church was entering the season of its greatest decadence, scandal, and shame. From Constantine (d. 337) till the birth of Wycliffe, the Roman Church was the center of every person's life in most of Western Christendom. The Church in England, which was Roman Catholic, was wealthy and powerful as the fourteenth century dawned, but already it exhibited signs of an invasive malignancy. Formal worship was magnificent, but as Langland and Chaucer later graphically revealed through their writings, an urgent need for religious renewal was desperately apparent. The Roman Catholic Church was becoming progressively more corrupt.

At the beginning of Wycliffe's century, Pope Boniface VIII (1294–1303) sat on the papal throne. He enriched his relatives at the expense of the Church, and both his personal character and orthodoxy were repeatedly called into question. Philip IV, King of France, called for a council to judge Boniface on charges of "heresy, blasphemy, murder, sodomy, simony and sorcery (including consorting with a familiar spirit or pet demon), and failure to fast on fast days."[12] He is reputed to have claimed that "sex with boys and women was no worse than rubbing one hand against another."[13] A notorious libertine, he once had a married woman and her daughter as his mistresses.[14] Even more disturbingly, he was said to have called Christ a "hypocrite," professed to be an atheist, rejected the resurrection, and claimed the only heaven and hell were here on this earth. In 1302 Boniface issued the bull *Unam Sanctum* which outrageously claimed that "it is altogether necessary for salvation for every human creature to be subject to the Roman Pontiff."[15]

Shortly after the death of Boniface, the French Pope Clement V transferred the papal court from Rome to Avignon

44

in France in 1309, where it remained for seventy years. Known as the "Babylonian Captivity," a metaphorical reference to the seventy-year Babylonian Captivity of the Jews, it was a time when the papacy continued its slide into spiritual and moral bankruptcy. After the Papal court returned to Rome, the Church was divided by the creation of antipopes.[16] Known as the Great Schism, the period lasted from 1378 to 1417. Two rival popes ruled at the same time, the first two being Urban VI in Rome and Clement VII in Avignon. Urban was violent, drank heavily, and told a cardinal who remonstrated with him that: "I can do anything, absolutely anything I like."[17] Like two mad bulls, the rival popes bellowed away at each other. All of Christendom was scandalized, and unbelievers scoffed at the sight of two competing "vicars of Jesus Christ" anathematizing and excommunicating each other, raising armies and slaughtering helpless women and children, each for his own enhancement. As the Great Schism unfolded, displaying the ugly state of the papacy, it only confirmed the accuracy of Wycliffe's uninhibited assessment of Church corruption.

In spite of the dissident movements inspired by Wycliffe— the Lollards and Hussites—whose aspirations were to rid the papacy of spiritual and moral perversion, the Roman Catholic Church continued its long slide into unbridled depravity. Before the fifteenth century came to a close, Rodrigo Borgia ascended to the papal throne by outbidding his rivals for the necessary votes.[18] Thereafter known as Alexander VI, he was a notorious seducer of women (he had ten known illegitimate children),[19] and during his reign the Vatican was as decadent, power hungry, and violent as any royal court.

Among Alexander's numerous concubines was his favorite, Vannozza Catanei, who bore him two children, Cesare and Lucrezia Borgia, two of the most infamous figures in history and considered by many contemporaries as monsters of lust and cruelty. Famed for her beauty, Lucrezia was a valuable pawn in the marriage game, and Alexander would use her to create one alliance after another. When her first husband no longer suited the Pope's needs, Lucrezia's virginity was restored by Papal decree (and her new maidenhood declared "miraculous"). "She was accused of poisoning the Pope's rivals, of incest with her brother and father, and of conspiring to kill her husbands."[20] Cesare was as bloodthirsty and rapacious a prince and military leader as has appeared on the pages of history. Machiavelli is said to have based his portrait of *The Prince* on him. Lucrezia and Cesare were only reflecting the amorality of their debauched Papal father. No sooner had Alexander achieved the papacy than he converted the Vatican, already no stranger to such revel, to a brothel. "There he frolicked with harlots, staged erotic exhibitions for the entertainment of himself, his children, and their friends, and looked benignly upon the orgies sponsored by his son Cesare."[21]

Not only was the pope lacking in respect from the populace, laymen took offense at the unfitness of the ordinary clergy. Priests were generally uneducated with little interest in their parishioners. Immorality was common among them. A priest could easily purchase from diocesan authority a license to keep a concubine. Erasmus speaks of priests "who by fraud or intimidation have been thrust into a life of celibacy in which they are allowed to fornicate, but not to marry, so that if they openly keep a concubine they are Christian priests, but if they take a wife they are burned."[22] Money could buy almost any kind of dispensation, one of the more popular being to legitimize children born illegitimately, the majority of whom were children of priests and prelates. Out of the 614 grants of legitimacy in the year 1342–43, 484 were to members of the clergy.[23] Many of the clergy were so debased that Wycliffe's contemporary, the poet Geoffrey Chaucer, feared for the souls of the common folk:

If golde ruste, what should iren do?
For if a preest be foul, on whom we truste
No wonder is a lewed man to ruste![24]

The pardoners,[25] commissioned by the Roman Catholic Church, sold absolution for any sin from gluttony to homicide, canceled any vow of chastity, remitted any penance for money, most of which they pocketed. Their mission was to peddle salvation, but in reality they took advantage of the people's need and credulity. The most detestable character in Chaucer's company of Canterbury pilgrims "is the Pardoner with his stringy locks, his eunuch's hairless skin, his glaring eyes like a hare's, and his brazen acknowledgment of the tricks and deceits of his trade."[26]Aeneas Sylvius, before becoming pope, wrote that everything was for sale in Rome, and that nothing could be had without money.[27] A generation later, the monk Savonarola called the Church of Rome a "harlot" ready to sell her favors for coin.[28] As one contemporary said, "It was as if God had given his sheep not to be pastured but to be shaven and shorn."[29]

Monks and itinerant friars were no less distinguished for their sacrilege than the pardoners. When first organized, the friars had been a mighty force for good, with their ideals of holiness, voluntary poverty, and powerful preaching. But in the course of time they had become degraded into idle vagrants and imposters. "They were notorious as seducers of women. Peddling furs and girdles for wenches and wives, and small gentle dogs 'to get love of them,' the friar in a fourteenth century poem 'came to our dame when the goode man is from home.' In the tales of Boccaccio . . . [and] in all popular literature of the time, clerical celibacy is a joke. 'Priests lived with mistresses or else went in hunt of them.'"[30] This shameless behavior explains why the friars were so often the object of intense hostility, sometimes even of physical

47

assault, because, as a chronicle of 1327 stated simply, "they did not behave as friars ought."

Absolved from the necessity of manual labor by the accumulation of wealth, "thousands of monks and friars neglected religious services . . . drank in taverns, and pursued amours."[31] A fourteenth century Dominican, John Bromyard, said of his fellow friars:

> Those who should be the fathers of the poor . . . covet delicate food and enjoy morning sleep. . . . Very few vouchsafe their presence at matins or Mass. . . . They are consumed in gluttony and drunkenness . . . not to say in uncleanness, so that now the assemblies of clerics are thought to be brothels of wanton folk and congregations of play-actors.[32]

Erasmus repeated the charge after a century: "Many convents of men and women differ little from public brothels."[33] Moreover, bishops added to their great incomes by taking bribes from wealthy adulterers. Such profligate behavior represented only the tip of the iceberg.

The immense wealth of the Roman Catholic Church created resentment among impoverished laypeople and pricked the conscience of Wycliffe who resolved to protest against it. The Church owned a third of all real estate in England. The Pope received as much money from taxes on the English as the King of England. The writer Petrarch pointed out in the 1340s that the popes, successors of "the poor fisherman of Galilee" were now "loaded with gold and clad in purple . . . I am living in the Babylon of the West," he said, where prelates feast at "licentious banquets" and ride on snow-white horses "decked in gold, fed on gold, soon to be shod in gold if the Lord does not check this slavish luxury."[34] Lavish expenditures had so depleted the central ecclesiastical treasury that the Pope issued demands for even more funds from the British. Parliament refused to comply with such orders, and Wycliffe stood by the government. The huge fortunes amassed by the dignitaries of the Church were the objects of some of Wycliffe's most determined assaults.

Priests fanned the flames of superstition by attributing credence to the worship of relics:[35] a splinter of wood from the true cross (Erasmus later charged they were "so numerous by now that a ship could not hold them all"),[36] a vial of milk from the Virgin Mary, a piece of the burning bush of Moses, straw from the manger at Bethlehem, the foreskin of Jesus, and a complete skeleton of one of the babies murdered by Herod the Great, to name just a few. Religious pilgrimages were made by many to view these relics, with the expectation that credulous pilgrims would pay generously to see them.

THE INQUISITION

The infamous Inquisition was in full force in European countries during Wycliffe's era. Instituted in the thirteenth century and lasting in some form for almost six centuries, the Inquisition was the Roman Catholic Church's official method of purging heresy. Even before the official launching of the Inquisition, Urban II had decreed at the end of the eleventh century that all heretics were to be tortured and killed.[37] The groundwork had been laid. It was Gregory IX (1227–41) who, in his attempt to stamp out heresy, approved the use of force against error in 1231, when he incorporated into canon law the imperial legislation that decreed the burning of convicted heretics by the secular power. In a series of actions from 1231 to 1235 Gregory instigated a formal organization and set of procedures whereby the apprehension and trial of heretics became the major responsibility of papal inquisitors. Gregory put the Inquisition in the hands of the friars, especially the Dominican and Franciscan Orders, whose relentless pursuit of heretics earned them the nickname *Domini canes*—"the hounds of the Lord."[38] Gregory is therefore often credited with having established the Inquisition.

The most inhumane torture methods were devised to elicit confessions from convicted heretics. These barbarisms were perpetrated simply because men and women refused to submit to the official Church viewpoint. Unrepentant heretics were handed over to the secular authorities to be punished in accordance with the law of the state. This normally meant burning at the stake. Milder punishments included imprisonment, confiscation of property, wearing distinctive crosses on clothing, fasting, flagellation, and pilgrimage. Thousands would suffer during this bloody holocaust. Although the Papal Inquisition was never formally established in England, many of the same frightening methods of torture were employed by English Church authorities to combat heresy.

WYCLIFFE'S OPEN CRITICISM OF ABUSES

Being an ardent student of Scripture, Wycliffe soon discovered within its pages the doctrinal errors of the Church, and he became increasingly bold in challenging them. His blistering criticisms of these abuses resonated with many of his countrymen. He would play a leading role in directing England out of the political and religious quagmire in which both church and state were embroiled. Debates at Oxford sharpened his skills and deepened his convictions, and his studies led him to value truth above tradition. In Oxford, "Wycliffe the fighter" was born, and his sword was, above all, the Bible. His intellectual struggle had brought him a new religious freedom under a new authority—the written Word of God. Notwithstanding he was a Catholic priest during the whole of his adult life, with his only desire being to reform the Church, Wycliffe suffered constant harassment from Roman authorities. His numerous polemical writings and scathing rebukes against the corrupt practices of the Church provoked the wrath of his superiors.

Beginning in 1376 and continuing until his death in 1384, Wycliffe published his theological system in a series of tracts, the main thesis being that Scripture is the foundation of all doctrine. This was a turning point of doctrinal history. Until then, tradition was placed alongside Scripture as a source of doctrine; but Wycliffe disputed this notion with devastating logic. Later John Huss, Martin Luther, as well as William Tyndale, Ulrich Zwingli and John Calvin, would adopt the revolutionary view of Wycliffe.

Wycliffe's great treatise on *Civil Dominion,* written in 1376, pulled no punches. He declared that "England belongs to no pope. The pope is but a man, subject to sin; but Christ is the Lord of Lords, and this kingdom is held directly and solely of Christ alone."[39] It was this book that incited Wycliffe's opponents to silence him.

A man of strong opinions, Wycliffe expressed them in bold, explicit language. Not one to be labeled "politically correct," Wycliffe was the first to call the Pope "antichrist." He described him in such colorful terms as "a poisonous weed," "a limb of Lucifer," "a simple idiot," and "a more horrible idol than a painted log."[40] Falsehood and sham anywhere and everywhere he despised and dared to expose. The cardinals he called "the hinges of the broad road that lead to the pit;" the bishops had become "dumb fools in the realm of hell," as well as "dumb hounds that may not bark in time of need;" the "pardoner" who went about selling indulgences was a "vile quack."[41] The Benedictines were "black dogs."[42] Needless to say, this graphic language did not endear him to church authorities.

But it was when Wycliffe denied the teaching of transubstantiation, also called "the real presence"—the central doctrine of the medieval Church—that he aroused the most animosity. Transubstantiation was of comparatively recent origin and could be dated to the time of Pope Innocent III (1198–1216).[43] It is the belief that the bread and wine, elements used in the Mass, when consecrated by the priest, are "transubstantiated" (transformed in substance) into the actual body and blood of Christ. Wycliffe called it "a pestiferous doctrine." In return he was called "a pertinacious heretic."[44]

William Courtenay, Bishop of London, resolved to call Wycliffe to account for such "wicked and damnable heresies."[45] He summoned him to appear before the Convocation assembled at St. Paul's Cathedral to answer charges of heresy. Wycliffe appeared before that august body on February 19, 1377, accompanied by his patrons, John of Gaunt, Duke of Lancaster, the actual ruler of England, and Lord Henry Percy, the king's marshal. The great cathedral was filled with people. A controversy arose as to whether Wycliffe should stand as a prisoner before the bar or sit as a doctor defending his arguments. Courtenay demanded that Wycliffe stand as long as the trial might last. Gaunt objected and threatened to drag the bishop out by the hair of his head if he did not show proper respect to Wycliffe. An altercation erupted and mass confusion ensued as everyone bolted towards the nearest exit. Wycliffe was dismissed with a warning to preach no more heresy. The feisty professor paid no heed to this warning but taught even more boldly than before. He denied that the pope was the head of the Church, affirming rather that Christ alone was its head.

Three months after the melee in St. Paul's, five papal bulls were issued by Pope Gregory XI against Wycliffe for heresy. These bulls condemned nineteen articles taken from his writings as dangerous to state and Church. Pope Gregory called on Archbishop of Canterbury, Simon of Sudbury, to imprison Wycliffe until the papal court should pass final sentence.[46] Addressing the chancellor of Oxford, the pope charged Wycliffe with vomiting out from the filthy dungeon of his heart most wicked and damnable heresies, by which he proposed to bring destruction upon church and state alike.[47] The pontiff likened him to "those arch-destroyers and heretics, Marsilius of Padua and John of Jandun."[48] The Roman Catholic Church in England tried him three times, two popes summoned him to Rome—he never went—but nothing could silence him.

Ecclesiastical authorities were unsuccessful in their attempts to execute Wycliffe, but they finally expelled him from his professorship at Oxford, forcing him to retire to his parish church at Lutterworth, a small market town in the English Midlands. Thinking such an act would demoralize him and mitigate his influence, they were later chagrined upon discovering that Wycliffe's last years were his most effective and far-reaching in influence. At Lutterworth he devoted all his energies to preaching the Gospel and helping the people of England understand the Bible. He accomplished this by overseeing a translation of the Bible—the very first complete Bible into the English language. Wycliffe fervently believed that ordinary laymen could understand Scripture if only it were translated into their native tongue.

Wycliffe's tract, *De Veritate Sacrae Scripturae (On the Truth of Holy Scripture),* which he completed in about 1378, "shook the fourteenth century English social structure to its roots. In this tract, Wycliffe refutes in the most scholarly of terms the time-honored doctrine of 'mediate dominion.'"[49] This is the belief that people can learn Bible truth only through the medium of a priest or some other Church authority. Man's relationship with God is "immediate," Wycliffe contended, and as there should be no barriers between *God* and his children, there should be no barriers between God's *Word* and His children.[50] Wycliffe asserted that no priest had more right to the Word of God than an ordinary layperson.

This tract established the Word of God as the basis of all truth, the source of all authority. What was not found there had no right to exist, in fact was the work of the devil. "Holy Scripture," Wycliffe wrote, "is the preeminent authority for every Christian and the rule of faith and of all human perfection."[51] Wycliffe insisted that all other teaching, including tradition, must be judged by reference to Scripture, and, if found wanting, must be rejected. This tract was Wycliffe's strongest statement about the supremacy of Scripture over tradition. "Were there a hundred popes and all friars turned to cardinals," he wrote, "their opinions in matters of faith should not be accepted except in so far as they are founded on Scripture itself."[52]

"The truth of Scripture above tradition" contradicted Catholic doctrine, which recognized tradition as equal to Scripture. By tradition is meant the expressions of faith, such as the Apostles' and Nicene Creeds; the conclusions of Church councils; the writings of Church Fathers such as Augustine, Jerome, and others; and decrees of the popes. Such traditions could therefore be said to justify doctrines not found in Scripture itself. But to Wycliffe the Bible was the supreme standard by which Church doctrine must be tested.

Others before Wycliffe, such as Peter Waldo and William of Ockham, had stressed the authority of Scripture, and though Wycliffe's emphasis was much the same, he added a new doctrine, the right of every person, whether cleric or layman, to examine the Bible for himself. To Wycliffe, there could be no better way to "educate a Christian or Christianize a pagan"[53] than to place the Bible before the eyes of everyone, great and small. He held that the best way to empower Christians to develop spiritually and to free their minds from the corrupt tyrannies of papal rule was to make the text of Scripture available to them directly; the result being that, like the Bereans in Acts 17, they could search the Scriptures for themselves to see if what they heard was true. Besides, if everyone was supposed to obey the Bible as God's law, then everyone ought to know what it said. The whole Bible should therefore be accessible to all in a form they could understand.

AUTHORITIES OBJECT TO WYCLIFFE'S BIBLE

Wycliffe's determined effort to put the Bible into the language of his countrymen would not be achieved without intense opposition from the powers that be (the Roman Catholic Church). First, the Church hierarchy looked upon English as a language of peasants, a gutter language incapable of expressing anything other than the crudest and most basic of matters. After the Battle of Hastings in 1066, when the Norman French defeated the English, French became the language of the elite in English society, the only language used by governmental officials and in the courts. Latin was the official language of the Catholic Church; only French and Latin were taught in the schools of the day, not English. Alleged by secular and ecclesiastical authorities to be a barbaric language, the English language could not do justice to such a sophisticated matter as the Bible. But a new day was dawning by the time Wycliffe began work on his translation. The English language was becoming increasingly popular as well as versatile, and Wycliffe, through his writings and translation of the Bible, would help to bring it to a higher level of acceptance.

Another reason authorities objected to a vernacular translation was that the Catholic Church believed Christ had given the Scriptures only to the clergy. Wycliffe's version was regarded by the Church as a deliberate attempt to "vulgarize" a literature of peculiar sanctity which required careful exposition by men of learning, meaning priests and other authorized leaders of the Church. The Bible was not intended for the laity. One of Wycliffe's enemies, Henry Knyghton, canon of Leicester, explained why he opposed an English translation of the Bible:

> The Gospel, which Christ delivered to the clergy and doctors of the church, that they might themselves sweetly administer to the laity and to weaker persons . . . this Master John Wycliffe translated it out of the Latin into

English, [not satisfied with leaving it in] the Angelic [Latin] tongue, and thus laid it more open to the laity and to women who could read, than it had formerly been to the most learned of the clergy—even to those of them that had the best understanding. And in this way the Gospel pearl is cast abroad and trodden under foot of swine; that which was before precious both to clergy and laity is rendered as it were the common jest of both. The jewel of the Church is turned into the common sport of the people, and what was hitherto the principal gift of the clergy and divines is made forever common to the laity.[54]

Knyghton stated the traditional medieval view of the Catholic Church, that Scripture was not for general consumption, especially for women and the uneducated.

Furthermore, though Wycliffe was a priest in the Catholic Church, his views were considered heretical, and someone with such aberrant beliefs could not be trusted to translate the Bible. Only those authorized by the Church had that prerogative. Catholic authorities were clever enough to know the Bible contradicted some of their cherished dogmas and many of their lucrative practices. To permit a vernacular translation to fall into the hands of ordinary laymen could result in efforts to challenge the Church's spiritual dominion, consequently undermining the old regime.

But Wycliffe pressed on in spite of opposition. He was determined in his mission because he was convinced he was working under a divine mandate. This was not a project he devised on his own. He felt called by God and sensed a divine urgency to accomplish his task. Like the apostle Paul he could say, "This one thing I do" (Philippians 3:13). That "one thing" for Wycliffe was to make the Bible understandable and accessible to the common Englishman.

Wycliffe insisted that the Bible should be put into the hands of the people. In opposition to popular ecclesiastical opinion, Wycliffe advanced the maxim that Scripture was the only true authority for belief and practice and that no special religious agent (priest, bishop, etc.) was required to interpret it. Wycliffe passionately believed that the true meaning of Scripture is always revealed to people yielded to the Holy Spirit and who possess humility of mind. Ordinary laymen could understand the Bible if only it was translated into the language they were accustomed to speaking. "The Sacred Scriptures," Wycliffe said, "are the property of the people, and one which no one should be allowed to wrest from them. . . . Christ and His apostles converted the world by making known the Scriptures to men in a form familiar to them, and I pray with all my heart that through doing the things contained in this book, we may all together come to the everlasting life."[55] Those who accepted this maxim and founded their convictions on an infallible book would die by the hundreds over the next two centuries for those convictions.

Generations of medieval Catholic scholars had paid lip service to the Bible. They mined it for individual texts to use in debates and sermons, even writing extravagant comments on passages within it. But their approach was most often that of the detached logician. They did not think of Scripture as a work that was alive and breathing, like the God who inspired it. It was a text suited only for priests—dusty, locked up in Latin, safely beyond the reach of the average Englishman. Religion had come to mean the Church and its traditions, with the Bible playing only a "bit role" in the drama.

To achieve his goal of making the Scriptures widely available in the vernacular, Wycliffe gathered around him a small band of scholars, notably Nicholas of Hereford and John Purvey, who assisted him in the work of translation. It is generally acknowledged that Wycliffe did not do all the translating himself, although he was the inspiration and driving force behind the project. He and his associates wisely translated into the Middle English dialect, the most widely spoken dialect of the time in England, and by so doing helped

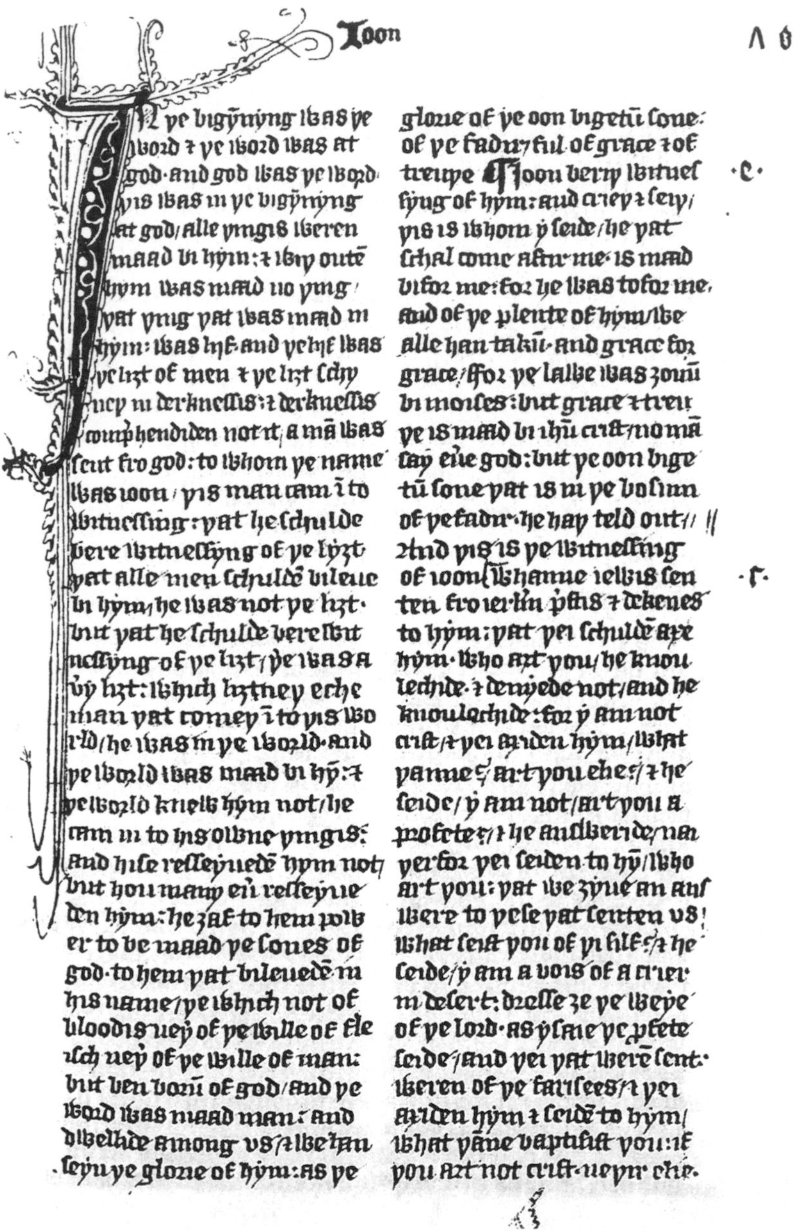
Ioon

[I]N ye bigynnyng was ye
word & ye word was at
god. and god was ye word.
yis was in ye bigynnyng
at god/ alle yingis weren
maad bi hym: & wiy outē
hym was maad no ying/
yat ying yat was maad in
hym: was lijf. and ye lijf was
ye li3t of men & ye li3t schy
neþ in derknessis: & derknessis
comphendiden not it/ a mā was
sent fro god: to whom ye name
was ioon/ yis man cam ī to
witnessing: yat he schulde
bere witnessyng of ye li3t.
yat alle men schuldē bileue
bi hym/ he was not ye li3t.
but yat he schulde bere wit
nessyng of ye li3t/ ye was a
vy li3t: which li3tney eche
man yat comey ī to yis wo
rld/ he was in ye world. and
ye world was maad bi hȳ: &
ye world knew hym not/ he
cam in to his owne yingis:
and hise resseyuedē hym not/
but hou many eu resseyue
den hym: he 3af to hem pow
er to be maad ye sones of
god. to hem yat bileuedē in
his name/ ye which not of
bloodis ney of ye wille of fle
sch ney of ye wille of man:
but ben born of god/ and ye
word was maad man: and
dwelhde among us/ & we han
seyn ye glorie of hym: as ye
glorie of ye oon bigetū sone:
of ye fadir/ ful of grace & of
treuye ¶ Joon beriþ witnes
syng of hym: and crieþ & seiy/
yis is whom y seide/ he yat
schal come aftir me. is maad
bifor me: for he was tofor me.
and of ye plente of hym/ we
alle han takū. and grace for
grace/ ffor ye lawe was 3ouū
bi moises: but grace & treuy
ye is maad bi ihū crist/ no mā
say euer god: but ye oon bige
tū sone yat is in ye bosum
of ye fadir. he hay teld out//
And yis is ye witnessing
of ioon/ whanne iewis sen
ten fro ierlm pstis & dekenes
to hym: yat yei schuldē axe
hym. who art you/ he knou
lechide. & denyede not/ and he
knoulechide: for y am not
crist/ & yei axiden hym/ what
yanne? art you elie?/ & he
seide/ y am not/ art you a
profete?/ & he answeride/ nai
yerfor yei seiden to hȳ/ who
art you: yat we 3yue an ans
were to yese yat senten us/
what seist you of yi silf?/ & he
seide/ y am a vois of a crier
in desert: dresse 3e ye weye
of ye lord. as ysaie ye pfete
seide/ and yei yat weren sent.
weren of ye farisees/ & yei
axiden hym & seidē to hym/
what yanne baptisist you: if
you art not crist. neyir elie.

The Gospel of John Chapter One from
Wycliffe's Bible, 1382

standardize and shape the future of our language. Wycliffe has been classed with Chaucer, Shakespeare, and Tyndale as one of the chief makers of the English language.

Wycliffe's Bible was not a translation from the original languages for two reasons: first, the manuscripts that later became available had not yet been discovered; furthermore, he was not a Greek and Hebrew scholar, as those languages were not commonly taught in England at the time. But Wycliffe and his associates were good Latin scholars, and the source for their translation of the Scriptures was Jerome's Latin Vulgate.

Almost three-quarters of a century would pass before the introduction of the printing press in Europe, hence all of Wycliffe's Bibles had to be handwritten. It took about ten months for a scribe to reproduce one copy of the Bible, and the cost of a copy was between 30 and 40 English pounds, an enormous sum of money in those days, considering the average yearly salary was only a fraction of that amount.[56] In spite of the cost and the small number available, the Wycliffe Bibles created a sensation among the common people of England. At last many of them could hear or read the Word of God for the first time in their own language. John Foxe in his *Book of Martyrs* wrote of people who provided a cartload of hay for the privilege of having the New Testament to read for just one day. Some would save for a month in order to purchase a single page of the Bible.[57]

A few years after Wycliffe's death in 1384, a revision was made by John Purvey, Wycliffe's close associate and personal secretary. Purvey's revision was more idiomatic than the earlier version that was somewhat stilted, especially in the Old Testament. Some of the Old Testament translation in the earlier edition was the work of Nicolas of Hereford, another of Wycliffe's associates. It was Purvey's version that was circulated as the Wycliffe Bible, and it is impossible to overemphasize its importance and influence.

THE LOLLARDS

Not only did Wycliffe oversee the first complete translation of the English Bible, he and his colleagues trained young itinerants, "poor priests" Wycliffe called them, and sent them throughout England, dressed in modest russet cloth, their backpacks stuffed with tracts and portions of the new translation of Scripture. Going out two-by-two according to the New Testament pattern, these courageous young men would read and explain the Bible to the common people at impromptu gatherings in churchyards, markets, open fields, and homes. Because their activity was forbidden by the English Church, men and women would gather clandestinely in illegal groups to hear the vernacular Bible read and discussed. The mission of these itinerants was to preach the revolutionary message that *salvation comes through faith in Christ alone* without the aid of meritorious works. In addition, they attacked the substitution of tradition for Scripture, clerical celibacy and immorality, transubstantiation, indulgences, image worship, religious pilgrimages, prayers for the dead, the wealth and endowment of the Church, the necessity of confession to priests, the worship of saints, and the papacy. It was to these young men the word "Lollard" was first applied. Intended as an expression of derision, it is believed to mean someone who "lolls around," is a "mumbler" or "mutterer."[58] In time the name stuck and those who were so designated proudly bore the name. Also called "Bible Men" (to many it would seem a complimentary label), it was a contemptuous term coined by the bishop of Chichester.[59]

As early as 1382 a monastic chronicler reported the Lollards "multiplied exceedingly, like budding plants, and filled the whole realm....You could scarce meet two men of the road but that one of them was a disciple of Wycliffe."[60] These itinerants were well trained in Scripture by Wycliffe and his associates. Indeed, in accordance with the Biblical command, they were prepared to give an answer to anyone who requested of them a reason for the hope that was in them (1 Peter 3:15). Wycliffe gave to his Lollard preachers an excellent guide to understanding the Scriptures that they were in turn to pass along to their listeners. [The spelling has been modernized.]

> It shall greatly help you to understand Scripture,
> If you mark not only what is spoken or written,
> But of whom,
> And to whom,
> With what words,
> At what time,
> Where,
> To what intent,
> With what circumstances,
> Considering what goes before,
> And what follows.[61]

It would be hard to improve on this as a brief summary, even in the modern era.

For more than a century before the first printed English New Testament, Lollards fearlessly circulated portions of handwritten manuscript copies of the Scriptures, and in so doing frequently put themselves in harm's way. Many were imprisoned, and some suffered martyrdom. In 1401, Henry IV and his Parliament issued the infamous statute *De haeretico combuerndo* ("concerning the burning of heretics"), *The Suppression of Heresy Act*: all persons declared by an ecclesiastical court to be persistent heretics were to be burned, and all heretical books were to be destroyed.[62] The intent was to destroy Lollardy.

William Sawtrey, a priest from Lynn in Norfolk, became the first martyr for Wycliffe's doctrine. Among other charges, he had been guilty of saying, "Instead of adoring the cross on which Christ suffered, I adore Christ who suffered on it."[63] On February 24, 1401, he was conducted to St. Paul's, where he was degraded from office, then handed over to the "mercy" of the state. Early in March, only days after *The Suppression of Heresy Act* was passed, Sawtrey was burned in Smithfield before a crowd of spectators. It was the first recorded burning of a heretic in England since that of a deacon convicted of converting to Judaism nearly two hundred years before.[64] Church authorities wanted everyone to understand, especially those with Lollard sympathies, that the new law had teeth; it was not meant to be a dead letter. From 1401, the work of the new Inquisition went rapidly forward. Before the Act was finally repealed in 1559 under Queen Elizabeth, hundreds of so-called "heretics" would suffer death by burning, many of them Lollards.

One of the most famous and influential Lollards was Sir John Oldcastle (c. 1378–1417), a remarkable knight from Herefordshire. He was rich, a soldier, and intimate of the king. Yet he abandoned a brilliant career to be a follower of Wycliffe's doctrines, using his wife's fortune to have Wycliffe's works copied and distributed. Incurring the displeasure of Thomas Arundel, Archbishop of Canterbury, for his Lollard sympathies, Oldcastle was accused of heresy in 1413. Summoned before Convocation, he was subsequently handed over to the civil authorities for trial. Courageously upholding Lollard beliefs, Oldcastle rejected transubstantiation and confession, denounced the pope as Antichrist, and denied the hierarchy's right to dictate what a man should believe. Proclaimed a heretic, he was sentenced to death and imprisoned in the Tower of London. The king gave him forty days to recant, but somehow Oldcastle managed to escape before their expiration. Conspiring with others after his escape, Oldcastle planned to seize the king and establish a Lollard government. The conspirators cared so intensely for the mission that they were willing to stake their lives and fortunes on the attempt to obtain freedom of conscience. The plot proved to be a desperate, ill-timed endeavor. The collapse of the mission resulted in the capture of many of the Lollards. Oldcastle evaded custody and remained in hiding until 1417. For four years he was the most wanted fugitive in the kingdom.[65] He was finally captured, conveyed on a litter to London under heavy guard, and brought before Parliament December 14, 1417. Condemned for treason, he was at once sentenced to immediate execution. "Taken to the tower, he was laid on a hurdle and dragged to St. Giles' Field where before a large crowd he was hanged by a chain from a new gallows, the 'Lollard gallows' as they came to be called, while a fire was lighted beneath him."[66] He was reputed to have been the basis of Shakespeare's famous character, Falstaff.[67] In the wake of Oldcastle's rebellion and death, the Lollards became an underground movement, and remained such until the Reformation.[68]

WYCLIFFE'S DEATH AND INFLUENCE

Remarkably, with his opposition to certain doctrines of the Church and his criticism of the corruption of the clergy, Wycliffe was never excommunicated during his lifetime, nor did he ever leave the Roman Catholic Church. In fact, he suffered a fatal stroke in the Lutterworth church while he was celebrating Mass as a parish priest. Three days later, he died peacefully at home in bed on New Year's Eve, 1384. In 1415, the Council of Constance condemned Wycliffe's doctrines and ordered his body to be exhumed and removed from sacred ground. Thirteen years later, in 1428, and forty-four years after Wycliffe's death, the still infuriated English church authorities had his body removed from sacred ground at the Lutterworth church, burned his bones, and scattered the ashes in the nearby River Swift. The River Swift is a tributary of the Avon River. Years later, someone wrote a moving eulogy to Wycliffe, suggesting his far-reaching influence:

> The Avon to the Severn runs,
> The Severn to the Sea,
> And Wycliffe's dust shall spread abroad,
> Wide as the waters be.[69]

British people took Wycliffe's new translation right to heart. Many were overjoyed to finally have a Bible in their own language; but ecclesiastical authorities were less than pleased. In 1408, laws were drawn up by Archbishop of Canterbury, Thomas Arundel, which decreed that "no one henceforth do by his own authority translate any text of Holy Scripture into the English tongue or into any other, by way of book or treatise; nor let any book or treatise now lately composed [meaning the Wycliffite version], be read in whole or in part, in public or private, under pain of the greater excommunication . . . He that shall do contrary to this shall likewise be punished as a favorer of heresy and error."[70] The "punishment" referred to involved execution by burning. In the fifteenth century the mere fact of owning and reading the Bible in English was presumptive evidence of heresy. Foxe relates how one mother was burned at the stake for teaching her children to recite The Lord's Prayer and The Ten Commandments in English.[71]

Archbishop Arundel was so frustrated by the people's determination to read the Scriptures in spite of his prohibition against it that he wrote Pope John XXII in 1412 blaming "that wretched and pestilent fellow John Wycliffe," for this sad state of affairs. Out of sheer "malice," Arundel said, Wycliffe "devised the expedient of a new translation of the Scriptures into the mother tongue." And "the crown of the offence," the archbishop complained, was "the translation were in a tongue comprehensible to all." To Arundel, this was unforgivable.[72] In 1414 a law was enacted that all persons who should read the Scriptures in the mother tongue should "forfeit land, cattle, life, and goods from their heirs forever."[73]

In spite of interdicts, papal bulls, threats and executions, British people continued for more than a century to read tattered fragments of Wycliffe's Bible, even though they had to smuggle its precious pages from hand to hand, farmhouse to farmhouse, village to village. In doing so, they kept alive the demand for an English Bible. Wycliffe had released an irresistible force into England.

Wycliffe's influence stretched far beyond his native land. No man during the Middle Ages was so independent in his thought or so fearless in his utterances as Wycliffe. Not even Luther was more merciless in his attacks on the existing Church order or more uncompromising in his assaults on the failings of popes. The dauntless written words of Wycliffe spread far beyond the borders of England. One of Wycliffe's devotees was Queen Anne, the wife of Richard II of England. Through the efforts of Anne, many young men in her native land of Bohemia (a region in western Czechoslovakia) were profoundly stirred by Wycliffe's writings. One of the young men affected was John Huss, who, like his mentor Wycliffe, would become a reviled but vastly influential reformer. When Martin Luther was summoned to appear before the Diet of Worms in April 1521, one of the charges leveled against him was that he had revived the old heresies of Wycliffe and Huss.[74]

All the major elements of the Reformation were in Wycliffe: the revolt against the worldliness of the clergy; the emphasis on an infallible Bible as opposed to the fallible traditions and dogmas of the Church; the rejection of indulgences, auricular confession, and transubstantiation; the appeal to the state to end its subordination to the papacy; and the attack on the wealth of the clergy. Before Huss, Luther, Zwingli, and Calvin, Wycliffe was "a voice crying in the wilderness" for the reform of the Roman Catholic Church, the one who justly merits the epithet, "The Morning Star of the Reformation."

In his famous defense before Parliament on the freedom of the press (1644), John Milton asserted:

> Why was this Nation chosen before any other, that out of her, as out of Sion, should be proclaimed and sounded forth the first tidings and trumpet of Reformation to all Europe? And had it not been [for] the obstinate perverseness of our prelates against the divine and admirable spirit of Wickliff,

to suppress him as a schismatic and innovator, perhaps neither the Bohemians Huss and Jerome, no nor the name of Luther or of Calvin, had ever been known: the glory of reforming all our neighbours had been completely ours.[75]

Chapter Four

THE SIGNIFICANT EVENTS THAT SHAPED THE ENGLISH BIBLE

etween the time of Wycliffe and the Great Reformation (1330–1517), sweeping events took place in the medieval world which helped to create a brand new intellectual and cultural climate in Europe. Moreover, these events worked in concert to prepare the way for the first printed English Bible, the first such to be translated from the original languages.

THE RENAISSANCE

The collapse of the Roman Empire plunged the Western World into what some have labeled "The Dark Ages." In A.D. 395 the Roman Empire split into two parts: a Western Empire with its capital in Rome, and an Eastern Empire with its capital in Constantinople (present-day Istanbul). Less than a hundred years later (A.D. 476), Germanic tribes conquered the Western Empire, and much of the old Roman civilization disappeared. Great cities fell into ruins, roads became overgrown with weeds, trade collapsed, and the widespread rule of Roman law ended.[1] For almost a millennium, the people of Europe huddled together for protection in small towns and villages in the countryside. Most barely eked out an existence from the soil as war, disease, and famine routinely spread over the land.

The Roman Catholic Church became pervasive during those years, disseminating knowledge as well as proscribing it. People were discouraged from challenging the accuracy of current knowledge, and curiosity about the world was stifled. Monks in monasteries laboriously copied books by hand, and few people were allowed access to them.[2] Books that were made available to the public usually ended up in the libraries of kings, queens and wealthy merchants. For a peasant to be literate was rare indeed, much less to have the means to purchase a book. The meager knowledge the ordinary citizen had of history, geography, medicine, and science (not to mention religion), was permeated with errors and superstition. Hence many of the artistic works and scientific discoveries of the ancient world were forgotten.

During the fourteenth century, scholars awakened interest in the classical art and literature of the ancient Greeks and Romans. Generally disregarding the stereotypical views of the Church towards these matters, they began to work out new ideas for themselves. This blossoming of the arts and sciences is called the "Renaissance," a French word meaning "rebirth."[3] Although artistic achievement and learning were not entirely dormant during the Middle Ages, not until the fourteenth century did the new learning take root and its impact become widespread.

Starting in Italy with the poet Francesco Petrarch (1304–74), this new Renaissance, which lasted from about the middle of the fourteenth century to the middle of the seventeenth century, led to a great flowering of the arts, and transformed science, learning, and religion throughout Europe. As more and more scholars began to examine original Greek and Roman texts, they discovered many ideas that had been lost to the West for a thousand years. This led to some startling changes in the way scholars thought about the world around them and to a passionate belief in the possibility of educating individuals and societies to higher levels of achievement.[4]

Known as "humanists," these scholars of the new learning proposed that every individual, commoner as well as king, was important in the eyes of God. They insisted that people should be free to think about the world, and that curiosity and discussions about ideas were no longer to be proscribed by a monolithic ecclesiastical organization that often contradicted itself. Unlike official Catholicism, humanists believed that people could examine several points of view and still follow the essential teachings of Christ and the Bible. "The belief that people could use art and literature for enjoyment as well as the glory of God, encouraged many talented individuals to experiment with new ideas."[5]

As Renaissance ideals penetrated the more northerly countries of Europe—Germany, France, and England—in the early years of the sixteenth century, the field of theology and Biblical studies became the focal point. The northern humanists were more interested in the Christian classics, the New Testament and the Church Fathers, than in pagan texts such as Plato and Aristotle. They were also concerned with reforming the Church according to apostolic principles. These scholars were generally called "Christian Humanists." Among their number were John Colet (c.1466–1519), Johannes Reuchlin (c.1454–1552), Thomas More (1478–1535), and the most noteworthy of all, Desiderius Erasmus (c.1467–1536), called "The Prince of the Humanists."[6]

Convinced that the purest text of the Bible was not to be found in the Latin version of Jerome (accepted as inspired by the Catholic Church), but in the languages in which the Bible was first written, Hebrew and Greek, Erasmus launched a project that would give to the world the first published Greek text of the New Testament. He accomplished this in 1516, using four Greek manuscripts that were available to him while in England,[7] and five or six Greek manuscripts that were accessible at the University of Basel library.[8] From Erasmus' text would come the first printed English New Testament.

THE DEFEAT OF CONSTANTINOPLE

When Constantine finally gained sole control of the ailing Roman Empire in A.D. 323, he immediately recognized that Rome was too far away to deal with the eastern problems of the Empire. His solution was to locate a city on the eastern perimeter that would be considered a "New Rome," and would serve as a second capital. At first, he planned to build on the site of ancient Troy, but soon saw the advantage of establishing the city on the site of the Greek city of Byzantium, a small trading town on a magnificently strategic site jutting into the sea of Marmara, which connected with the Black Sea to the north and the Aegean to the south. It was one of the most momentous decisions in the history of Western civilization. The site gave the city control over all commercial vessels entering or leaving the Black Sea, thus placing it in a very powerful position. On May 11, 330, after forty days and nights of festivities, Constantine dedicated his new capital, calling it "Constantinople,"[9] and heralded the beginning of one thousand years of Byzantine civilization. The ensuing centuries witnessed the development of one of the world's great cities.

Beginning in the seventh century, Muslims began crossing the Bosphorus in an attempt to gain control of the city. Constantinople survived these periodic Muslim blockades for almost 800 years. But at daybreak on May 27, 1453, after a two-month siege from land and sea, an assault on the city was launched that proved to be crushingly effective. With their superior armaments and numbers, the Turks managed to breach the ancient walls and flood into the city, causing terror and panic among the helpless inhabitants and inflicting heavy casualties. The bodies of the fallen warriors, Christians and Muslims alike, were thrown into the Hellespont, where "they were carried along in the current like melons."[10] According to the Italian Niccolo Barbaro, "the Turks sought out the convents and took the nuns out to ships in the harbor to dishonor them before selling them as slaves."[11] By Tuesday, May 29, the city of Constantine had become Muslim, and the Church of St. Sophia, for almost a thousand years the largest, most celebrated church in Christendom, after proper "purification," was transformed into a mosque. All its Christian symbols were removed, and its mosaics were whitewashed into oblivion for five hundred years.

The defeat of Constantinople shook every throne in Europe. The city that had provided protection for Europe from Asian hordes for over a thousand years had fallen. Trade routes once open to Western vessels were now in alien hands. The papacy, which had dreamed of all Greek Christianity submitting to the rule of Rome, saw with dismay the rapid conversion of millions of southeastern Europeans to Islam, mostly by force.

One positive outcome emerged from this calamitous event. Many of the eminent Bible scholars of the East fled to the great cities of Europe—Paris, Geneva, Basel, and Zurich—bringing with them their Greek New Testament manuscripts. These scholars stirred up a whirlwind of Biblical studies on the Continent and in England. Several of these manuscripts would form the basis of the first printed Greek New Testament and the first printed English Bible.

THE INVENTION OF PRINTING

The marvelous new printing presses developed in Europe played a significant role in the evolution and diffusion of the English Bible. Johann Gutenberg is credited, at least in the West, with the remarkable invention that changed the world—printing from moveable type. Printing from blocks and moveable type was known in the Far East long before Gutenberg, but for a variety of reasons, social and political rather than technological, the invention did not take root and have the profound impact there that it was to have in Germany and the rest of Europe.[12]

Though born in Mainz, Germany (c. 1397), an uprising in the city in Gutenberg's early manhood resulted in the family's move to Strasbourg. Gutenberg's first experience as a tradesman was as a goldsmith in Strasbourg from 1434 to 1444. It was there that we get the first hint that Gutenberg was beginning his experiments with printing. Returning to Mainz in 1448, he set up a foundry and press, borrowing money for the venture from the banker Johann Fust.[13] Significantly, the very

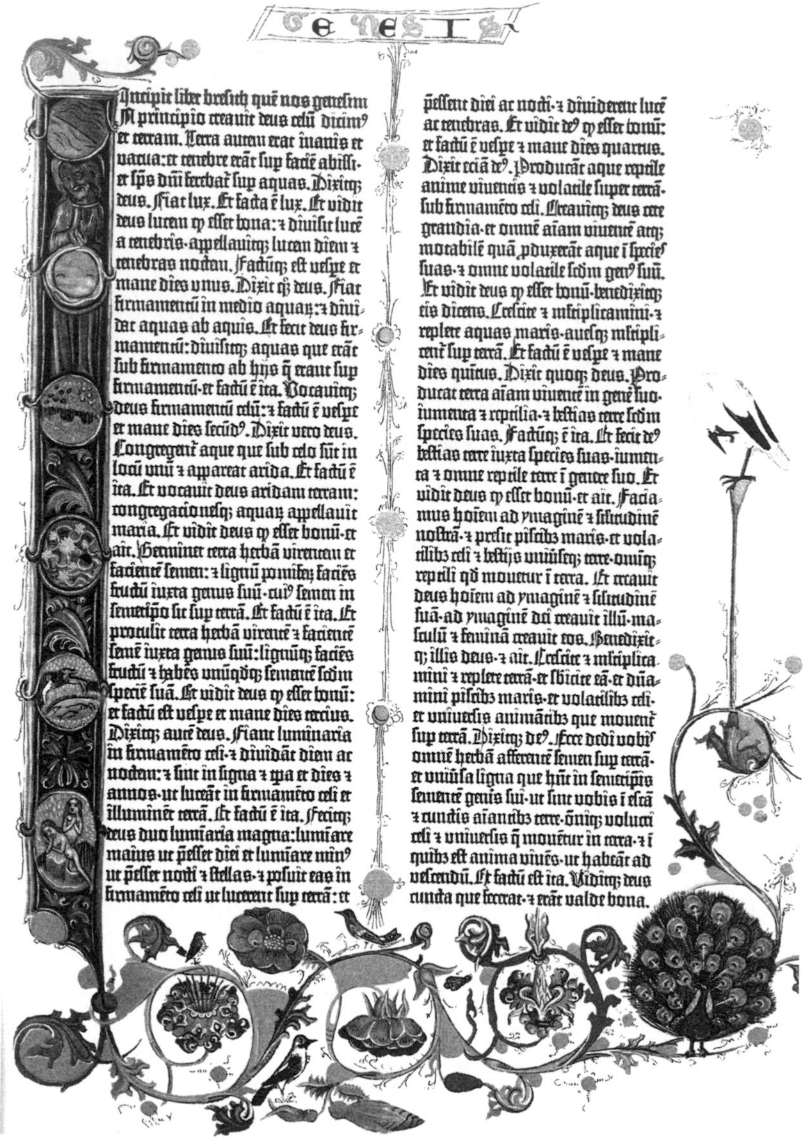

Sample Page from the Gutenberg Bible, c. 1455

first book printed on Gutenberg's revolutionary press in Mainz, was the Bible—the Latin Vulgate, c. 1454/55. These remarkable Bibles were later nicknamed "the Mazarin Bible," owing to the discovery of one of them in the library of Jules Mazarin. Out of the enormous revenues he collected as a Roman Catholic cardinal from various rich ecclesiastical offices, Mazarin amassed a huge fortune, part of which he devoted to his famous library that included a copy of this rare and extremely beautiful first printed edition of the Bible.[14] Also technically designated by bibliographers as "the 42-line Bible," the Gutenberg Bible was printed in double columns, forty-two lines to a column, and in two folio volumes.[15] Gutenberg only produced about 180 copies of his famous Bible, some 135 on paper and the rest on vellum. Each vellum copy used the skins of 170 animals; hence, it comes as no surprise that paper prevailed as the print medium of choice. In the opinion of many critics, it is one of the most beautiful books ever produced. Today about forty of these Bibles are known to exist, most of them in famous museums.

Gutenberg could not have fully comprehended the enormous significance of his achievement. Few inventions in history have so profoundly affected human education and culture. It was a communications revolution that transformed the way humans were able to connect with one another. Even in the primitive days of printing, it was possible to print more in a day than was formerly written in a year. The emergence of the new technology meant that for the first time Bibles and other literature could be mass produced and made available to the general public at a reasonable cost.

The world quickly awakened to the advantages of Gutenberg's invention. The practice of printing spread rapidly as eager entrepreneurs began attempting to duplicate and even improve on Gutenberg's invention. About twenty years after Gutenberg printed the first book, William Caxton brought the printing process to England. "Before 1500, the total number of books printed throughout Europe was about 35,000, most of them in Latin. Between 1500 and 1640, in England alone, some 20,000 items in English were printed, ranging from pamphlets to folios and Bibles."[16]

The invention of the printing press changed the world more rapidly than any previous invention. Literacy became much more common as books proliferated. John Foxe attributed "this gift of printing" to direct divine intervention.[17] He alleged that a readily available and inexpensive Bible would help to dispel false doctrine among the masses of England. Some in the Roman Church, however, were not so enthusiastic about the new invention. The Catholic, Rowland Phillips, lamented: "Either we must root out printing, or printing will root us out."[18] Thomas Beard, Oliver Cromwell's mentor and friend, echoed Foxe in seeing divine Providence behind the coincidence in time of the invention and development of the printing press and the translation of the Bible into English.[19]

THE APPEARANCE OF ERASMUS' GREEK/LATIN NEW TESTAMENT

Erasmus of Rotterdam epitomized the Renaissance in the Northern European countries. Born illegitimately to a widow and a priest (in orders at the time) in or near Rotterdam sometime between 1466 and 1469,[20] Erasmus became a widely acclaimed savant and prolific author whose biting satire often targeted the abuses of the Catholic Church. Of his many contributions to the literature of the Renaissance, none excels in significance his Greek/Latin text of the New Testament. By the time he left England after his first visit there in January of 1500, he had formed his resolve to study and edit the Greek text of the New Testament. This, he believed, embodied "the distilled essence of that real Christianity which in the judgment of reformers and humanists alike, had been overlaid and concealed by the dogmas and accretions of centuries."[21]

Over a decade later Erasmus presented to Johann Froben, a printer in Basel, the manuscript of his monumental critical

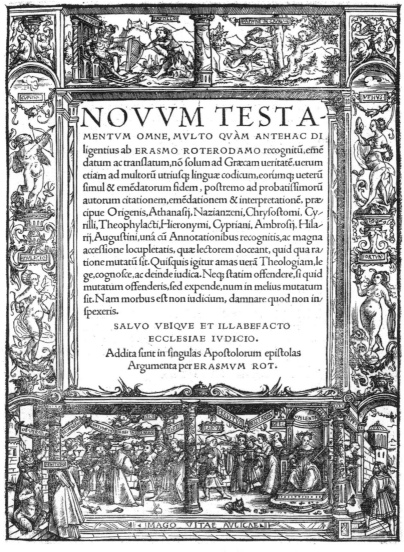

The Title Page from Erasmus' Greek/Latin New Testament,
1519

revision of the Greek Text of the New Testament, with a new Latin translation and a commentary. Published in February of 1516, it was a risky venture for author and publisher alike, considering how unyielding the Catholic Church was about approving versions other than the standard Vulgate. Even though the volume was dedicated to Pope Leo X, who was obviously pleased with such recognition by Europe's greatest scholar, this fact did not save it from the scrupulous guardians of the Vulgate. From that time on, much of Erasmus' time was occupied with defending his Greek Testament, and especially his Latin translation.[22] Though containing numerous typesetting errors, it was a *tour de force* for Erasmus, representing the most enduring monument to his knowledge and skill, while marking the first time a printed Greek/Latin New Testament had ever been published.[23]

Called by Erasmus *Novum Instrumentum*,[24] his Greek Testament, in spite of all its faults and the hostility of some modern scholars, was the *textus receptus* for the great edition of the French scholar-printer Robert Estienne (Stephanus) in 1550, and it was not seriously challenged until the late nineteenth century. The Latin phrase, *textus receptus,* was first used in the preface of the Greek Testament issued at Leiden in 1633 by the Elzevir press; it was essentially the text of Erasmus. The Latin phrase means, "a text received by all."

Erasmus' second edition *Novum Testamentum* (1519) served as a basis for Luther's German New Testament (1522). Luther used both the Greek and Latin texts of Erasmus in his work. The first English New Testament, also based on Erasmus, was translated by William Tyndale and printed at Worms in 1526. All subsequent English New Testament translations for almost four centuries, including the KJV, were based on Erasmus. The Hungarian versions of Benedek Komjati (1533) and Janos Sylvester (1540), the Spanish of Francisco de Enzinas (1543) and many more were based on Erasmus.

Like Wycliffe, Erasmus expressed his strong support for vernacular renderings of sacred Scripture. He wrote in the preface to his New Testament:

> I would have the weakest woman read the Gospels and the Epistles of St. Paul . . . I would have those words translated into all languages, so that not only Scots and Irishmen, but Turks and Saracens might read them. I long for the plowboy to sing them to himself as he follows the plow, the weaver to hum them to the tune of his shuttle, the traveler to beguile with them the dullness of his journey. . . . Other studies we may regret having undertaken, but happy is the man upon whom death comes when he is engaged in these. These sacred words give you the very image of Christ speaking, healing, dying, rising again, and make him so present, that were he before your very eyes you would not more truly see him.[25]

Traditionalists, on the other hand, did not share this view, fearing people would develop their own interpretations of the Bible if they read it in their own language. They assumed the Church would lose control of what people believed. But Erasmus and others similarly inclined did not think this would lead to anarchy. They wanted the Bible to be available to all, not just to scholars.

Though a devout Catholic all of his life, Erasmus relentlessly satirized numerous Catholic practices and beliefs that failed to meet Scriptural criteria. At first Erasmus seemed pleased by the "new learning" introduced by the young German reformer Martin Luther. In a letter to Luther, he commented approvingly on the position Luther had taken: "I have turned over a few pages of your *Commentaries on the Psalms,*" he told him. "They please me exceedingly."[26] When Duke Frederick, elector of Saxony, questioned Erasmus about Luther's orthodoxy, Erasmus remained silent for a moment as the benign old man watched him. At last he replied: "Luther has erred on two points: attacking the crown of the pope and the bellies of the monks."[27] But Erasmus never developed into the bold reformer Luther hoped he would. In a letter to the famous humanist in the spring of 1524, Luther hinted at his disappointment with the man's timidity: "For we observe that the Lord has not granted you sufficient courage or steadfast intention" to proceed against the Church of Rome "freely and confidently. . . . We do not presume to demand of you what is beyond your powers and talents . . ."[28] Only when the Roman Church pressured him to take a stand against Luther did Erasmus relent, attacking him on the issue of the freedom of the will. As the years passed Luther's disdain for Erasmus became more and more belligerent in tone.

However, Erasmus' contribution to the formation of the English Bible, as well as to the Reformation, was incalculable and leaves us all in his debt. Perhaps unwittingly, Erasmus made a significant contribution to the Reformation in his Latin translation of the New Testament which was printed alongside his Greek text in parallel columns. The Latin text differed from the Vulgate in numerous places which is why it was so harshly attacked by critics. One example will serve to illustrate this. In Matthew 3:2 the Greek *metanoeo* is translated in the Vulgate as *"penitentiam agite,"* which tends to obscure the original thought. Latin had only one word for "repentance," and "penance" did not satisfy the full force of the Greek. The traditional Catholic interpretation inclined toward "do penance," which buttressed the Sacrament of Penance, and in effect the whole sacramental system. Erasmus did not accept the Vulgate translation and instead substituted either *"resipiscite"* or *"ad mentem redite,"* that is, "be mindful" or "come to your senses." Shoeck comments, "The leaven of this new rendering worked so powerfully in Luther's mind that it became the starting point of the Reformation and thus permeated the whole loaf of Christendom.[29] Erasmus is said to have "laid the egg that Luther hatched!"[30]

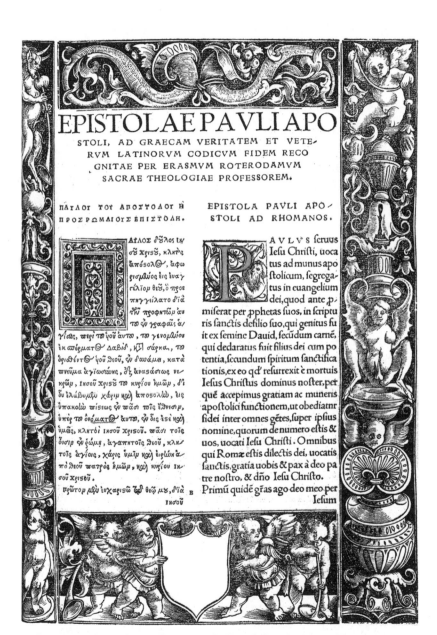

Romans One from Erasmus' Greek/Latin New Testament,
1519

THE REFORMATION

In 1517 a great "heretic" arose in Germany—"a wild boar in the vineyard," in the words of the bull *Exsurge domine* by which Pope Leo X excommunicated Martin Luther in 1520. "It was when the spirit of Renaissance individualism reached the realm of theology and religious conviction within the Roman Catholic Church in the person of the German Augustinian monk, Martin Luther, that there erupted in Europe the momentous Protestant Reformation."[31] Although Luther is recognized as the presiding genius and initiator of the Reformation, the way was prepared for him by a host of illustrious men—John Wycliffe (c. 1330–84) in England, John Huss (c.1369–1415) and Jerome of Prague (c.1371–1416) in Bohemia, Girolamo Savonarola (1452–98) in Italy, Erasmus (1466–1536) in Holland, and by various others who detested the corruptions they ridiculed and lamented, yet were unable to remove. Antipapal sentiment only smoldered until fanned into flames with the posting of Luther's Ninety-five Theses on the door of the Wittenberg Church on October 31, 1517. Precipitated by the papacy's attempt to finance the building of St. Peter's Basilica in Rome by the theologically dubious means of selling indulgences, Luther's daring act became "the hammer blow heard around the world."

The Medici Pope, Leo X, had authorized John Tetzel, a traveling friar, to sell indulgences in Germany to finance the building of the largest, most ornate church in Christendom. The practice of selling indulgences allowed the Church not only to raise money for building cathedrals and hospitals, but also to finance crusades against the Muslims. At first applied only to penalties imposed by the Church in this life, by Luther's time, indulgences were being granted to remit penalties imposed by God in the afterlife, including immediate release from purgatory.[32] Tetzel devised a clever little jingle that provoked added incentive to his sale of indulgences: "As soon as the coin in the coffer rings, the soul from purgatory springs."[33]

But beyond the matter of indulgences lay more urgent reasons to revolt against the established order. The flagrancy of those evils was becoming ever more apparent: papal authoritarianism and the frauds on which it was based; the long-developing secularism of the Church hierarchy; the ignorance, superstition and dissolute lives of the clergy; the worship of images; masses for the dead; the substitution of legends for Scripture (which was not translated or read by the people); religious pilgrimages; the worship of relics; the grinding spiritual despotism of popes, bishops, and priests, keeping the human mind in bondage and suppressing intellectual initiative. This is to say nothing of the massacres, poisonings, assassinations, fornications, and abominations of which history accuses many of the pontiffs who sat on papal "thrones." But a deeper factor behind the Reformation was the lack of emphasis on the simplicity of Biblical truth as the sole basis for faith and practice.

Ever aware of his own sinfulness, Luther as a young monk desperately sought for God's acceptance and redemption. He failed to experience God's grace through his own "monkery" or in his own works, nor did he find it in the Church—its sacraments, traditions, rituals, religious pilgrimages, or indulgences. It was finally in *the truth of justification by faith* that Luther experienced the assurance of salvation. And upon that exclusive rock he built his new movement of a reformed Christianity. Initially believing he could restore the Church from within, through much soul-searching he reluctantly concluded, given that the Church hierarchy remained intransigent to such reform, "only complete schism and independence from an institution he viewed as the seat of Antichrist would prove effective."[34]

All the accretions brought into Christianity by the Roman Church that were not found in the New Testament were now solemnly questioned, criticized, and often purged altogether by Luther and his fellow reformers—sacraments, rituals, complex organizational structures, the priestly hierarchy, belief in purgatory, papal infallibility, clerical celibacy, transubstantiation, the popular worship of the Virgin Mary, and finally the Mother Church herself. All these had become contrary to the individual Christian's primary need for faith in Christ's redemptive grace. They were merely human attempts to merit what could never be merited but only received, the grace of God. Justification occurred by faith alone.

The only source of theological authority now lay in the literal meaning of Scripture, not in some capricious interpretation of it or in tradition. No longer would it be necessary to attempt to comprehend Scripture according to the commonly accepted, complex method of interpretation. Medieval theologians proposed a fourfold sense in Scripture: literal, moral, allegorical, and anagogic (the mystical or spiritual meaning of words). This method of interpretation enabled the reader to draw any meaning he pleased from any portion of Scripture. It made it almost hopeless to know precisely what the Bible taught.[35]

In the reformer's vision, true Christianity was founded on "faith alone *(sola fide),*" "grace alone *(sola gratia),*" and "Scripture alone *(sola Scriptura)."* Special emphasis was given to the exclusive authority of Scripture. Luther made this amply clear in his impassioned defense before the imperial Diet of Worms on April 18, 1521: "Unless I am convinced by Scripture and plain reason—I do not accept the authority of popes and councils, for they have contradicted each other—my conscience is captive to the Word of God. I cannot and I will not recant anything, for to go against conscience is neither right nor safe.[36] God help me. Amen."[37]

Luther's exalted view of Scripture and antipathy for religious sham would soon filter into other countries, influencing William Tyndale of England, Ulrich Zwingli of Zurich, John Calvin of Geneva, and John Knox of Scotland. **With a renewed emphasis on "Scripture alone," and a deep-rooted belief in the Bible as the primary source of spiritual growth and maturity, it became incumbent on Luther and the reformers** in lands outside of Germany to provide translations of the Bible in the everyday language of the people.

THE PUBLICATION OF MARTIN LUTHER'S BIBLE

The fundamental concept that convinced Martin Luther to take his historic stand against the established Church—that the Word of God is the final authority in all matters of faith and practice—imposed on him the necessity to render it into the vernacular of his fellow Germans. A little over twelve years he toiled with his co-laborers in completing the translation, thereby opening the Book and making it accessible to the common people of his native land. Stimulated by the example of Luther's translation and by the impetus it gave to Bible study, scholars in other countries, notably William Tyndale in England, soon engaged in its translation into their native tongues. And by no means has Bible translating and revising spent its force. The appearance of Luther's German New Testament in 1522 remains one of the most noteworthy and far-reaching events in the history of the Christian world, indeed, in the history of the world. His Bible introduced mass media, unified a nation, and set the standard for future translations.

The best known statue of Luther depicts him reverently clasping a Bible in his arms. The entire career of the great reformer pointed logically to his translating the Bible into the language of the people. Besides, it was only through the Bible that he had become what he was. It was *to* the Bible that he owed the source of his own religious convictions. It was *through* the Bible that he escaped the confinement of scholastic theology, and it was *in* the Bible that he rediscovered the heart of the Gospel.

The Bible was Luther's chief weapon in his struggle against a thousand-years-old system. By translating the Scriptures into the vernacular, he would be giving to the German people access to the fountain from which he himself was drinking. Now if they followed Luther's teaching, everyone could search the Scriptures for themselves, not only for spiritual guidance, but to see if what they heard from religious authorities was true. The priesthood of the believer was a note sounded repeatedly by Luther and other reformers. By searching the Scriptures for themselves, believers would be exercising their chief duty and the principal birthright of *all* Christians—to function as priests unto God. Luther was convinced that if the common people had the Scriptures in a language they understood, they could hear God speaking to them directly in its pages, and could go to Him for comfort, warning, or instruction.

Luther placed an infallible Bible over against an alleged infallible Church, and reassigned to Scripture the same kind of infallibility that had been presumed to belong to the Roman Catholic Church. In medieval times, people accepted decisions of popes and councils as the last decisive utterance on all matters of controversy in doctrine and morals. In placing the Bible where these popes and councils had been, Luther revealed his conviction that the last and final appeal should be made to its pages. In making the Bible the only rule of faith and practice, Luther rejected the authority of tradition, and consistently gave to the writings of the Church Fathers, the creeds, and devotional literature a subordinate place. He even belittled his own works and those of his co-workers as tending to obscure the Bible itself. All such, he contended, were human productions with no claim to a direct or special inspiration of the Spirit, making their value secondary.

Luther was many things: preacher, teacher, orator, translator, theologian, musician, composer, and family man. But of the many great and noble deeds he accomplished, perhaps none is greater than his translation of the Bible. No other work has had a stronger impact on a nation's development and heritage as has this book. It marks the beginning of a great era of Bible translation, and takes its place among the eminent Bible translations of all time. It was the one event that contributed more to the cause of the Reformation than any other. Prior to the appearance of Luther's New Testament in 1522, numerous German Bibles had circulated, but none of these earlier Bibles or fragments met Luther's two requirements for an acceptable translation: "It should be based on the original texts and should use a German comprehensible to all."[38] Furthermore, Luther insisted in his typically candid manner that "it is no use trying to find out from the Latin how to speak German, as those asses [previous translators] did. You must be guided by their language [ordinary Germans], the way they speak, and do your translating accordingly."[39] Determined that his Bible would be as accurate as possible, Luther based his translation on the original languages—Hebrew and Greek—not the Latin Vulgate as previous German translators had done. Desiring it to be accessible to everyone, he rendered it into idiomatic German.

On his way home from his courageous performance at Worms in 1521, Luther was "kidnapped" by friendly forces and spirited away to the Castle of Wartburg. Condemned as a heretic at the Diet and put under the ban of the Empire, his life was in serious jeopardy. Fearing for his safety, the Elector of Saxony, Frederick the Wise, arranged for Luther to be abducted to the famous old castle for safekeeping. In his voluntary exile, Luther assumed the dress of a knight, grew a beard, and went by the name of "Junker Georg." Only a few trusted friends knew of his whereabouts or even that he was still alive. Now secure in that historic fortress perched on a mountaintop overlooking nothing but vast stretches of woodland, Luther would at last be afforded the necessary leisure from other duties to occupy himself with his greatest achievement—the translation of the New Testament into German. However, the first few months of his exile were spent in study, correspondence with a variety of friends, and polemical treatises dealing with popular issues of the day.

On December 4, 1521, still disguised as Junker Georg, Luther made a brief, clandestine trip to Wittenberg to settle some of the diverse opinions that emerged among co-workers during his absence. While there, his friend Philipp Melanchthon, professor of Greek at Wittenberg University, urged him to pursue his translation of the New Testament.[40] Shortly after returning to the Wartburg, Luther set to work on his projected version. The literary and Biblical tools so necessary to the scholar for so great a task were limited in those days, especially since Luther was isolated from almost all the necessary materials needed for translation work [Greek grammars, Greek dictionaries, commentaries, concordances, etc.]. Compare this with the story of the translation of the King James Bible by about fifty eminent scholars who had access to all the accumulated Bible translations of over two centuries. Luther had two books—the Hebrew Bible and the Greek New Testament—rescued from among his things at the moment of ambush near Altenstein,[41] and only a small sampling of other reference works. The study of the Greek language had only recently been introduced into Western Europe, and the first Greek New Testament (that of Erasmus in 1516) had been published only five years before.

Luther used some of his leisure time at Wartburg to cultivate his knowledge of the Biblical languages, Hebrew and Greek. In a letter to Georg Spalatin early on in his exile, he wrote: "I am both very idle and very busy here. I study Hebrew and Greek and write without ceasing."[42] Moreover the German language was in such a chaotic condition that in no two parts of the country was it spoken or written in the same way. Luther's task would not be an easy one. It is no wonder that he often spoke of the great difficulty with which he was confronted in making inspired men of old speak in the German language. Though faced with a monumental task, Luther was equal to it in every way. His genius was such that in spite of limited helps and the great difficulty of producing a Bible in a language understandable to the majority of Germans, like a man obsessed, he worked so rapidly that within eleven weeks his first draft of the New Testament translation from Greek to German was completed.

The Title Page from Luther's German Bible, 1541

The finished volume, an edition of 3,000 copies (some say 5,000), issued from the press on September 21, 1522, the very day Luther had set for its publication.[43] It is because of its appearance in September that it has been frequently labeled the "September Bible." When a second edition of the New Testament became necessary, it was not Luther's intention to permit a mere reprint of the text. The December edition contains no less than 574 improvements over the first edition.[44] Not only did he correct the typographical errors of the September edition, he also translated many single words altogether differently. Bainton notes that Luther "went to incredible pains to find the right words."[45] Sometimes when at a loss for terms he would set out in quest for words. "In order to name the precious stones in the twenty-first chapter of Revelation he examined the court jewels of the elector of Saxony. For the coins of the Bible he consulted the numismatic collections in Wittenberg.[46] In many instances he changed the word order of the sentences and made improvements in syntax and style. With unwearied diligence Luther labored to perfect his translation. It demonstrated his devotion to his subject and his reverence for the inspired Word of God. Luther continued revising it to the day of his death in 1546.

Not surprisingly, while Luther's New Testament received a warm welcome among the general public, the ecclesiastical authorities in Germany were outraged that a pronounced heretic should tamper with the Bible. They were conspicuously envious that Luther had beaten them to the punch. Cries of protest were heard all the way to Rome. But by this time Luther reveled in his role as provocateur and had become somewhat immune to hostility. He received the criticism with a mixture of resolve and resignation. Ever aware of Rome's obsessive scrutiny of his every word and action, he once commented, "If I break wind in Wittenberg, they hear it in Rome!"[47] Almost immediately, so as to counter the popularity of Luther's Bible, Catholics began producing translations of their own, mostly replicating Luther's text word-for-word except in those sections that needed a Catholic slant.

Luther's New Testament translation was based primarily on the second edition (1519) of Erasmus' Greek New Testament. As Erasmus is credited with publishing the first Greek New Testament (1516), Luther's New Testament has the distinction of being the first version in a modern European language based on the original Greek, not on the official Latin Vulgate.

Work on the Old Testament was begun even before the first edition of the New Testament had left the press. Not long after commencing his work on the Old Testament, Luther made an amusing comment that hinted at the difficulty a translator experiences who attempts to translate from one language to another: "Now I know what it means to translate and why no one has attempted it until now without concealing his name."[48]

Luther's initial step in translating was to comprehend clearly the literal meaning of the Hebrew words. In this his remarkable memory and his rare gifts of distinguishing fine shades of meaning in the use of words served him well. The next step was to express the Hebrew meaning in idiomatic German. "I endeavored," he said, "to make Moses so German that no one would suspect he was a Jew."[49] None of his contemporaries questioned Luther's remarkable command of his native tongue. Even one of his worst enemies, George, Duke of Saxony, said of Luther, "One thing about that absconding monk is you can learn the use of German from him right well."[50]

But Luther found the going much slower in the Old Testament than in the New. In one letter he wrote: "We are now working on the Prophets; great heavens, what a huge and wearisome task it is to make the Hebrew writers speak German. How they dig their toes in, and how unwilling they are to leave their Hebrew ways and follow the coarse German ones. It is like asking a nightingale to abandon its sweet melody and imitate a cuckoo."[51]

Always desirous of finding or coining the right term, Luther would spare no expense or effort to be accurate. When he undertook to translate the second half of the Pentateuch with its detailed laws regarding sacrifices, which carefully differentiated between the various internal organs of the sacrificial animals, his difficulties increased enormously. The solution to his dilemma came when he went to see a butcher, watched him slaughter a few sheep, and carefully noted the familiar German designations for every organ and part as the butcher named them.[52] When he arrived at the building of Solomon's temple, he said: "We shall have our work cut out with this beastly building. . . . How I dislike building Solomon's temple!" But no difficulty dissuaded him. He visited craftsmen in their workshops to get them to explain their tools to him.[53] He endeavored to put the Bible into "pure and clear German, and it often happened that we sought and inquired for a single word for a fortnight, or three or four weeks, and sometimes even then we did not find it . . ."[54]

Looking back over the completed translation, Luther wrote: "Philipp Melanchthon, Matthaeus Aurogallus, and I had to work so hard at this translation that sometimes we could barely translate three lines in four days. Gracious, now that it is translated into German and finished, anyone can read it and get the meaning out of it, peruse three or four pages and find no difficulties; but he doesn't realize with what hardships we had to struggle before we arrived at the translation. Where the reader glides along smoothly, as over a polished surface, we had to sweat and worry to clear the track of obstacles and to fill up the ditches."[55]

Even after Luther put the final touches on his translation, he did not consider his work completed. Presently he formed a special commission which he jokingly dubbed "the Sanhedrin," enlisting the members to join him in revising his translation thoroughly. This was in keeping with his belief that Bible translators should not work alone unless the situation demanded it. "Translators must never work by themselves," he once wrote. "When one is alone, the best and most suitable words do not always occur to him."[56] The revision that resulted represented the combined efforts of the commission. According to minutes of some of these meetings, the commission labored in every instance to find the most accurate and fitting German expression with which to convey to the reader the full meaning of the Hebrew original.

The mere reproduction in German of the literal meaning of every Hebrew word was not considered the ideal translation. Aiming for something better than that, they sought to express the Hebrew words and phrases, as well as the personal attitude of the speaker, in idiomatic German. Gritsch notes that Luther was guided not only by the way German was spoken at the Saxon court; he flavored his translation with words ordinary people used in the marketplace and with "the dialects prevalent along the trade routes and rivers, such as the Meissen German spoken along the River Main."[57] Luther's spirit motivated and guided "the Sanhedrin" in producing a translation that was not woodenly literal. He wanted his Bible to be in spoken rather than bookish or written German.[58]

Frequently there were lively debates about the manner in which a passage should be translated. After the various possibilities had been championed and discussed, Luther would make the final decision. However, in spite of all the painstaking effort to find the correct wording, Luther would sometimes complain, "This is what the Hebrew means, but you can't express it in German."[59] This much can be said with certainty: the committee meetings did much to improve Luther's translation.

When Luther translated the Bible into his Saxon dialect, no standard German existed. He performed his job with such skill that his Bible formed a linguistic rallying point for the formation of the modern German language. Unconsciously he became the creator of the modern German language. Because his Bible sounded natural when spoken as well as read, it remains a popular version among Protestants throughout Germany almost five centuries after it was first published.

As might be expected, the German Bible's impact reached well beyond the borders of Germany. It was the direct source of Bible translations in Holland, Sweden, Iceland, and Denmark, and its influence was felt in many other countries as well.[60] But most important, Luther's Bible, especially his New Testament, left a permanent impression on William Tyndale of English Bible fame. It is incorrect to assert, as Thomas More and other opponents of Tyndale have done, that his translation is merely a reproduction of Luther's German Bible and not from the Greek or Hebrew. It is equally unwarranted to claim that he never used or was not significantly influenced by Luther's translation. Tyndale especially utilized Luther's New Testament in the rendering of some of the Greek idioms.[61] Furthermore, the arrangement of the text on the printed page and the headings minutely follow Luther's lead. In the placement of the New Testament books Tyndale followed Luther, as have almost all English Bible translators since. Two entire pages of Tyndale's "Prologge" (Preface) itself are a literal translation of what constitutes over one-half of Luther's Preface.

Like Luther, Tyndale eschewed the Latinized ecclesiastical terms in favor of those more in conformity with the actual meaning of the Greek term: "repent" instead of "do penance;" "congregation" rather than "church;" "elder" in the place of "priest;" and "love" rather than "charity" for the Greek *agape*. Luther's enduring influence on the "Father of the English Bible" is unmistakable.

Without Luther's Bible, the Reformation in England might never have occurred; indeed the history of the development of the English Bible would have been vastly different. It was Luther more than any other single individual who emboldened Tyndale and his fellow reformers and translators to provide the English-speaking people with a Bible in their native tongue, the result being the inflicting of a lethal blow to Roman Catholic hegemony in England.

THE REIGN OF THE TUDORS

The first of the Tudor monarchs, Henry VII, died in 1509 after a reign of twenty-four years. His flamboyant eighteen-year-old son succeeded him, and would thereafter be known as Henry VIII. Foreign ambassadors vied with each other in praising the handsome and athletic young king, "his auburn hair, his golden beard, his extremely fine calf."[62] Thomas More said of him that he "has more learning than any English monarch ever possessed before him."[63] Henry's accession was hailed as the dawn of a golden age. By his actions in domestic and foreign affairs, he would bring about the most sweeping religious and social changes of the sixteenth century in England.

Six weeks after Henry's accession, he married Catherine of Aragon, his older brother's widow. Henry's elder by six years, Catherine was the daughter of Ferdinand and Isabella of Spain. The marriage was arranged before Henry VII died in order to forge an alliance between England and Spain against France. However, Catherine failed in the most important duty incumbent on a queen in those days: she gave Henry no son to inherit the throne. Only one of her children survived infancy and that was Mary, who would later as queen undertake to suppress the Reformation and establish Catholicism once again as the state religion.

Meanwhile, when Henry turned thirty-four and was in the prime of his young manhood, Catherine was forty and had grown withered and unattractive, looking much older than her years. Henry had become infatuated with Anne Boleyn, a dark-haired lady-in-waiting to the Queen. Whereas Catherine was a devout Catholic, Anne had imbibed Protestant ideas as a young girl while studying in France. Anne's sister Mary had earlier been the mistress of Henry, and now that that relationship had cooled, Henry sought after a new paramour and set his sights on Anne. But strong-willed Anne possessed enough moral courage to inform the King that if she could not be his wife, she would not share his bed. She maintained this resolve for a number of years before succumbing to the King's advances, but only after he pledged matrimony.

After resolving to marry Anne, Henry ordered Cardinal Thomas Wolsey, Chancellor of the Realm and Papal Legate to England, to hasten to Rome and secure a papal annulment of his marriage to Catherine. Annulments were not uncommon in this era; monarchs often received them as political favors from popes. But in this instance Pope Clement VII was being pressured from another quarter. Holy Roman Emperor Charles V was loath to sever the fragile link he had with England through his Aunt Catherine, Henry's wife. With his army stationed in Italy, Charles threatened violence if the Pope sanctioned the divorce. The Pope wavered between his two options, then decided to postpone the decision. When Wolsey returned to England empty-handed, Henry dismissed him from office in 1529 and took matters in his own hands.

Henry now proceeded cautiously but quickly to make the break from Rome. The kings of England had long been disenchanted with the papacy, since so much English money flowed into the pope's coffers. For reasons other than the unwillingness of the Pope to grant an annulment, Henry knew that now was the propitious time to act. Sometime in November, 1532, Henry and Anne were secretly married. Contrary to Catholic rumour, she was not pregnant at the time. Henry then appointed a new Archbishop of Canterbury, Thomas Cranmer, a friend of the Boleyn family, whom he instructed to declare his marriage to Catherine void on the grounds that it had been illegal in the first place. Cranmer obliged and on May 28, 1533, Anne was crowned Queen of England. Pope Clement retaliated by excommunicating Henry (July 11, 1533), declaring his new marriage null and void, and its future offspring illegitimate. On September 7, the future Queen Elizabeth was born.

By the Act of Supremacy on November 11, 1534, Henry had Parliament name him and his successors supreme head on earth of the Church of England, giving him the right to make all ecclesiastical appointments, and requiring all clergymen to swear allegiance to him instead of the Pope. By the Act of Dissolution Henry dissolved most of the monasteries, a not too unpopular decision, because for years the wealth and moral laxity of these religious houses provoked criticism among the rank and file. The monks were given the option of joining the few monasteries that remained, or of entering the secular clergy. Most of the spoils of the monasteries went to the Crown or to the Tudor nobility and gentry. Thus began the slow process of moving the state away from the iron clutches of Roman Catholicism.

Queen Anne Boleyn, with her strong Protestant sympathies, deserves more credit than is usually given her for the ultimate triumph of Protestantism in England. In fact, it is not too much to say that she was more instrumental than Henry in setting the tone for this major religious upheaval in England; and it was the chief reason she was so hated and slandered by Catholic authorities. Staunch Roman Catholic, Sir Thomas Tresham of Rushton, admitted Anne's influence:

> Anne Boleyn, the bane of that virtuous and religious Queen Katherine, the ruin of many pious, worthy and famous men who favored not that unlawful marriage, the first giver of entrance to the Protestant religion . . .[64]

John Foxe echoes a similar sentiment:

> What a zealous defender Anne was of Christ's gospel all the world doth know, and her acts do and will declare to the world's end."[65]

Anne was twenty-six years old when she became Queen and only twenty-nine when she was executed for treason against the King. Her brief reign of just under three years prompted the well-known nickname, "Anne of the Thousand

Days." The seven or eight years she spent in France as a young, impressionable student transformed her into an extremely committed and articulate advocate of the "new faith" (as it was termed before "Protestantism" became the common label). These revolutionary ideas came to her from a French Bible, from French commentaries on Scripture, and from the Reformist poetry of Clement Marot.[66]

Active in promoting Christian education and scholarship, she often read and discussed Protestant literature and especially the Bible with other educated women at court. In the short span of time she served as Queen, her convincing proposals to Henry regarding policy matters of great moment affected extraordinary changes in England for centuries to come. Her contemporaries believed that she swayed Henry to dissolve the monasteries, and saw her as a key figure in the reforming group around the King.[67] She was a strong supporter of Thomas Cromwell and Thomas Cranmer, the first the head of state, the other of the church, and both eager to institute the new Reformation principles.

Especially noteworthy is Anne's influence in championing the dissemination of a vernacular Bible for her English subjects to read.[68] A copy of Tyndale's revised 1534 New Testament, bound in vellum, was presented to her with her coat of arms stamped on the title page. Although a banned book at the time, the Queen must have treasured it, else it almost certainly would have been destroyed. Thomas Cromwell, Thomas Cranmer, and no doubt Anne herself were instrumental in persuading Henry to allow the publication in England of a vernacular Bible. Anne was said to be "the principal cause of the spread of Lutheranism in [England]."[69] In fact, some of her Catholic adversaries would go so far as to call Anne "the Martin Luther of England." Her religious policies made her the bitter antagonist of the Catholic Church. Soon they began spreading malicious rumors about her supposed moral indiscretions. Convinced the rumors were true, Henry confined

Anne to the Tower where she would be eventually beheaded. It is no exaggeration to say that Anne Boleyn was one of the most influential people in the history of the English-speaking world.

Though Henry was somewhat ambivalent toward and even opposed to certain aspects of the Reformation, nevertheless, he was the first monarch to fully authorize the printing and distribution of an English Bible, the Great Bible of 1539. In May 1541, a royal proclamation ordered every parish church to have a copy for public use of the Great Bible.

The Bible continued to be published and distributed in England after the death of Henry, but not for long. Henry's young but fragile son, Edward VI, succeeded to the throne in 1547 at the tender age of nine. His advisors were staunchly Protestant, assuring the free flow of Scripture during his brief six-year reign. Things would change radically when Mary Tudor, the daughter of Henry VIII and Catherine, ascended the throne in 1553. Instructed by strict Catholics in her youth, Mary determined to censor Protestants and prevent the distribution of Scripture. Using threats of imprisonment and capital punishment to those who opposed her, Mary was able in part to succeed in rolling back the effects of Protestantism. Labeled "Bloody Mary" because of the almost 300 Protestants who were burned at the stake during her reign, mercifully she only lived five years after her coronation.

Next in line to the throne was Elizabeth, Mary's half-sister and the daughter of Henry VIII and Anne Boleyn. The last monarch of the Tudor dynasty, Elizabeth reigned from 1558 to 1603. Her long reign is remembered for many reasons, chief of which was the reinstitution of Protestantism as the state religion in England. She set in motion once again the reforming policies of her mother, and to some extent of her father. With the defeat of the Spanish Armada in 1588 (an attempt by the Spanish to reclaim England for Roman Catholicism), Protestantism took firm root in England for the first time. Though not sympathetic to the Puritan element in the Church of England (those who sought to "purify" the Church of Roman Catholic tendencies), she sought to be tolerant of most of those who objected to her policies. Like her mother, Anne Boleyn, Elizabeth was a devoted student of Scripture and gave encouragement to the distribution of the English Bible among her subjects. The Geneva Bible (1560) was dedicated to her and went through sixty editions during her reign. The Bishops' Bible (1568) had a large portrait of Queen Elizabeth on its title page. Both of these actions were indicators that the ones responsible for those versions believed they had a person who lent strong support to their efforts.

These noteworthy events: *the Renaissance, the defeat of Constantinople, the invention of printing, the appearance of Erasmus' Greek/Latin New Testament, the Reformation, the publication of Martin Luther's Bible, and the reign of the Tudors,* all joined in concert to serve as useful allies of William Tyndale and future English Bible translators.

Chapter Five

THE FATHER OF THE ENGLISH BIBLE

Beginning in about 1517, according to tradition, a group of college lecturers and students began to meet regularly at the White Horse Inn, a tavern near Cambridge University, in England. They met there to talk about the stirring events just beginning to take place in Germany, led by the brilliant young monk Martin Luther. Luther's writings were the main topic of conversation. There seems to have been no secret about their meetings, for the inn became known as "Germany," or "Little Germany" to all the university.[1] The young men among the group were fired by the prospects of change and reform; as Thomas More put it, "yonge scolers be somtyme prone to new fantasyes" and become "newfangly mynded."[2]

From this little group of Cambridge men would come some of the outstanding leaders of the Protestant Reformation. Among the "obscure" students were Robert Barnes, Thomas Bilney, John Frith, John Lambert, and Rowland Taylor, all of whom were to be burned at the stake; future bishops, Hugh Latimer, Nicolas Ridley, Miles Coverdale, Richard Cox, and future archbishops Thomas Cranmer and Matthew Parker. Latimer, Ridley, and Cranmer would also be consigned to the flames. But no figure in this group would make a more indelible mark on the future of the English Church, the English Bible and the English language than an earnest young student of Scripture named William Tyndale.

Born in about 1494 to a prosperous family in Gloucestershire near the Welsh border, Tyndale spent his early childhood years in obscurity. Nothing of certainty is known of that formative period of his life. Even the exact location of his birth has been a matter of dispute for centuries, with several villages in the Cotswold district claiming bragging rights as the legitimate place.[3] At age twelve, in about 1506, the young prodigy went up to the University of Oxford, to Magdalen Hall. There, according to historian John Foxe, Tyndale,

> by long continuance increased in the knowledge of tongues and other liberal arts, [and] especially in **the knowledge of the Scriptures, whereunto his mind was singularly addicted;** insomuch that he, [residing] then in Magdalen College, read privily to certain students and fellows of Magdalen College some parcel of divinity, instructing them in the knowledge and truth of the Scriptures. His manners and conversation, being correspondent to the same, were such that all they that knew him reputed him to be a man of most virtuous disposition and of life unspotted.[4]

Tyndale's lifelong love of the Bible and his earnest desire to share its truths with others were nurtured at Oxford. The first undisputed fact that emerges from his stay was that he received his B.A. in July 1512, and his M.A. in Philosophy in 1515. On the record books at Oxford he is listed as William Hychyns, a name used by some of his family.[5]

Sometime around 1517 Tyndale left Oxford for Cambridge. No one knows precisely why Tyndale chose to leave Oxford to further his training at the rival school. The most plausible explanation seems to be that Cambridge was more favorably disposed than Oxford to Reformation ideas recently imported from Germany. Furthermore, Erasmus, the famous Renaissance scholar, had taught at Cambridge from 1510 to 1514, infusing humanism among both students and professors. Apparently Tyndale had already been exposed to the writings of Erasmus and Luther; now he desired additional exposure, prompting him to remove to Cambridge. Little is known of Tyndale's stay in Cambridge except for a brief blurb in Foxe, "Spying his time, [Tyndale] removed from thence [Oxford] to the University of Cambridge, where he . . . made his abode a certain space. Being now further ripened in the knowledge of God's word . . ."[6]

Though Tyndale never referred to his reasons for attending Cambridge, his sojourn there proved to be a defining time in his life. During those days, a fire began to burn within him to translate the Bible into English from the original languages—Hebrew and Greek. No one had ever done that before. His reason for pressing to get the Bible into the English tongue was simple and direct:

> **I perceived by experience how that it was impossible to establish the laypeople in any truth, except the Scripture were plainly laid before their eyes in their mother tongue, that they might see the process, order, and meaning of the text . . . else whatsoever truth is taught them, these enemies of all truth quench it again . . . with apparent reasons of sophistry and traditions of their own making, founded without [basis] in Scripture; and partly in juggling with the text, expounding it in such a sense as is impossible to gather of the text.[7]**

We can only assume that Cambridge is where Tyndale learned the necessary fundamentals of Biblical Greek, a knowledge that served him well during his future work on the New Testament. While Tyndale resided at Cambridge, Luther's revolutionary view on *the doctrine of justification by faith* was spreading like wildfire through the campus, unsettling some and confirming the faith of others. This teaching, that Christ gives salvation to those who turn to Him directly and place their total trust in Him without any mediation of priests or penances imposed by a hierarchical church, became the rallying cry for Tyndale and other English Reformation leaders. Furthermore, it served as a compelling reason for every person to be able to understand the Bible as directly as possible without hindrance of language or tradition.

TYNDALE BECOMES A PRIVATE TUTOR

It may have been shortly after Tyndale was ordained a priest, sometime around 1521, that he left the university world to join the household of Sir John Walsh at Little Sodbury where he served as a private tutor to the Walsh children. Little Sodbury was north of Bristol and not too many miles from Tyndale's birthplace. Some of the local clergy often came to dine at the Walsh manor house, which gave Tyndale ample opportunity to witness firsthand their ignorance of the Bible and to become engaged in theological disputes with them. Many have testified of the gross ignorance of the clergy in those days. Some years later in the reign of Edward VI, Bishop Hooper of Gloucester examined 322 clergy. Of these, "168 were unable to repeat the Ten Commandments, 31 could not tell where they came from, 40 were unable to repeat the Lord's Prayer, and about 40 could not name the author."[8]

The Constitutions of Oxford in 1408 had expressly forbidden the translation of any portion of Scripture into English or the reading of such a translation without the approval of the bishop, an approval not likely to be granted. Hence, it comes as no great surprise that the clergy were ignorant of basic Bible doctrines. The Bible was not even a part of the preparatory study of priests. Tyndale expressed his own disappointment with the theological training he received at Oxford. McGrath notes that Tyndale's professors "seemed to give the study of Aristotle priority over mastering the Bible. In an autobiographical fragment, Tyndale recalled how the Oxford authorities 'ordained that no man shall look in the Scripture until he be nuzzled in heathen learning eight or nine years and armed with false principles with which he is clean shut out of the understanding of Scripture.'"[9]

On one occasion in Little Sodbury, a certain unlearned and biased clergyman who had heard of Tyndale's intention to translate the Bible into the English tongue, confronted him and insolently voiced his objection: "It were better to be without God's laws [the Bible] than the Pope's." Tyndale came back with his famous response, "I defy the Pope and all his laws; and if God spare my life, ere many years, **I will cause a boy that driveth the plow to know more of the Scripture than thou dost.**"[10]

The outspoken young scholar caused many anxious moments for his hostess, Lady Anne Walsh, who reminded him that well-paid, respected bishops and abbots held views contrary to his, and "were it reason, think you," she said, "that we should believe you before them?"[11] In order to strengthen his position with his cautious hostess, Tyndale chose to translate Erasmus' *Enchiridion militis Christiani* ("*Handbook of a Christian Soldier*") for the sole purpose of winning her, her husband Sir John, and other skeptics over to his viewpoint. Erasmus' fame was resounding throughout Europe at the time, and his words were sure to lend credence to Tyndale's attempt to persuade Sir John and Lady Anne. Tyndale's plan had its desired effect. Walsh and his wife were won over to his point of view, and the clergy were no longer invited.[12]

Tyndale did not play the part of a cloistered monk while remaining with the Walsh family. He would often preach in the nearby little church of St. Adeline and even on St. Austin's Green in Bristol, about fifteen miles distant. The clergy fiercely attacked his straightforward preaching. "When they come together to the alehouse," said Tyndale, "which is their preaching place, they affirm that my sayings are heresy. And besides that they add to of their own heads which I never spake" [i.e., "they accuse me of saying things I never said."][13]

The situation in Gloucestershire became increasingly precarious for Tyndale. According to Foxe, the priests hounded him continually, charging him with heresy in philosophy, logic and theology. They secretly accused him before the Chancellor of the diocese, who, when Tyndale appeared before him, "threatened me grievously," he said, "and reviled me, and rated me as though I had been a dog."[14] Tyndale promptly went to Walsh and asked permission to leave his service. Not only was it hazardous for him to stay; he wisely recognized it might prove to be risky for his host as well.

Tyndale was aware that his desire to "English" the Bible resonated with the common people of England. Many of them aspired to have a Bible they could read and understand on their own, that was affordable and could be kept in their homes. But it was still illegal in England to own an English Bible, a result of the law imposed more than a hundred years earlier (1408). Faced with this anomaly, Sir Thomas More, Tyndale's chief antagonist and the Pope's leading apologist in England, suggested that small sections of the Bible might be loaned to carefully selected people. But they were not to get together so that someone could see the whole Bible in English, for to do so could result in death by burning. More and his Catholic accomplices were afraid that if laypeople were allowed to read the Bible, they might discover that profitable Church practices such as indulgences, purgatory, and the adoration of relics, were not in the Bible at all.

Tyndale resented the fact that people were deprived of a Bible. In his book *The Obedience of a Christian Man* he censures the Church for its "threatening and forbidding lay people to read the Scripture." The Church was not motivated in this attitude by love for the souls of their parishioners, "which they care for," Tyndale caustically notes, "as the fox doth for the geese."[15]

In his preface to *The Five Books of Moses* (1530), Tyndale wrote,

> A thousand books had they (Catholics) rather to be put forth against their abominable doings and doctrine, than that the Scripture should come to light. For as long as they may keep that down, they will so darken the right way with the mist of their sophistry . . . and with wresting the Scripture unto their own purpose clean contrary unto the process, order and meaning of the text; and so delude them in [commenting] upon it with allegories, and amaze them

expounding it in many senses before the unlearned lay people (when it hath but one simple literal sense whose light the owls [biased priests] cannot abide), yet couldst thou not solve their subtle riddles.[16]

The law banning English translations of the Bible unless authorized by the Church proved to be a huge obstacle for Tyndale. He would need ecclesiastical approval to get his Bible published, or he likely could be accused of heresy and possibly burned. Although he had differences with Catholic doctrine and tradition, he was a priest and he intended if possible to go through the proper channels to accomplish his purpose.

TYNDALE SEEKS A BISHOP'S PATRONAGE

Tyndale went to London to obtain an interview with Bishop of London, Cuthbert Tunstall, hoping for his patronage. In the preface to his Pentateuch, he gives his reason for doing so:

As I thought, the bishop of London came to my remembrance whom Erasmus (whose tongue maketh of little gnats great elephants and lifteth up above the stars whosoever giveth him a little exhibition) praiseth exceedingly among other in his annotations on the new testament for his learning . . . And even in the bishop of London's house I intended to have done it (i.e., the translation of the Bible) . . .[17]

Tunstall had assisted Erasmus with the second edition of his Greek New Testament and even loaned him a Greek New Testament manuscript. It therefore seemed likely to Tyndale that the Bishop would look with favor on his translation project.

To demonstrate his ability as a translator of Greek, Tyndale brought to London a translation he had done of an oration of Isocrates. He gave the copy to Harry Gilford, the King's controller, and requested that he give it to the Bishop, which he did. Tyndale then went himself to the Bishop's residence and spoke of his intentions. Not surprisingly, Tyndale's request fell on deaf ears. The Bishop's rebuff greatly disillusioned Tyndale. Later, after his translation was published and he could reflect on the Bishop's refusal to grant patronage, as well as on the deplorable religious state in London, Tyndale wrote:

> But God which knoweth what is within hypocrites saw that I was beguiled, and that that counsel was not the new way to my purpose. And therefore he got me no favor in my lord's sight. . . . And so in London I abode almost a year, and marked the course of the world, and heard our praters, I would say, our preachers, how they boasted themselves and their high authority, and beheld the pomp of our prelates . . . and saw things whereof I defer to speak at this time, and understood at the last not only there was no room in my lord of London's palace to translate the New Testament, but also that there was no place to do it in all England, as experience doth now openly declare.[18]

In Little Sodbury, Tyndale was exposed to the ignorance of the clergy. In London, he witnessed the corruption and hypocrisy of clerics, which he vividly denounces in his book, *The Practice of Prelates,* written in 1530. He was as outspoken as Wycliffe had been, calling the monks and friars "caterpillars," "horseleeches," "drone bees," and "draff" [refuse]. The bishops he called "bishaps" (half-man, half-mishap).[19] Vulgarity was common in Tyndale's day and he was not loath to use it. He reminded bishops that "to preach is their duty only and not to offer their feet to be kissed."[20] He described Cardinal Wolsey as "this wily wolf, and raging sea, and shipwreck of all England."[21] This is not the sort of language moderns expect from one who translates the Bible, but Tyndale, though brilliant, was a plainspoken man whose language was always direct and to the point. His New Testament would reflect his liveliness and candor.

In 1523, when Tyndale attempted to obtain the sanction of Bishop Tunstall to translate the Bible into English, England remained the only European country without a printed vernacular translation of the Bible. In fact, by the time Luther finished his translation of the New Testament in 1522, more than fifteen German translations of the Bible were already in circulation. To Tyndale, the lack of a printed English Bible from the original languages was an intolerable deprivation that he intended to rectify.

LEAVES ENGLAND FOR GERMANY

Not one to give up easily, Tyndale found lodging in the home of wealthy London cloth merchant Humphrey Monmouth who was sympathetic to his cause. No doubt Tyndale worked on his translation during the year or so that he lodged with Monmouth. With the financial backing of Monmouth and other wealthy English merchants, Tyndale resolved to leave the country and engage in the work of translation on the Continent. In 1524 he sailed across the Channel to Germany, never to see his native land again. Because of a bounty on his head, he developed an uncanny ability to dodge the persistent Roman Catholic authorities, living a hand-to-mouth existence, always managing to stay a step ahead of his dogged pursuers. Like the apostle Paul, Tyndale could say, "I die daily."

First he journeyed to Hamburg, then "he made his way to the little town [Wittenberg] that had suddenly become the sacred city of the Reformation. Students of many nations were flocking there with an enthusiasm that resembled that of the Crusades."[22] "As they came in sight of the town," a contemporary tells us, "they returned thanks to God with clasped hands, for from Wittenberg, as previously from Jerusalem, the light of evangelical truth had spread to the utmost parts of the earth."[23] Here it is likely he consulted with Luther, and may even have attended Wittenberg University for a period of time to study Hebrew. Such a visit could only embolden Tyndale's determination to face the poverty, exile, bitter absence from friends, great dangers, and other innumerable difficulties that would accompany his work.

The ᵃ* Gospell of Saint
Mathewe.

❡ The first Chapter.

❡ The Genealogie of Chryst, and maryage of
his mother Mary. The Aungell satisfieth
Josephes mynde.

The ᵇ* Boke of the generation of Jesus Chryst, the sonne of Dauid, the sonne of Abraham.

The Gospell on the Sund. after Chrystmas.

Abraham begat Isaac.
Isaac begat Jacob.
Jacob begat Judas and his brethren.
Judas begat Phares and Zaram of ᶜ* Thamar.
Phares begat Hesrom.
Hesrom begat Aram.
Aram begat Aminadab.
Aminadab begat Naasson.
Naasson begat Salmon.
Salmon begat Booz of ᴰ* Rachab.
Booz begat Obed of Ruth.
Obed begat Jesse.
Jesse begat Dauid the kyng.
Dauid the kyng begat Salomon, of her that was the wyfe of Urye.
Salomon begat Roboam.
Roboam begat Abia.
Abia begat Asa.
Asa begat Josaphat.
Jesaphat begat Joram.

A.i.   Joram

Chapter One of Matthew's Gospel from Tyndale's
New Testament, 1562

108

All this time Tyndale worked on his translation of the New Testament, assisted by his amanuensis, a lapsed friar by the name of William Roye.[24] The Testament was ready for the press by the following year (1525). He and Roye moved to Cologne, where they found a printer by the name of Peter Quentell and the pages began to roll off the press. But one of the printers drank too much one night and spoke a little too freely to an opponent of Tyndale's, Johann Cochlaeus, who was also having work done at the same print shop. Cochlaeus notified authorities who arranged for a raid on the press, but Tyndale had been warned just in time. Seizing the pages already printed and barely escaping capture, Tyndale and Roye moved up the Rhine River to Worms, a city whose Lutheran sympathies made the atmosphere more conducive to his translation work.

THE FIRST PRINTED ENGLISH NEW TESTAMENT

It was in Worms that the first complete New Testament printed in English was published in February, 1526. These pocket-sized New Testaments could not be shipped to England through ordinary channels. Considered contraband goods, they had to be smuggled in bales of cloth, sacks of flour, and other goods of trade; then ferried by boat down the Rhine and across the Channel to English ports.

Almost immediately the New Testaments caused a furor. The people wanted to read them and the Church wanted to burn them! Only weeks before the New Testaments were first off-loaded at English ports, Edward Lee, Henry VIII's almoner[25] and a future archbishop of York, wrote the king, warning him of the imminent arrival of the contraband New Testaments and the grave consequences should people be allowed to read them:

> Please it your highness moreover to understand that I am certainly informed as I passed in this country, that an Englishman, your subject, at the solicitation and instance of

Luther, with whom he is, hath translated the new testament into English, and within four days intendeth to arrive with the same imprinted in England. I need not to advertise your grace, what infection and danger may ensue hereby, if it be not withstood. This is the next way to fill your realm with Lutherans, for all Luther's perverse opinions be grounded upon bare words of scripture not well taken nor understood, which your grace hath opened in sundry places of your royal book. All our forefathers, governors of the Church of England hath with all diligence forbade and eschewed publication of English Bibles, as appeareth in constitutions provincial of the Church of England. Now sir as God hath endued your grace with Christian courage to set forth the standard against these Philistines, and to vanquish them, so I doubt not that he will assist your grace to prosecute and perform the same . . . I thought my duty to advertise your grace thereof, considering that it toucheth your high honor, and the wealth and integrity of the Christian faith within your realm which cannot long endure, if these books may come in . . .[26]

Soon after the New Testaments began to circulate among the English, Cardinal Wolsey and the bishops consulted together on the subject of Tyndale's translation, and published a prohibition against it in all their dioceses. Charging it with false and heretical glosses brought in to corrupt the Word of God, they demanded that it and all "untrue translations" should be burned.[27] Sir Thomas More especially objected to its anti-ecclesiastical slant. Tyndale substituted "congregation" for "church," "elder" for "priest," "love" for "charity,"[28] and "repentance" for "do penance."[29]

Because London was the most affected by the distribution of the New Testament, Bishop of London, Cuthbert Tunstall, issued an injunction to his archdeacons on October 24, 1526:

Certain children of iniquity, maintainers of Luther's sect, blinded by extreme wickedness, declining from the way of truth and the orthodox faith, have with crafty trickery translated the holy gospel of God into our vulgar English tongue, intermingling certain articles of heretical depravity and pernicious erroneous opinions, pestilent, scandalous, and seductive of simple minds, and have endeavored by their nefarious and crooked interpretations to profane the hitherto undefiled majesty of holy scripture, and cunningly and perversely to abuse the most sacred Word of God, and the right sense of the same. Of which translation many books, containing the pestilent and pernicious poison in the vulgar tongue, have been dispersed in great numbers throughout our diocese; which truly, unless it be speedily foreseen, will without doubt infect and contaminate the flock committed to us with the pestilent poison and deadly disease of heretical depravity, to the grievous peril of the souls committed to us and the most grievous offence of the divine majesty.[30]

Tunstall particularly disliked Tyndale's marginal notes, some of which were critical of the pope and the Roman church. A rousing sermon against the new translation was preached by Tunstall at St. Paul's Cross in London,[31] warning the people of the consequences of reading it, hearing it read, or possessing it. He decreed that all Tyndale's New Testaments be destroyed. A vigorous attempt was made by Church authorities to confiscate as many of them as possible. Hundreds of the New Testaments were ritually consigned to the flames at St. Paul's Cross in London in the autumn of 1526. Other such ritual burnings took place at Oxford and Antwerp. The campaign was so successful that, of the six thousand copies printed in 1526, only three copies remain today: one in the British Library, complete except for the title page; an incomplete textual copy in St. Paul's Cathedral; and a third copy in the Stuttgart Museum in Germany, the only complete copy extant.

Hollywood canonized Sir Thomas More as a courageous, genial man of conviction and restraint in the award-winning movie, "A Man for All Seasons;" and more often than not More exhibited those qualities. But More displayed his dark side when

Tyndale's Testament invaded England. He detested the new translation and became Tyndale's bitterest critic and the Pope's foremost apologist against Reformation principles in England. In his *The Dialogue Concerning Tyndale* he labeled Tyndale "a beast," discharging a "filthy foam of blasphemies out of his brutish mouth;" "the great master antichrist;" "a shameful, shameless, unreasonable, railing ribald;" "a hellhound" fit for "the hogs of hell to feed upon;" and "the son of the devil himself."[32] He claimed that the translation was not the New Testament at all, but rather "a cunning counterfeit, perverted in the interests of heresy."[33]

Meanwhile Bishop Tunstall devised a plan to thwart Tyndale's attempts to get his Testaments in the hands of the people. He determined to buy up the whole supply and destroy them before they could be distributed in England. On a trip to Antwerp, the bishop met with London merchant, August Packington, who was thought to know the sources of supply of the Testaments. The bishop told Packington of his proposal and promised to pay him generously for every copy he could get his hands on; for, as the bishop said, "the books are erroneous and naughty, and I intend surely to destroy them all, and to burn them at St. Paul's Cross."[34]

Packington assured the bishop he would assist him in carrying out his plan. What the bishop did not know was that Packington was acquainted with and had a high regard for Tyndale. When Tyndale heard from Packington of the bishop's scheme, his response was quite unexpected. "Well, I am gladder," he said, "for these two benefits shall come thereof: I shall get money of him for these books to bring myself out of debt, and the whole world shall cry out upon the burning of God's Word. And the overplus of the money that shall remain to me shall make me more studious to correct the said New Testament and so newly to imprint the same once again." "And so," the story goes, "forward went the bargain. The bishop had the books, Packington had the thanks, and Tyndale had the money."[35] Tyndale's plans were unwittingly fulfilled—at the Catholic Church's expense. Whether this quaint story is altogether true no one knows for certain. Mozley concludes that the story doesn't agree with itself about who owns the books that are being sold; but that little discrepancy aside, the story definitely has the ring of truth about it.[36]

No sooner had Tyndale finished translating the New Testament than he began revising it. The new edition appeared in 1534, the same year Martin Luther's complete German Bible was published. Tyndale's revised New Testament with corrections and revisions was printed in Antwerp, not Worms, as the first edition was.

In the meantime, Tyndale continued working on his translation of the Old Testament. In 1531, his translation of the Book of Jonah was finished. According to Foxe in his *Book of Martyrs,* when Tyndale was shipwrecked on the Dutch coast, he lost his translation of Deuteronomy. But he continued on to Antwerp, where he retranslated Deuteronomy and finished translating the Pentateuch. It is believed Tyndale also completed the historical books through 2 Chronicles.[37] Tyndale's prepared notes on other Old Testament books were used by his friend, John Rogers, in the so-called Matthew's Bible, published in 1537.

It is doubtful if anyone of that era was better qualified as a linguist than Tyndale. Buschius, a humanist and contemporary of Tyndale's referred to him as "an Englishman . . . who is so skilful in seven tongues, Hebrew, Greek, Latin, Italian, Spanish, English, French, that whichever he speaks, you would think it his native tongue."[38] His knowledge of Greek and Hebrew enabled him to translate directly from those original languages, with occasional references to the Latin Vulgate and Luther's German translation.[39] His style was simple and intended for the ordinary layperson. He kept his original aim to make the Bible accessible to "plowboys," not merely to the religious elite.

The Title Page from Tyndale's New Testament, 1550

BETRAYED AND ARRESTED

In Antwerp, Tyndale met a man named Henry Phillips, a devout Roman Catholic, who professed to be an ardent supporter of the Reformation. Using that ruse, he insinuated himself into Tyndale's life, finally becoming his close confidant. Phillips was a man of questionable reputation who robbed his own father and would stoop to almost anything to obtain money to pay his gambling debts. Because of the bounty, Phillips was eager to collect the money promised to the person responsible for turning Tyndale over to authorities. Phillips betrayed Tyndale directly into the hands of the imperial authorities who arrested him, charged him with heresy, and confined him in the prison at Vilvorde Castle, an impregnable fortress just north of Brussels, where he remained for exactly five hundred days before being executed.

We are given only one glimpse of him during his incarceration, but it is a very moving one. It was a letter written in Latin and addressed to the Marquis of Bergen as the winter of 1535/36 drew on:

> I believe, most illustrious sir, that you are not unaware of what has been decided concerning me. I therefore beg your lordship, and that by the Lord Jesus, that if I am to stay here through the winter, you will ask the officer to be good enough to send me from my goods which he has, a warmer cap. I suffer greatly from cold in the head, and have a perpetual catarrh, which is made worse in this cell. A warmer coat too, for the one I have is very thin, and also a piece of cloth with which to patch my leggings. My overcoat is worn out, and so are my shirts. He has a woolen shirt of mine, if he will be good enough to send it. Also he has my leggings of thicker material to go on top, and my warmer night cap. I ask to be allowed to have a lamp in the evening, for it is wearisome to sit alone in the dark. But most of all I beg and beseech your clemency to be urgent with the commissary, that he will kindly permit me to have my Hebrew Bible, Hebrew Grammar and Hebrew

Dictionary so that I may pass the time in that study. And in return may you be granted your greatest desire, so only that it be for the salvation of your soul. But if before winter is over any other decision has been made about me, I will be patient, abiding the will of God to the glory of the grace of my Lord Jesus Christ, whose Spirit (I pray) may ever direct your heart. Amen. W. Tindalus.[40]

Whether or not his requests were granted we do not know, although the plea that he might have his Hebrew Bible, grammar and dictionary may well have been approved. Tradition has it that even in the unfriendly confines of the prison, Tyndale pressed forward with his translation work. During this time he may have completed a manuscript translation of Joshua, Judges, Ruth, Samuel, Kings, and Chronicles, and perhaps even other Old Testament books.

Foxe claims that Tyndale was not too preoccupied with the discomfort of his confinement or his studies in prison that he neglected to witness to his captors. He was able to convert his keeper and his keeper's daughter. Others among the castle staff, impressed by his fortitude and sincerity, said to one another that if Tyndale "were not a good Christian man, they could not tell whom they might take to be one."[41] Even Pierre Dufief, the ferocious prosecutor, agreed that "his prisoner was *homo doctor, pius et bonus,*" a learned, pious and fine man.[42]

About a year after penning the prison letter, in early August of 1536, Tyndale was brought to trial for heresy. He acted as his own lawyer during the trial, no doubt making an impassioned plea for justification by faith and the urgent need for a translation in the vernacular. But his words fell on deaf ears. Under the Decree of Augsburg (1530), "death was to be imposed on anyone subscribing to justification by faith." Condemned as a heretic, he was defrocked, and delivered to the secular authorities for punishment. Thomas Poyntz, who ran the English merchants' house where Tyndale lodged in Antwerp, made a valiant attempt to secure Tyndale's release, endangering his own life in the process, but it proved to be futile. Henry VIII, who always thought of Tyndale as an enemy, did nothing to help the reformer; hence, Tyndale's execution was inevitable. Had not Anne Boleyn been executed a few months earlier, Tyndale's life might well have been spared. A staunch advocate of Bible distribution, Anne could have possibly used her influence to save Tyndale from his fate.

MARTYR

Tradition has it that on the morning of October 6, 1536, after local officials took their seats, Tyndale was led to the place of execution in the middle of the Vilvorde town square. Among the curious crowd that day there must have been some of Tyndale's Antwerp friends. They were surely moved to pity mingled with admiration as the frail, disheveled figure walked with a firm and dignified step towards the pile of wood. Tyndale ascended the platform, where his outer garments were stripped from him. Forced to stand in front of a large wooden stake, he was bound to it by a chain around his upper body and another around his legs to prevent escape. At neck level in the stake, a hole had been drilled, through which a hemp rope was threaded around the neck of the victim. Tyndale was given one last chance to recant. He refused to do so. Historian John Foxe in his *Book of Martyrs* revealed that Tyndale's last words were a prayer, "Lord, open the King of England's eyes."[43] When the procurer-general gave the signal, the executioner immediately tightened the rope, mercifully snuffing the life out before the fire was kindled.

In a matter of hours, this great and noble man was reduced to a heap of ashes; however, let it never be thought that his mission was terminated and his influence forever extinguished. His words would live on; indeed his death conferred validity to the dictum, "The blood of the martyrs is the seed of the church." He had not finished what he set out to do, but in no sense of the word can it be said that his mission was stillborn. His death created a sensation that inspired many of his countrymen with a

Sozatꝛ, ꝭ ꝭ ꝭ ꝭ
taꝛeth.

at that tyme about rii. oꝛ riii. weakes, so he taried not the commyng agayne of the messenger, but in a nyghte by a meane he conueyed hym selfe. And so by Gods helpe at the openyng of the towne gate in the moꝛnyng gatt alway. And whē it was perceyued that he was gone, there was hoꝛse sent out after hym, but by the meanes that he knewe well the contrey escaped and came into Englande. But what moꝛe trouble folowed to Poyntꝛ of the same, it serueth not foꝛ this place to rehearse. Maister Tyndall styll remayning in pꝛyson,

was pꝛoffered an Aduocate and a Procurour, foꝛ in any cryme there, it shall be permitted to counsell to make aunswere in the lawe, the whiche he refused to haue anye, but sayde, he would make aunswere foꝛ hym selfe, and did. But it is to be thought his aunswere wyl not be put foꝛth, notwithstandyng he had so pꝛeached to them there who hadde hym in charge, and suche as was theyꝛ conuersaunt with him in the Castel, that they repoꝛted of hym, that if he were not a good Chꝛistian man, they knew not whom they myght take to be one.

☞ The description and manner of the burning of Maister Wylliam Tyndall.

And the same moꝛnyng he was hadde to the fyer, he delyuered a letter to the chief keper of the Castel, whiche the keper hym self bꝛought to Poyntꝛ house in Andwarpe shoꝛtly after, who repoꝛted hym there as though he myght be compared to be feelowe with the Apostles beyng in pꝛyson, conuertyng the people, bethe foꝛ his conuersation and otherwyse pꝛeaching to them. That Traytour woꝛse then Judas to mans iudgement, in the acte doyng (only not comparyng to Chꝛiste, and that the scriptures hath already iudged Judas) otherwyse not so good, foꝛ Judas after he had betrayed his maister and frende, was soꝛy, acknowled-

ged and confessed his facte openly, declared his Maister to be the very trouth, despysyng the monye that he hadde receyued foꝛ doynge the acte, bꝛought it agayne and cast it befoꝛe thē. This traytour Phylippes contrarywyse, not lamentyng but reioysing in that he had done, not declaring the honest goodnes ꝭ trouthe of his frende, but applyed in all that he could deuise, to declare him to be false and sedicious, not despysyng the money that he had receiued, noꝛ bꝛyngyng it agayn, but pꝛocured ꝭ receiued moꝛe, wherewith to followe the suyte against that innocent bloude to the deathe, the whiche endured about one whole yeare ꝭ 1535. ii.   a halfe

Depiction of the Execution of William Tyndale from Foxe's
Book of Martyrs, 1563

fervent determination to bring his work to fruition and to see that the English Bible was openly available to all.

TYNDALE'S INFLUENCE

We all quote Tyndale's words without being aware of it, erroneously concluding that they originated in the King James Version. A master of the concise phrase, Tyndale coined such well-known sayings as:

> "Let there be light" (Genesis 1:3)
> "Am I my brother's keeper" (Genesis 4:9)
> "The fat of the land" (Genesis 45:18)
> "Let my people go" (Exodus 5:1)
> "Forever and ever" (Exodus 15:18)
> "The apple of his eye" (Deuteronomy 32:10)
> "The salt of the earth" (Matthew 5:13)
> "Cast pearls before swine" (Matthew 7:6)
> "Ask and it shall be given you" (Matthew 7:7)
> "Eat, drink, and be merry" (Luke 12:19)
> "A law unto themselves" (Romans 2:14)
> "Filthy lucre" (I Timothy 3:3)
> "Fight the good fight" (I Timothy 6:12)
> (See Appendix Five)

These words ripple through time and have etched themselves into our subconscious. Their alliteration, cadence, and word repetition convey in simple, direct language the exact meaning of the message we intend to communicate. Even those who never read the Bible often use these phrases with no awareness of their origin.

Besides succinct phrases and sentences, Tyndale coined or revived many words that are still in use. He formed the term "Jehovah" from an old Hebrew construction in the Old Testament. It was Tyndale who named the Jewish holiday "Passover." We use his word when we say that someone is being made a "scapegoat." "Beautiful" is another common word Tyndale originated, as is the word "peacemaker." Tyndale's phrases are more widely used than Shakespeare's, because the Bible has been read by a far greater number than have read Shakespeare's works. Most of the words Tyndale used were of Anglo-Saxon origin. It is no exaggeration to say that Tyndale was one of the primary architects of today's English language.

In the time Tyndale's Testament circulated in England, it won a permanent place with the people. Its wordings were fresh and lyrical, conveying the pure meaning of Scripture as never before in English. The simplicity of the translation went straight to the heart. Tyndale proved that a translation intended for the "plowboy" could be pleasing to the senses as well as true to the originals.

Years before his execution, Tyndale responded to the call of God and set himself to the task of translating the whole Bible into English. In pursuit of this vision, Tyndale would defy the combined powers of emperor, king, pope, and bishops; and though he would be hounded for the last twelve years of his life, finally to be betrayed, imprisoned, and executed for it, he would persevere and publish in the English language a masterful translation of the New Testament and much of the Old. His translation would have an incalculable effect, not only on subsequent English translations, but also on English society over the next several centuries, and through English, upon the entire world.

Chapter Six

THE LATER ENGLISH BIBLES
OF THE 16TH CENTURY

William Tyndale's last words were as much a prophecy as a prayer: "Lord, open the King of England's eyes." At the very moment Tyndale uttered those words, Henry VIII's eyes were in fact being opened to the value of publishing—and even to putting his royal stamp of approval on—Tyndale's Bible. Thomas Cranmer, Tyndale's friend from Cambridge days, had recently become Archbishop of Canterbury (1533); and he, along with Thomas Cromwell, Royal Secretary and chief advisor in all ecclesiastical matters to Henry VIII, had advocated Tyndale's English Bible.

COVERDALE BIBLE

After Tyndale's New Testament, a series of versions were published in rapid succession. This was due in part to England's break with Rome in 1534. Moreover, the government began to recognize the practical value of providing the people with a Bible in their own language. With the backing of Cranmer and the tacit approval of King Henry VIII in 1535, about a year before Tyndale's martyrdom, Miles Coverdale (1488–1569) published the first-ever, complete printed edition of the Bible in English.

Born in Yorkshire in 1487 or 1488, and a graduate of Cambridge University, Coverdale was ordained in 1514 and became an Augustinian friar. Under the influence of the reformer, Robert Barnes, he embraced Lutheran teaching and left the order. He may also have met Tyndale in Cambridge at the White Horse Inn, which was frequented by scholars open

121

to the new Lutheran ideas. It was reported of him, "he was one of the first to make a pure confession of Christ. Other men gave themselves in part; he gave himself wholly to the propagating of Christ's gospel."[1] His forceful preaching and open rebuttal of Catholic theology endangered his life, and in 1528 he was compelled to flee England. He joined Tyndale at Hamburg, where he worked with him on the Pentateuch.[2]

Most likely he arrived in Antwerp in 1534, at about the same time as John Rogers,[3] the chaplain of the English House. In Antwerp Coverdale worked as "corrector" for the printer Merten de Keyser.[4] Coverdale's famous Bible was printed in 1535, the same year Tyndale was confined at Vilvorde Castle. Not gifted with such a lively and vigorous style, nor so great a scholar as Tyndale—his knowledge of Hebrew and Greek was limited—Coverdale did know Latin and German well, and had a marvelous command of the English language. In preparing his translation, he made considerable use of Tyndale's translation, the Latin Vulgate, Luther's German Translation, *Santi Pagnini,* and the Zurich Bible of 1530.[5]

Some of the cherished ecclesiastical terms, such as "penance," "charity," and "priest," omitted by Tyndale were restored by Coverdale. Unlike Tyndale's New Testament, the margins were free of combative notes. "I have neither wrested nor altered so much as one word for the maintenance of any manner of sect," Coverdale wrote, "having only manifest truth of the Scripture before mine eyes."[6] It was the first English version to use the word *"biblia,"* or Bible. The title reads as follows: *Biblia: The Bible, that is, the holy Scripture of the Olde and New Testament, faithfully and truly translated out of the Douch [German) and Latyn into English, M. D. XXXV.* It was the first Bible to introduce chapter summaries, and, following Luther, to separate the Apocrypha from the rest of the Old Testament, placing them between the books of Malachi and Matthew. A number of Coverdale's fine phrases passed into subsequent English versions: "The pride of life"

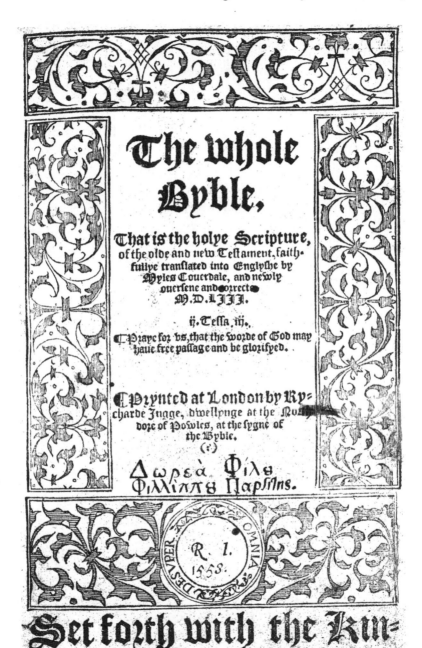

The Title Page from the Coverdale Bible, 1553

(1 John 2:16); "The world passeth away" (1 John 2:17); "Enter thou into the joy of the Lord" (Matthew 25:21,23). It is to Coverdale that we owe "tender mercies," "respect of persons," and the phrase "the valley of the shadow of death" in the Twenty-third Psalm.[7]

Undertaking the printing of Coverdale's Bible in England would have been extremely dangerous due to the fluctuating political situation. The printing would have to be done elsewhere; but where? For many years the scholarly consensus leaned toward Christopher Froschauer, the master printer of Cologne. Before that the favored town was Zurich. In A.D. 2000, Guido Latre presented compelling evidence suggesting the Coverdale Bible was printed in Antwerp.[8]

Coverdale dedicated the new Bible to King Henry VIII, and when a copy was presented to the king, Henry asked his bishops to review it as quickly as possible. At length they told the king it had many faults. "Well," said the king, "but are there any heresies maintained thereby?" They had to confess there were none. "If there be no heresies," cried Henry, "then in God's name let it go abroad among our people."[9] The Bible was immediately put into limited circulation, and Henry's second wife, Queen Anne Boleyn, laid a copy of it open on a desk at court for all to read.[10]

Since the "Lutheran" influences in Coverdale's Bible were readily discernible, why should so vigorous an opponent of Lutheranism as King Henry have permitted its circulation? F.F. Bruce observes, "The answer may be found in the influence exercised over him by Queen Anne Boleyn, until her fall from favour and execution in May, 1536. The queen certainly manifested a keen interest in Coverdale's version, and but for her sad fate, this version might have been approved before long for setting up in the parish churches of England."[11]

In addition to the version bearing his name, Coverdale produced the Great Bible of 1539, the Psalter of 1540, the

English translation of Erasmus' Paraphrase of the New Testament of 1549, and the 1550 reprint of his 1535 Bible. Some believe he may have had some part in the preparation of the Geneva Bible published in 1560. He lived long enough to see the publication in 1568 of the Bishops' Bible, dying on January 20, 1569, at the age of 81. As Decherd Turner notes, "One of the most remarkable feats of Coverdale's life was that he managed to live so long, and died in bed [i.e., not by execution]. Biblical translation in the years of Henry VIII and his children was in many cases not conducive to long life or peaceful death."[12] No person other than Wycliffe and Tyndale is owed a greater debt by those who love the English Bible than Miles Coverdale. A good part of his life was devoted to making the English Bible accessible to his fellow countrymen.

MATTHEW'S BIBLE

Meanwhile, another English Bible was being readied for the press. Issued in 1537, the title page lists Thomas Matthew as the translator, although the name is considered a pseudonym. The actual editor was John Rogers (1500–55), a former associate of Tyndale's. Most likely because Tyndale's translation had been condemned and Tyndale put to death as a heretic, Rogers thought it best not to connect his name with the new translation; hence the title page states that the Bible was "truly and purely translated into Englysh by Thomas Matthew."[13]

Born in about 1509 near Birmingham, Rogers was educated at Pembroke Hall, Cambridge. After ordination as a priest, he was from 1532 rector of a London church; then in 1534 became chaplain to the English merchants in Antwerp. Here he met William Tyndale, then engaged in his translation of the Old Testament. Foxe relates how Rogers' association with Tyndale and Miles Coverdale ripened his views "little by little," and "day by day," until at length "he embraced evangelical truth in its fullness."[14] This friendship could not

The New Testament Title Page from the Matthew's Bible,
1537

have lasted more than a few months, for Tyndale was martyred on October 6, 1536. Before Tyndale's martyrdom, he entrusted Rogers with all his materials, including his nearly completed translation of the Old Testament.[15] A careful editor, Rogers "preserved Tyndale's prologue to Romans, added the Prayer of Manasses to the Apocrypha (which Coverdale, following the Zurich Bible, had omitted), and corrected the numbering of the Psalms to agree with the original Hebrew."[16] Hoping for royal approval, he dedicated the work to King Henry VIII and his third and current wife, Jane Seymour.

Rogers printed fifteen hundred of these Bibles in Antwerp and sent an advance copy to Cranmer in England. The archbishop immediately told Cromwell, "I like it [the Bible] better than any other translation heretofore made."[17] Cranmer urged Cromwell to get the King to license it right away. Never suspecting that the "Matthew's Bible" was a disguised Tyndale Bible, the King, persuaded by Cromwell, permitted the Bible to be sold throughout England. In one of the strange ironies of English history, within twelve months of Tyndale's martyrdom (a result of his "heretical" Bible), and ten years after the burning and denouncing of his first New Testament at St. Paul's Cross, that same Bible under an assumed name was now republished and distributed in his native land with royal approval. The first English Bible distributed under a "royal license," it appeared with the words on the title page, "Set forth with the King's most gracious lycense."

Although a composite work and not a new translation, the Matthew's Bible was destined to produce lasting results. And since it formed the basis for the Great Bible and ensuing versions down to contemporary versions, it can be called "the Parent of the English Bible." Like his friend and mentor, William Tyndale, Rogers would also suffer martyrdom. He was the first Protestant leader burned at the stake at Smithfield under orders from Queen Mary in 1555.

This fortitude of mynd, which perchaunce is rare and not vsed among the Spaniardes, whē fryer Iohn sawe, thinking it came not of fortitude but of desperation (although suche maner exãples which ar of the like cõstancie haue bē much common here in England) ranne to the Lord Willias of Tame, crying that the Arch byshop was vexed in mynde, and died in great desperation. But he whiche was not ignozãt

of his countrimēs cõstancie, being vnknowē to the Spaniardes, smyled only, and as it wereby silence rebuked the fryers folie. And this was the ende of this learned Archebyshoppe, whome lest by euill saying he should haue perryshed by well recanting, God preserued, and lest he should haue lyued to shame, he died happely to the glorie of Gods name.

¶The burning of Tharchbishop of Cant. D. Tho. Cranmer, in the town dich at Oxford, with his hand first thrust into the fyre, wher with he subscribed before.

L. Receiue my spirit.

Frier Iohn.

Thus haue you the full storye concernynge the lyfe and death of this reuerend Archebyshop and Martyr of God, Thomas Cranmer, and also of all other the best learned sorte of Christes Martyrs burned in Quene Maries tyme, of whome this Archebyshop was the last, being burnt about the very myddle tyme of the reigne of that Quene, and almoste the very middle man of all the Martyrs, whiche were burned in al her reigne besydes. Diuers bookes and treatises he wrote both in pryson & out of pryson. Among the whiche especially he had a mynd to the aunswere which he made to M. Antonius Constantius. Which boke was the chiefest cause why he made his appeale, (as he wryting to a lawyer cõfesseth him self, pag.) and peraduenture was some cause also why he recanted, to haue leasure and time to finishe that booke. Of the whiche boke two

partes yet be ertant, and peraduenture (if God geue time and life) may hereafter be published: the third part, some same also was wrytten & afterward lost at Oxford, which if it be so, it is great pitie. Maister Ridley also, as it is testified, made an answer to the said M. Antonius Constant. with a cole in the margent of the booke, for lack of inke & paper, and I trust also that the same will come to our handes.

About the time that this good Archbyshop was thus cruely dispatched and burned at Oxford, there were twoo honest Matrones, Agnes Potten, the wyfe of Robert Potten of Ipswich in Suffolk, & the wyfe of one Spyebel Trochfield a shomaker in psame town, burnt at the said Ipswich the 19 day of Feb. An. 1556. Their opinion or rather certaine perswasion was, that in the Sacrament there was the memoriall of Christes death and passion.

1556. February. 19.

The answere of Cranmer to M. An tonius Cõstantius.

Two matrones burnt at Ipswych.

SSS.ii. Foz

Burning of Thomas Cranmer from Foxe's
Book of Martyrs, 1563

TAVERNER'S BIBLE

Born in Brisley, Norfolk, in 1505, Richard Taverner studied at Cambridge and Oxford. In his youth at Christ Church, Oxford, he got into trouble and was briefly imprisoned for reading Tyndale's New Testament, which was being circulated and promoted there by Thomas Garret.[18] In February, 1528, Cardinal Wolsey sought to apprehend Garret, but he escaped temporarily with the help of his friend, Anthony Dalaber. When he was brought back to Oxford, Garret and Dalaber participated in a public act of penance along with Taverner and others who would later play a prominent role in the coming struggle of the Reformation. One part of their punishment was to throw a book into the fire. In due course, Taverner recanted his recantation and became actively engaged in producing works designed to encourage the Reformation in England.

Although a lawyer by profession, the overriding ambition of Taverner's life was to become a recognized Greek scholar, a task he pursued with unwavering diligence. He annoyed his fellow law students by quoting legal items to them in Greek. He became a licensed lay preacher, escaping persecution during Queen Mary's reign by entering retirement. Upon her death he emerged again as a preacher under the more sympathetic regime of Queen Elizabeth I.

His Bible came suddenly and unexpectedly on the scene probably only a short time before the appearance of the Great Bible in 1539. Knowing very little Hebrew, the modifications Taverner made in the Old Testament reflect the influence of the Latin Vulgate. With his knowledge of Greek, numerous alterations were made in the New Testament from previous translations. We owe to Taverner the term "parable" (a Greek root), where Tyndale and Coverdale used "similitude," (a Latin root). This change was kept in the Authorized Version as were others, such as: "because of their unbelief" (Matthew 13:58), "ninety and nine" (Matthew 18:12), "the Israel of God"

(Galatians 6:16), "I stand in doubt of you" (Galatians 4:20), and "the express image of his person" (Hebrews 1:3). The disputed clauses in 1 John 5:7 are printed in smaller type.[19]

In addition to his love of Greek, Taverner had a passion for Saxon words, and he introduced several Saxon terms to replace Latinisms. In Matthew 24:12, he wrote, "the love of many shall wax cold." Tyndale and Coverdale had, "the love of many shall abate." Taverner even coined new words such as "spokesman" for *parakleton* ("advocate"), and "mercystocke" for *hilasmos* ("propitiation"), in 1 John 2:1–2.

Taverner's Bible was basically a revision of Matthew's Bible, the principal difference being the absence of a large proportion of the marginal notes found in the latter. While Taverner did not completely omit Matthew's notes, he excluded all that were in any way offensive (especially the anti-Catholic comments).[20] Taverner's Bible was almost immediately overshadowed by the publication of the Great Bible, which made its appearance shortly after Taverner's, causing the sales of the latter to diminish. Taverner's Bible has the distinction of being the first complete Bible to be printed in England.[21]

Opinions differ as to the real worth of Taverner's version. A.W. Pollard dismisses it too imprudently "as attaining little success at the time and having no influence on the version of 1611."[22] B.F. Westcott, however, feels that Taverner's version demands more study and is not to be too lightly regarded: "The work of Taverner is different from that of any of the revisers noticed before, and stamped with a very distinct individuality. . . . Throughout he appears to aim at vigorous and idiomatic language, and his New Testament deserves more attention than has yet been paid to it."[23]

GREAT BIBLE

Although many of the more traditional in the English Church were opposed to the Tyndale, Coverdale, and Matthew

The first boke
of Moses, called Gene-
sis oz generacion.

The creacyon of the wozlde.

The fyrst Chapter.
☞ By the wozde al thinges be create of God,
of mans creation, rule and substenaunce.

IN the begyn-
ninge * created
God heaue and
earth. The earth
was vopde and
and emptie, and
darcknesse was
vppon the depe,
and the * spi-
rpt of God was
boine vppon the
waters. And god
saide: lette there be lyghte: and there was
lyghte. And God sawe the lyghte that it
was good, And deuided the lighte from the
darcknes, and called the light the dap, and
the darknes the night: and the eueninge and
mozninge was made one dape.
God also saide: let there be a fyimament
betwene the waters, and lette it deuide the
waters a sunder. Then God made the spimamente, and parted the waters whyche
were vnder the spimamente, from the waters aboue the spimamente: And so it was
doone. And God called the fyimament hea
uen: And the eueninge and moznpnge was
made the seconde dape.
And God sapde: * Let the waters vnder
heauen be gathered together in one place,
that the dzye lande mape appeare. And so it
was doone. And God called the dzye lande
the earthe, and the gatherynges togpther
of waters called he the sea. And God sawe
that it was good.
And God sapde: lette the earthe bzpnge
fozthe the grene grasse and that beareth sede,
and fcutful trees bearpge frute euery one
in his kinde, hauing thepz seede in them sel
ues vpon the earthe. And it was done. And
the earthe bzought fozth herbes grasse that
that bare seede euery one in hys kinde, and
trees beringe frute, and hauing their seede
in them selues, euery one in his kinde: And
God saw that it was good: & the eueninge
and moznpnge was made the thpzde dape.
Then sapde God: * be there lightes in
the spimamente of heauen to deupde dape
from npghte that they mape be foz signes,
seasons, daies and peres. And * let them be
lightes in the spimamente of heauen, too
shpne vpon the earthe: And so it was done.
And God made * two great lightes: A grea
ter lpght to rule the dape, and a lesse lpght
to rule the npghte: and made sterres also.
And God set them in the firmament of hea

The .i. Chapter.

uen to shpne vppon the earthe, and to rule
the dape and the nighte, and to deupde the
lpghte from darckenes . And God sawe
that it was good: and the euenpnge and
mozning was made the fourth dabe.
And God sapd: * let the waters bzpnge
fozth creatures that moue and haue lpfe, &
foules foz to flpe ouer the earthe vnder the
spimament of heauen . And God created
greate whales, and all maner of creatures
that liue & moue, whych the waters bzought
fozth in their kindes, and all maner of fe-
thered foules in thepz kpndes. And God
sawe that it was good, and * blessed them,
saping: Encrease and multiplpe, and fpll
the waters of the seas, & let the foules mul
tiplie vpon the earth. And the euenpng and
moznpng was made the fpfth dape.
And God sapd: let the earth bzpng fozth the
liupnge creatures in their kpndes, cattell
and wozmes, and beastes of the earthe in
their kindes, and so it was. And God made
the beastes of the earth in thepz kindes, and
cattell in thepze kpndes, and all manner
wozmes of the earthe in thepz kpndes: and
God sawe that it was good.
And God sapde * let vs make man too
our similitude and after our likenesse: and
let hpm haue rule ouer the fpshe of the sea,
and ouer the foules of the apze, and ouer
cattell, and ouer all the earth, and ouer all
wozmes that creepe on the earth. And God
created manne after hps likenes, after the
lpkenes of God created he him: male and
female, created he them.
And God blessed them, and sapd: Grow
and multiplp, and fil the earth, and subdue
it, and haue dominion ouer the fishes of the
sea, and foules of the apze, and ouer all the
beastes that moue on the earthe.
And God sapd: Se, I haue geuen you al
hearbes that beare sede vpon the earthe, &
al maner trees that haue fruit in them and
beare seede: to be meate foz you and foz all
beastes of the earthe, and vnto al foules of
the apze, and vnto al that moue in the erth,
and wherein is lpfe, that they mape haue
al maner herbes and grasse fozto eate, and
so it was done. And * God behelde al that
he hadde made, and lo, they were exceedpng
good: and the eueninge and moznpng was
made the sixte dape.

The .ii. Chapter.

☞ The Chapter befoze is repeted againe: the
halowing of the Sabboth: the .iii. suddoe of
pezadpse: The setting in of man in pezadise
the tree of knowledge is fozbpdden by the
creatió of Eue: the institutió of mariage.

THus was heauen and earthe finished
with al their * furniture, and in the se-
uenthe dape God ended his wozcke
whiche he hadde made, and rested in the se-
uenthe dape frome all his wozckes that he
made . And blessed the seuenth dape, and
* sanctified it, foz in it he ceased frō all his
workes

Bibles (for the most part because of the outspoken anti-Catholic tone of their notes), the license that King Henry VIII granted to Matthew's Bible in 1537 and Coverdale's second edition in the same year, removed the official barrier to their circulation in England. Nevertheless, it was commonly believed among traditionalist churchmen that another revision was required. This would have to satisfy not only the scholars (Coverdale's translation was not based on the original languages), and the ecclesiastical English clergy (they were offended by Matthew's prefaces and notes), but also the King. Although he had broken with the Pope, Henry VIII did not abandon his cherished Catholic views and was not yet ready to adopt radical doctrinal reforms.

Having convinced King Henry of the need for a new English Bible, Thomas Cromwell turned to Miles Coverdale, who was in England in the early part of 1538, to undertake the revision of Matthew's Bible. Known as a skillful compromiser and editor, Coverdale seemed to be the best choice to satisfy the King's desire for a universally acceptable text. The King's one major requirement was a version free of all controversial annotations.

Although the new Bible would later advertise on its title page that it was "truly translated (out) of the Hebrew and Greek texts by the diligent study of diverse excellent learned men, expert in the aforesaid tongues," Coverdale merely edited Tyndale's text—integrating it with that of Matthew's (1537), leaving out all the controversial notes and prefaces. The "diverse excellent learned men" were simply the translators, editors and other scholars whose works Coverdale consulted.[24]

The process of revision took only a matter of months, and when completed, Coverdale and publishers Edward Whitchurch and Richard Grafton journeyed to Paris where the Bible was to be printed. Whitchurch and Grafton had the responsibility of overseeing the work. The new translation was first entrusted to Francis Regnault, the renowned Paris printer,

6th Great Bible. 5 parts

The Title Page from the Great Bible, 1541

but by the end of 1538, the relations of France and England had become strained, the printing house was seized and the printed sheets of the Bible confiscated. Cromwell somehow arranged to have Coverdale and Grafton get

> the presses, letters and servants of the aforesaid Printer, and [bring] them to London, and there they became printers themselves (which before they never intended) and printed out the said Bible in London [1539], and after that printed sundry impressions of them.[25]

The result was a magnificent edition, the largest, most attractive English Bible ever printed to that date, hence called the "Great Bible" because of its size and adornment. The large title page woodcut, printed in black with red text, depicts the Word of God being presented by King Henry VIII to Cranmer and Cromwell. They in turn distribute the Bibles to the English people, who shout, *"Vivat Rex"* or "God save the kynge." "The Almighty looks down upon King Henry and speaks the words of Acts 13:22, 'I have found a man after my own heart, who shall perform all my desire.' Thus, to paraphrase Tyndale's dying words, it appeared that 'the Lord opened the King of England's eyes.'"[26]

Lacking all of Rogers' contentious notes, Henry at once agreed to put the stamp of "royal authority" on it, making it the first fully authorized English Bible. It rapidly became the favored Bible for use in the churches. Every parish church in England was required to have a copy in order to comply with the injunction of September 5, 1538. The injunction charged the clergy that they should provide,

> one book of the whole Bible of the largest volume in English, and the same set up in some convenient place within the said church that ye have cure [care] of, whereas your parishioners may most commodiously resort to the same and read it; the charges of which book shall be rateably [proportionately] borne between you, the parson

and the parishioners aforesaid, that is to say, the one half by you and the other half by them . . . Ye shall discourage no man privily or apertly [openly] from the reading or hearing of the said Bible, but shall expressly provoke, stir and exhort every person to read the same, as that which is the very lively Word of God, that every Christian person is bound to embrace, believe, and follow, if he look to be saved; admonishing them nevertheless to avoid all contention and altercation therein, but to use an honest sobriety in their inquisition [investigation] of the true sense of the same, and to refer the explication of obscure places to men of high judgment in scripture.[27]

The Bible was to be chained to a table or podium in the churches for safekeeping, hence it became known as "The Chained Bible." The common people began to take up Scripture reading with enthusiasm. Older people learned to read just so they could read God's Word. Bishop of London, Edmund Bonner, "set up six Bibles in certain convenient places of St. Paul's Church" with the warning "that it not be read with noise in time of divine service; or that any disputation or contention be used at it."[28] But the people paid little heed to the warning. The Bibles were conveniently placed in the narthex to serve the crowds who would come to read or listen to the Bible being read. The babble of people reading aloud and discussing the texts became so clamorous the clergyman speaking in the main service could not be heard. This prompted Bishop Bonner to threaten to remove the Bibles: "Diverse willful and unlearned persons," he writes, "inconsiderately and indiscreetly . . . read the same especially and chiefly at the time of divine service . . . yea in the time of the sermon. . . . Wherefore I intend, and especially for the said abuses, to take down the said Bibles [if the matter is not speedily rectified]."[29]

The first open reading of the Bible caused a sensation in England. Churches and homes were divided over the issue. On the one side were the traditionalists of the old school to whom

A Chained Bible, 1578

change seemed to be the harbinger of libertinism where each person would decide for himself what the correct interpretation should be. On the other side were the eager and restless young, burning with enthusiasm to expand the spiritual freedom which they had so recently glimpsed. In the middle were the unassertive who preferred not to align with either faction, fearing spiritual despotism if one side prevailed and anarchy if the other emerged as the majority party.

GENEVA BIBLE

Two months after the publication of the Great Bible[30] Thomas Cromwell was thrown into prison. His ecclesiastical enemies had at last orchestrated his downfall. The leader of the Protestant Reformation in England and chief architect of the plan to publish Tyndale's Bible was beheaded in July of 1540. After his death, the Church of England took a more traditional turn. Certain prominent bishops made a determined attempt to disparage the Protestant versions and remove them from circulation in an endeavor to restore the Latin Vulgate to its former place.[31]

The remainder of Henry VIII's reign was a period of turning back to the old ways. Following the King's instructions, Convocation in 1542 decided to revise the Great Bible "according to that Bible [the Vulgate] which is usually read in the English Church."[32] Cranmer managed to foil the conspiracy, and nothing more was heard of the attempt. So dangerous to the Church did some leaders consider the unrestricted reading of the Bible that Parliament in 1543 issued restrictions based on a class and property basis. Certain high government officials were permitted to read the Bible as they were accustomed to doing, but others less titled, such as noblemen and noblewomen, could only read the Bible in private. No artificers, apprentices, journeymen, servingmen of the degrees of yeomen, husbandmen or labourers were to read the New Testament to themselves or to any other, privately or openly, on pain of one month's imprisonment. All ordinary women were not even allowed to read the Bible in the privacy of their homes.[33]

In July, 1546, a Royal decree was even stricter in tone, stipulating that no man or woman, regardless of position in government or society, was "after the last day of August, to receive, have, take, or keep, Tyndale's or Coverdale's New Testament."[34] In his last speech to Parliament, the King with tears in his eyes lamented that the Bible "was disputed, rhymed, sung and jangled in every alehouse and tavern."[35]

The most pathetic testimony to this denial of an open Bible was written by a shepherd in 1546 on the flyleaf of a book he bought and would read while watching his sheep. He was accustomed to reading the Bible, but the recently enacted law forbade him to do so: "When I kepe Mr. Letymers shepe, I bout [bought] thys boke [book] when the Testament was oberragated [abrogated], that shepeherdys myght not rede hit. I pray God amende that blindness. Wryt by Robert Wyllyans, keppyng shepe upon Seynbury hill. 1546."[36]

Henry VIII was the father of three children by three different wives. His first wife, Catherine of Aragon, was the mother of Mary, while his second wife, Anne Boleyn, was the mother of Elizabeth. Finally, Henry's third wife, Jane Seymour, gave him the son who would be heir to the throne. When Henry VIII died in 1547, Edward became king at the tender age of nine. Protestantism again flourished during Edward VI's brief six-year reign, and the open Bible came once again into favor. But when he died of tuberculosis at the age of 15, an intense, short period of turmoil ensued. Protestants and Roman Catholics vied to place their candidate on the vacated throne. Protestants ignored Henry VIII's two daughters, Mary and Elizabeth, and chose to crown Lady Jane Grey, a niece of Henry, as the new queen. After reigning only nine days, she was arrested and beheaded by Catholic supporters of Mary who arose as an army and seized the throne for their chosen candidate.

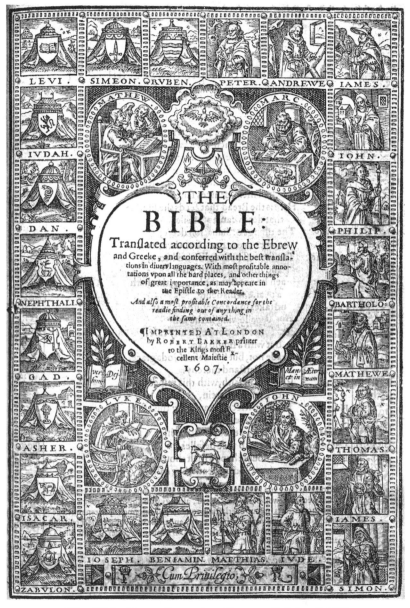

The Title Page from the Geneva Bible, 1607

As a devout Catholic, Mary was determined to roll back the Reformation and reinstate Catholicism in England. She married the Catholic king of Spain, Phillip II, and induced Parliament to recognize papal authority once more. The freedom and openness enjoyed during her brother, Edward VI's, reign speedily came to a dramatic and violent end. What followed was a reign of terror, a blood bath of persecution in which at least 300 martyrs to the Protestant cause were burned at the stake at Smithfield, earning Mary the nickname, "Bloody Mary." The first to die was John Rogers, Tyndale's close friend and associate, who had translated the Matthew's Bible in 1537. Thomas Cranmer was burned in 1556.

John Foxe meticulously chronicled this period without sparing any of the gory details. His famous book, *Acts and Monuments of matters happening in the Church,* commonly known as *Foxe's Book of Martyrs,* extolled the heroism and endurance of the Protestant martyrs of Mary's reign. First published in English in 1563, the book with its vivid descriptions and chilling illustrations of the sufferings imposed on the victims of Papist tyranny, gained wide popularity and helped insure the continued growth and stability of Protestantism in England.

The persecution of Protestants in the five-year reign of Mary resulted in a flood of exiles to the Continent, many of whom ended up at Geneva. For centuries the city of Geneva, perched high in the Alps on the border between France and Switzerland, was a haven for political and religious refugees. Among these English exiles were some of the outstanding Bible scholars of the age. According to most authorities, it was William Whittingham, John Calvin's brother-in-law, and John Knox, both hard core Calvinist, who first became interested in producing a new Bible translation.[37] The two met in Frankfurt, and after being expelled for their radicalism, ended up in Geneva.

Led by the brilliant theologian, John Calvin, Geneva was alive at this time with the thrill of Bible scholarship. At the very time the English exiles arrived in Geneva, the French exiles were laboring over a new Bible translation to send home. A group of notable English scholars, led by Whittingham, produced a Bible in 1560 that was to set the standard for English Bibles for years to come. The Geneva Bible, as it was called, quickly became the most popular Bible among English-speaking people.[38]

A number of innovative features set this Bible apart from previous English Bibles:

First, it was small and inexpensive, not huge and unafford-able like the Great Bible.

Second, it was the first English Bible to be printed in the more legible Roman type, not the harder-to-read Gothic or black print. Erasmus in his Greek/Latin New Testament was the first to establish Roman type as a viable type for Bible usage. Roman type is to be found in virtually all Bibles today.

Third, verse divisions were adopted for the first time in an English Bible. Each verse was printed as a separate unit or paragraph. The verse divisions for the New Testament first appeared in the fourth edition of Stephanus' Greek Testament in 1551. The chapter divisions, which earlier English versions used, were believed to have been worked out by Stephen Langton (1150–1228), and used in Latin versions. Prior to the introduction of verse numbering, marginal markers often assisted location within a chapter: A, B, C, etc., every 10 to 15 lines.

Fourth, the New Testament used italics to display English words not in the original Greek but necessary to make sense in English.

Fifth, it had copious annotations that served as a commentary to explain the meaning of the text. It was the first "Study Bible," as similar Bibles are called today.

Sixth, each chapter had a summary statement at the beginning of the chapter.

46 15 Then Nathanael sayd vnto him, Can there any good thing come out of Nazareth? Philip said to him, Come, and see.

47 20 Iesus sawe Nathanael comming to him, and said of him, Behold in deede an Israelite, in whom is no guile.

48 21 Nathanael saide vnto him, Whence knewest thou me? Iesus answered, and said vnto him, Before that Philip called thee, when thou wast vnder the figtree, I saw thee.

49 Nathanael answered, and said vnto him, Rabbi, thou art that Sonne of God: thou art that King of Israel.

50 Iesus answered, and said vnto him, Because I said vnto thee, I saw thee vnder the figge tree, beleeuest thou? thou shalt see greater things then these.

51 And he said vnto him, Verely, verely I say vnto you, Hereafter shall ye see heauen open, and the Angels of God + x ascending, and descending vpon that Sonne of man.

CHAP. II.

1 *Christ turneth water into wine,* 11 *which was the beginning of his miracles.* 12 *Hee goeth downe to Capernaum:* 13 *From thence he goeth vp to Hierusalem,* 15 *and casteth the merchandise out of the Temple.* 19 *Hee foretelleth that the Temple, that is, his body shall bee destroyed of the Iewes.* 23 *Many beleeue in him, seeing the miracles which he did.*

ANd the a third day, was there a marriage in Cana a towne of Galile, and the mother of Iesus was there.

2 And Iesus was called also, and his disciples vnto the mariage.

3 Now when the wine failed, the mother of Iesus sayd vnto him, They haue no wine.

4 Iesus sayd vnto her, Woman, what haue I to doe with thee? mine b houre is not yet come.

5 His mother sayd vnto the seruants, Whatsoeuer he sayth vnto you, doe it.

6 And there were set there, sixe waterpots of stone, after the maner of the purifying of the Iewes, conteining two or three u firkins apiece.

7 And Iesus sayd vnto them, Fill the waterpots with water. Then they filled them vp to the brimme.

8 Then he sayd vnto them, Draw out now, and beare vnto the gouernour of the feast. So they bare it.

9 Now when the gouernour of the feast had tasted the water that was made wine, (for hee knew not whence it was, but the seruants which drew the water, knew) the gouernour of the feast called the bridegrome,

10 And said vnto him, All men at the beginning set foorth good wine, and when men haue e well drunke, then that which is worse: but thou hast kept backe the good wine vntill now.

11 This beginning of miracles did Iesus in Cana a towne of Galile, and sheweth foorth his glory: and his disciples beleeued on him.

12 After that, he went downe into Capernaum, hee and his mother, and his f brethren, and his disciples: but they continued not many dayes there.

13 3 For the Iewes Passeouer was at hand. Therefore Iesus went vp to Hierusalem.

14 4 And hee found in the Temple those that sold oxen, and sheepe, and doues, and changers of money sitting there.

15 Then hee made a scourge of small cordes, and draue them all out of the Temple with the sheepe and oxen, and powred out the changers money, and ouerthrew their tables,

16 And said vnto them that sold doues, Take these things hence: make not my fathers house, an house of merchandise.

17 And his disciples remembred, that it was written, + The g zeale of thine house hath eaten me vp.

18 5 Then answered the Iewes, and sayd vnto him, What h signe shewest thou vnto vs, that thou doest these things?

19 Iesus answered and said vnto them, + Destroy this Temple, and in three dayes I will raise it vp againe.

20 Then said the Iewes, Fourtie and six yeeres was this Temple a building, and wilt thou reare it vp in three dayes?

21 But he spake of the i temple of his body.

22 As soone therefore as hee was risen from the dead, his disciples remembred that hee thus said vnto them: and they beleeued the Scripture, and the word which Iesus had said.

23 Nowe when hee was at Hierusalem at the Passeouer in the feast, many beleeued in his name, when they saw his miracles which he did.

24 6 But Iesus did not commit himselfe vnto them, because he knew them all,

25 7 And had no need that any should testifie of man, for he knew what was in man.

CHAP. III.

1 *Christ teacheth Nicodemus the very principles of christian regeneration.* 14 *The serpent in the wildernes.* 23 *Iohn baptizeth,* 27 *and teacheth his that he is not Christ.*

THere 1 was now a man of the Pharises named Nicodemus, a a ruler of the Iewes.

2 This man came to Iesus by night, and sayd vnto him, Rabbi, wee know that thou art a b teacher come from God, for no man could doe these miracles that thou doest, c except God were with him.

3 2 Iesus answered and said vnto him, Verely, verely I say vnto thee, Except a man bee borne againe, he cannot d see the e kingdome of God.

4 Nicodemus said vnto him, How can a man be borne which is olde? can he enter into his mothers wombe againe, and be borne?

5 Iesus answered, Verely, verely I say vnto thee, except that a man be borne of water and of the Spirit, hee cannot enter into the kingdome of God.

6 That which is borne of the flesh, is g flesh: and that that is borne of the Spirit, is spirit.

7 Marueile not that I said to thee, Ye must be borne againe.

8 The winde bloweth where it h lusteth, and

thou

The Gospel of John Chapter Two from the Geneva Bible, 1607

The Geneva Bible became the most popular version simply because it was the best English version available in its day. It was never authorized, but the people put their stamp of approval on it. It was also called the "Breeches Bible" because of its translation of Genesis 3:7, "They sewed fig leaves together and made themselves *breeches."* Our modern word "britches" is a form of the Old English word "breeches."

The Geneva Bible was the Bible of Oliver Cromwell, the Puritans, Shakespeare, John Bunyan, and even most of the King James translators. It was the Bible quoted by Miles Smith in the Preface of the first edition of the King James Version. The Geneva Bible continued to be the most popular version of the Bible for a generation after the King James appeared in 1611. The first English Bible brought to America (to Jamestown in 1607 and by Pilgrims on the Mayflower in 1620) was the Geneva Bible.

At the Hampton Court Conference in 1604, King James I demanded that all dissenters conform to the Church of England; those who refused to do so, he would "harry out of the land." The Pilgrims who came to the New World were Puritan separatists who declined to conform to the Church of England. They were willing to brave a treacherous ocean and an uncharted wilderness to find a place of refuge where religious liberty could flourish. Not surprisingly, they did not think too kindly of King James, so the Bible they brought to America was the Geneva Bible, the Bible favored by the Puritans, not the new Bible that bore the name of the king that forced them to leave their homeland in the first place.

In describing the dramatic effect the Geneva Bible exerted on the English population, historian J. R. Green made this perceptive observation:

> England became the people of a book, and that book was the Bible. It was as yet the one English book which was familiar to every Englishman; it was read at churches and read at home, and everywhere its words, as they

fell on ears which custom had not deadened, kindled a startling enthusiasm. . . . Day after day the family group that hung on the words of the Geneva Bible in the devotional exercises at home, were leavened with a new literature. . . . The power of the book over the mass of Englishmen showed itself in a thousand superficial ways, and in none more conspicuously than in the influence it exerted on ordinary speech [and literature]. . . . But far greater than its effect on literature was the effect of the Bible on the character of the people at large. . . . A new moral and religious impulse spread through every class.[39]

BISHOPS' BIBLE

Though the Geneva Bible was the people's choice, most of the leaders in the Church of England were dissatisfied with it. There were two reasons: first, it was not an authorized Bible, hence not the Bible that was read from the pulpit. Second, its Calvinistic notes were sometimes inflammatory which made it unsuitable for official church use. After Mary's death in 1563, her half-sister, Elizabeth, became queen and began her long reign of forty-five years. Elizabeth was sympathetic to the Protestant cause, so once again Bible publishing was allowed and Protestantism flourished.

Recognizing the ideological drift away from the tenets of the Church of England caused by the growing popularity of the Geneva Version of the Bible, Archbishop of Canterbury, Matthew Parker, with Elizabeth's blessing, set in motion plans to create a revision of the authorized Great Bible in 1564. His aim was to produce an official Bible that would displace the Geneva Bible. Portions of the text were assigned to various revisers, which included nine bishops. Parker supervised the work, but there does not appear to have been any organized system of collaboration or revision, and the results proved to be unequal. The scholarship shown in the New Testament "is on a much higher level" than that of the Old Testament.[40]

conteynyng the olde
Teſtament and the newe.

The Title Page from the Bishops' Bible, 1568

After about four years of work, in 1568 the translation work was completed. Because bishops, or men who would become bishops in the Church of England, prepared the translation work, the new Bible became known as *The Bishops' Bible.* Although the translators were said to have been inclined to counter the Calvinistic undertones of the Geneva Version, they were instructed "to make no bitter notes upon any text, or yet to set down any determination in places of controversy."[41] As a result, the Bible achieved a perceived tone of dignity, a feature that was mirrored in its noble appearance. No expense was spared to make it attractive; and in typography, illustration, and paper, this was the most impressive of the English Bibles produced in the sixteenth century. The Convocation of Canterbury in 1571 instructed churchwardens to place copies in their churches; and in this way the Bishops' Bible succeeded to the role and function previously accorded to the Great Bible. Ecclesiastical dignitaries were also instructed to place the Bible in halls or dining rooms for the use of servants and visitors.

Between 1568 and 1602, the Bishops' Bible went through seventeen editions. This was the Bible generally used in pulpits until 1611. But the Geneva Bible remained the favorite for home and personal use and far outweighed the Bishops' Bible in both popularity and longevity.

RHEIMS/DOUAY BIBLE

After the death of Queen Mary in 1558, a new climate favorable to Protestantism arrived with the accession of Elizabeth I as queen of England. The Protestants returned from exile and a new era of the English Bible began. Two new English Bibles were published during her long reign, one by bishops of the Church of England, as we have already seen, and the other by Roman Catholics. Elizabeth's Protestant sympathies prompted many staunch Roman Catholic scholars

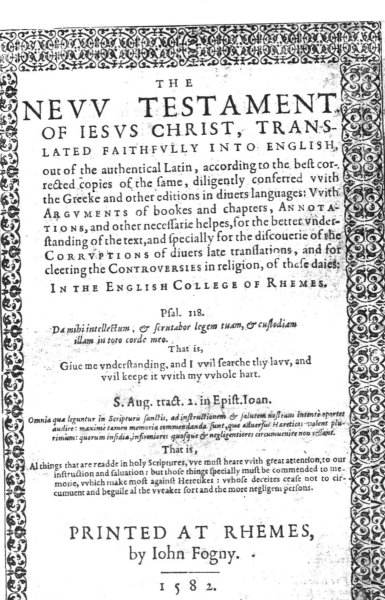

THE

NEVV TESTAMENT

OF IESVS CHRIST, TRANS-
LATED FAITHFVLLY INTO ENGLISH,

out of the authentical Latin, according to the best corrected copies of the same, diligently conferred vvith
the Greeke and other editions in diuers languages: Vvith
ARGVMENTS of bookes and chapters, ANNOTA-
TIONS, and other necessarie helpes, for the better vnderstanding of the text, and specially for the discouerie of the
CORRVPTIONS of diuers late translations, and for
cleering the CONTROVERSIES in religion, of these daies:

IN THE ENGLISH COLLEGE OF RHEMES.

Psal. 118.

*Da mihi intellectum, & scrutabor legem tuam, & custodiam
illam in toto corde meo.*

That is,

Giue me vnderstanding, and I vvil searche thy lavv, and
vvil keepe it vvith my vvhole hart.

S. Aug. tract. 1. in Epist. Ioan.

*Omnia quæ leguntur in Scripturis sanctis, ad instructionem & salutem nostram intentè oportet
audire: maximè tamen memoria commendanda sunt, quæ aduersus Hæreticos valent plu-
rimùm: quorum insidiæ, infirmiores quosque & negligentiores circumuenire non cessant.*

That is,

Al things that are readde in holy Scriptures, vve must heare vvith great attention, to our
instruction and saluation: but those things specially must be commended to me-
morie, vvhich make most against Heretikes: vvhose deceites cease not to cir-
cumuent and beguile al the vveaker sort and the more negligent persons.

PRINTED AT RHEMES,
by Iohn Fogny.

1582.

CVM PRIVILEGIO.

The Title Page from the Rheims New Testament, 1582

to flee the country, fearing retaliation because of Mary's previous treatment of Protestants.[42] Most of the Catholics who fled England settled in Catholic-dominated France where they established a college at Douay in 1568, the very year the Bishops' Bible was published.

William Allen, an Oxford Scholar and former canon of York, initiated the proposal to create the institution. It would ultimately become the intellectual center of the covert Catholic missionary movement to England. Affiliated with the University of Douay, the school was founded for the express purpose of training young priests in Scripture (as Catholicism interpreted it) who could then assist in the work of restoring England to the Roman fold. A century earlier, such familiarity with the text of Scripture was considered superfluous. Now with the proliferation of Protestant Biblical studies, it was deemed imperative for Catholics to become more knowledgeable of Scripture if they were to repatriate the alleged heretics who now dominated their English homeland.

This represented a compelling reason for Catholics to produce a Bible for the faithful in the English language, one that would compete with and hopefully displace popular Protestant versions. In a letter to Dr. Venderville in September of 1578, William Allen described the rationale behind the proposal for the version they wished to prepare:

> Catholics educated in the academies and schools have hardly any knowledge of the Scriptures except in Latin. When they are preaching to the unlearned and are obliged on the spur of the moment to translate some passage into the vernacular, they often do it inaccurately and with unpleasant words, or it does not occur to them at the moment. Our adversaries, however, have at their finger tips from some heretical version all those passages of Scripture which seem to make for them, and by a certain deceptive adaptation and alteration of the sacred words produce the

effect of appearing to say nothing but what comes from the Bible. This evil might be remedied if we too had some Catholic version of the Bible, for all the English versions are most corrupt. . . . If his Holiness shall judge it expedient, we ourselves will endeavor to have the Bible faithfully, purely, and genuinely translated according to the edition approved by the Church, for we already have men most fitted for the work. . . . And [because] there is often also such need of reading Scriptures in order to confute our opponents, it is better that there should be a faithful and Catholic translation than that men should use a corrupt version to their peril or destruction.[43]

This proposal represented a break from the long-held position of the church, that a vernacular translation was *not* essential to convince people of the Catholic viewpoint. Allen's remarks imply that the time had come when it was unlikely any churchgoer would be convinced of the validity of Catholic Church doctrine without such a translation.

Gregory Martin, scholar of St. John's College, Oxford, became the main translator for the Catholic project. A lecturer at the college in both the Hebrew language and in Scriptural interpretation, after refusing to conform to the Reformation theology, he fled to Douay in France in 1570, where he taught at the new school established by Allen. In 1578 he removed to Rheims, where he soon began work on the new translation. In order to complete the project as quickly as possible, Martin made a practice of translating two chapters daily. In a little over three years the work was completed. The finished product received a final revision by William Allen and Richard Bristow (Moderator of the college). The New Testament was published in Rheims in 1582. Though translated first, because of lack of funds, the Old Testament was not published until 1609–10 at Douay, hence the name, "Rheims/Douay Bible."[44]

The translation is based on the Latin, not the original languages, Hebrew and Greek. "We translate the old Vulgar Latin text, not the common Greek text."[45] Several reasons are alleged in the Preface for adopting this policy:

> The antiquity of the Vulgate; its correction by Jerome according to the Greek; its continuous employment since that time in the Church's services; because the Church Fathers used and expounded it; because the Council of Trent had declared it authentic; because in places where the Latin and Greek disagree the Latin is better than the Greek text—the proof adduced being that 'most of the auncient heretikes were Grecians, and therefore their Scriptures in Greeke were more corrupted by them, as the auncient fathers often complaine.'[46]

Although the quality of the translation may be said to be excellent in certain places, overall it suffered from being excessively literal and incorporating too many Latinisms (for example: azymes, carbona, parasceve, donaries, hostes, repropitiate, commessation, condigne).[47] Some extremely quaint renderings never fail to elicit a smile: "a young man clothed with sindon on the bare" (Mark 14:51); "If thou be a prevaricator of the law, the circumcision is become prepuce" (Romans 2:25); "His mother looked out at a window and howled; and she spoke from the dining room" (Judges 5:28); "He exinanited himself" (Philippians 2:7); "coiquination and spottes, flowing in delicacies, in their feastings rioting with you" (2 Peter 2:13).

These few oddities aside, the influence of the Rheims New Testament on the Authorized Version is considerable, as James G. Carleton demonstrates in his book, *The Part of Rheims in the Making of the English Bible*. The King James' revisers took over from the Rheims' version such expressions as "this wicked generation" (Matthew 12:45); "salted with salt" (Mark 9:49); "the things that are Caesar's" (Mark 12:17); "in the shambles" (1 Corinthians 10:25).[48] A single Epistle (that to the Romans) furnishes the following list of Latin words which King James' translators have taken from the Rheims Testament: "separated," "consent," "impenitent," "approvest," "propitiation," "remission," "grace," "glory (in tribulations)," "commendeth," "concupiscence," "revealed," "expectation," "conformable," "confession is made (to salvation)," "emulation," "concluded," "conformed," "instant," "contribution."[49]

In the epistle of Hebrews 11:1, Tyndale and the Great Bible have "Faith is a sure confidence of things that are hoped for;" the Bishops' Bible has "Faith is the ground of things that are hoped for;" and the Rheims New Testament has "And faith is the substance of things to be hoped for." The panel translating for King James finally decided upon "Now faith is the substance of things hoped for," thus showing that they were not afraid to use a translation from a rival version, even though it did not convey the thought as well as Tyndale.

One can readily see the similarity between the KJV in the first eight verses of 1 Corinthians 13 and the Rheims quoted below: (spelling modernized)

1. If I speak with the tongues of men and of angels, and have not charity, I am become as sounding brass, or a tinkling cymbal.
2. And if I should have prophecies and should know all mysteries, and all knowledge, and if I should have all faith, so that I could remove mountains, and have not charity, I am nothing.
3. And if I should distribute all my goods for meat for the poor, and if I should deliver my body so that I burn, and have not charity, it doth profit me nothing.
4. Charity is patient, is benign: charity envieth not, dealeth not perversely; is not puffed up.
5. Is not ambitious, seeketh not her own, is not provoked to anger, thinketh not evil.

6. Rejoiceth not upon iniquity, but rejoiceth with the truth;

7. Suffereth all things, believeth all things, hopeth all things, beareth all things.

8. Charity never falleth away: whether prophecies shall be made void, or tongues shall cease, or knowledge shall be destroyed.

Though not often consulted or published today, the Rheims New Testament now circulates in Bishop Richard Challoner's much later revision of the text. Challoner produced numerous revisions of the Douay Bible between 1738 and 1772.

Chapter Seven

THE NOBLEST MONUMENT
OF ENGLISH PROSE

The fascinating story behind the most famous and enduring English Bible translation must begin with the King without whose sanction and support the new translation would never have seen the light of day. More commonly known in England as "The Authorized Version," millions in the United States know this translation simply as "The King James Version." But just who is this king who is celebrated primarily because of the Bible that bears his name?

When James became King of England at age 36, he had already served as King of Scotland for almost 35 years. His beautiful and frivolous mother, Mary Queen of Scots, a staunch Catholic, was forced to abdicate the throne of Scotland when implicated, along with her lover, in the murder of her husband, Lord Darnley. Only thirteen months old when declared the new Scottish King on July 29, 1567, Prince James would thereafter be known in Scotland as James VI. Reformation leader John Knox preached the coronation sermon in the parish kirk at Stirling, and two of the great lords took oaths on the infant James' behalf that he would defend the Protestant faith. James could not in later life remember a time when he had not borne the title of "King."

For forty-five years, Elizabeth, daughter of Henry VIII and Anne Boleyn, had been England's monarch. Her death in the early hours of Thursday, March 24, 1603, would bring about significant changes to England, and especially to James. Within eight hours of Elizabeth's death, there was a proclamation at Whitehall Gate declaring James VI of Scotland the new King of England. Sir Robert Carey had arranged for horses to be posted

The 1611 King James Bible With Original Boards

along the North Road to enable him to be the first to break the news to the new monarch at Edinburgh. Despite an ugly fall from his horse, Carey knocked at the gate of Holyroodhouse on Saturday night, was quickly brought to James' chamber, knelt before him, and saluted him as the new King of England. James was in bed at the time Carey arrived but not asleep. A lengthy conversation ensued as James peppered Carey with questions about the situation in England and the kind of reception he could expect as the new King. No longer would he be known as James VI of Scotland; his new title would be James I of England and Scotland. Long at odds with each other, the two countries were now united under one head.

James was not caught by surprise when news reached him of Elizabeth's passing. For two years medical reports had been conveyed to him almost weekly telling of her deteriorating physical condition. Elizabeth's chief minister, Sir Robert Cecil, had maintained a secret correspondence with James in order to prepare in advance for a smooth transition. This gave James ample time to soberly reflect on his future elevated social and political standing.

No one had been more prepared intellectually and socially for kingship (or as he would have put it, "king-craft") than James. The "epistle dedicatory" in the KJV describes him as having been enriched by God's heavenly hand "with many singular and extraordinary graces." It was no ordinary prince who had written, besides sonnets and other works, a "Paraphrase on the Revelation of St. John" before the age of twenty.

During his childhood and youth, James was exposed to the finest classical education. His principal tutor was George Buchanan, the greatest of the Scottish humanists, a supporter of the Reformation of the Scottish Church, and in the year of James' birth, Moderator of the General Assembly of the Church of Scotland. Buchanan made every effort to build an excellent library for the King's use. While James was still a schoolboy he had at his disposal some six hundred volumes, probably the largest collection in Scotland at the time. The Greek and Latin classics were purchased in large numbers, along with grammars and works on pronunciation. Collections of maxims and moral tales such as the familiar sayings of Plutarch, the couplets of Cato, and the fables of Aesop formed the first source for the King's store of wise sayings and aphorisms.

Buchanan also bought histories of most of the countries of Europe, lives of the Roman emperors and the popes, as well as treatises on government and on the education of princes. There were many books of theology—both medieval and modern— the writings of the Protestant reformers, and the *Augsburg Confession.* Works on geography, cosmography, natural history and mathematics, as well as on logic and dialectics were included. The majority of these books were written in Latin, many were in French, some in Greek, Spanish and Italian, surprisingly few in English.[1]

Buchanan and other tutors were determined to make their small pupil a royal paragon of scholarly achievement. "A king," said Buchanan, "should be the most learned man in his dominions." The tutors found that James was highly intelligent, that he learned with ease and possessed an excellent memory. They pushed him very hard. Training in Latin was a prime objective of the tutors, and James learned the language well, writing and speaking it with ease. The King later remarked that he could speak Latin before he could speak his native tongue. Other languages such as French and Italian were added to his storehouse of knowledge. Minister James Melville tells in his autobiography how he and his Uncle Andrew visited Stirling in 1574 when James was eight years of age. He told how the young King "read a chapter of the Bible out of Latin into French, and out of French into English, [and he read so well that] few men could have added anything to his translation."[2]

James was taught to know the Bible thoroughly, and it was his custom to have a chapter of the Scriptures read and discussed at every meal. James Gordon, a Catholic with whom

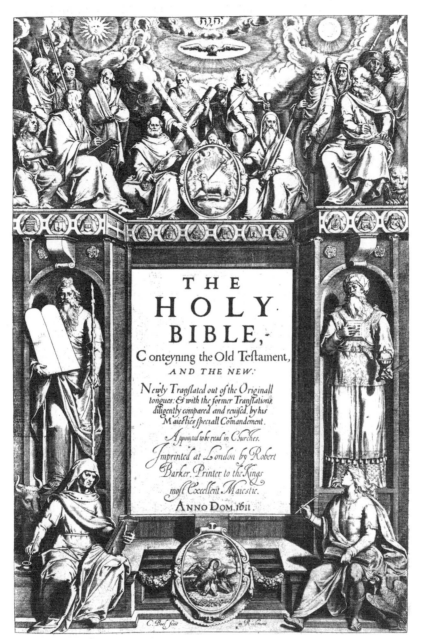

The Title Page from the 1611 King James Bible

James disputed in 1588, declared that the King "is naturally eloquent, has a keen intelligence, and a very powerful memory, for he knows a great part of the Bible by heart. He cites not only chapters, but even the verses in a perfectly marvelous way."[3]

Like all kings, James had his detractors as well as supporters. Sir Anthony Weldon, a contemporary of James, spoke uncomplimentary of the King. "He never washed his hands, only rubbed his finger-ends slightly with the wet end of a napkin." He spoke of the King's "weak legs, clumsy gait, circular walk, large rolling eyes and his tongue [that was] too large for his mouth."

Nineteenth century historian Thomas Babington Macaulay, basing his description of James on biased and hostile contemporary writers, portrayed the King as a slobbering pedant whose lack of statesmanship undermined the monarchy that was to fall under his son, Charles I. It is true that his stubborn attachment to the doctrine of the Divine Right of Kings set the Stuarts not only above criticism, but above the law of the land. Another fault that elicited much public disapproval was James' excessive spending habits. He was inclined to spend more money than was available either in the Treasury or from Parliament. His Danish wife, Anne, was also known for her too great extravagance. James was bitterly assailed for his failure to assist his son-in-law, the elector Frederick of the Palatine, which allowed Bohemia to fall into Catholic hands and trigger the Thirty Years War. Another flaw of James, often discussed by his subjects and criticized by his enemies, was his inordinate vanity and narcissism.

While some of the criticism was justified, much of it was undeserved. James had been a remarkably successful King of Scotland before 1603, often in very difficult circumstances— in many ways the most successful king Scotland ever had— and he was not an altogether ineffective King of England. In the past two decades historians have reassessed the accomplishments of James. He is portrayed as an able ruler

THE TRANSLATORS
to the Reader.

ZEale to promote the common good, whether it be by deuising any thing our selues, or reuising that which hath been laboured by others, deserueth certainely much respect and esteeme, but yet findeth but cold entertainement in the world. It is welcommed with suspicion in stead ot loue, and with emulation in stead of thankes: and if there be any hole left for cauill to enter, (and cauill, if it do not find a hole, will make one) it is sure to be misconstrued, and in danger to be condemned. This will easily be graunted by as many as know storie, or haue any experience. For, was there euer any thing proiected, that sauoured any way of newnesse or renewing, but the same endured many a storme ot gaine-saying, or opposition? A man would thinke that Ciuilitie, holesome Lawes, learning and eloquence, Synods, and Church-maintenance, (that we spake of no more things ot this kinde) should bee as safe as a Sanctuary, and ‖ out of shot, as they say, that no man would lift vp the heele, no, nor dogge mooue his tongue against the motioners of them. For by the first, we are distinguished from bruit-beasts led with sensualitie: By the second, we are bridled and restrained from outragious behauiour, and from doing of iniuries, whether by fraud or by violence: By the third, we are enabled to informe and reforme others, by the light and feeling that we haue attained vnto our selues: Briefly, by the fourth being brought together to a parle face to face, wee sooner compose our differences then by writings, which are endlesse: And lastly, that the Church be sufficiently prouided for, is so agreeable to good reason and conscience, that those mothers are holden to be lesse cruell, that kill their children assoone as they are borne, then those noursing fathers and mothers (wheresoeuer they be) that withdraw from them who hang vpon their breasts (and vpon whose breasts againe themselues doe hang to receiue the Spirituall and sincere milke of the word) liuelyhood and support fit for their estates. Thus it is apparent, that these things which we speake of, are of most necessary vse, and therefore that none, either without absurditie can speake against them, or without note of wickednesse can spurne against them.

Yet for all th .t, the learned know that certaine worthy men haue bene brought to vntimely death for none other fault, but for seeking to reduce their Countreymen to good order and discipline: and that in some Common weales it was made a capitall crime, once to motion the making of a new Law tor the abrogating of an old, though the same were most pernicious: And that certaine, which would be counted pillars of the State, and paternes ot Vertue and Prudence, could not be brought for a long time to giue way to good Letters and refined speach, but bare themselues as auerse from them, as from rocks or boxes ot poison: And fourthly, that hee was no babe, but a great clearke, that gaue foorth (and in writing to remaine to posteritie) in passion peraduenture, but yet he gaue foorth, that hee had not seene any profit to come by any Synode, or meeting of the Clergie, but rather the contrary: And lastly, against Church-maintenance and allowance, in such sort, as the Embassadors and messengers of the great King of kings should be furnished, it is not vnknowen what a fiction or fable (so it is esteemed, and for no better by the reporter himselfe, though superstitious) was deuised; Namely, that at such time as the professours and teachers of Christianitie in the Church of Rome, then a true Church, were liberally endowed, a voice torsooth was heard from heauen, saying; Now is poison powred downe into the Church, &c. Thus not only as oft as we speake, as one saith, but also as oft as we do any thing of note or consequence, we subiect our selues to euery ones censure, and happy is he that is least tossed vpon tongues; for vtterly to escape the snach of them it is impossible. If any man conceit, that this is the lot and portion of the meaner sort only, and that Princes are priuiledged by their high estate, he is deceiued. *As the sword deuoureth as well as the other,* as it is in *Samuel;* nay as the great Commander charged his souldiers in a certaine battell, to strike at no part of the enemie, but at the face; And as the King of *Syria* commanded his chiefe Captaines *to fight neither with small nor great, saue onely against the King of Israel:* so it is too true, that Enuie striketh most spitefully at the fairest, and at the chiefest. *Dauid* was a worthy Prince, and no man to be compared to him for his first deedes, and yet for as worthy an acte as euer he did (euen for bringing backe the Arke of God, in solemnitie) hee was scorned and scoffed at by his owne wife. *Solomon* was greater then *Dauid* though

Miles Smith's Preface to the 1611 King James Bible

who extended royal power in Scotland, preserved his kingdoms from war throughout his 57 year reign, and encouraged English trade and colonization. At the beginning of James' reign, there were no British colonies. At the end of his reign a quantity would already have come into existence. Jamestown, the first permanent English settlement in the New World, was named after him in 1607.

James' reputation, both during his life and after his death, has been largely influenced by comparisons between him and his predecessor. Elizabeth's revered memory, sometimes much embellished, often prevents justice being done to the memory of James. However, there was some truth in the aphorism of the day that "King Elizabeth" had been succeeded by "Queen James," principally because James appeared, in the estimation of some, to lack the manliness and heroic attributes that many expected in a king. Elizabeth and James are unusual among English monarchs in their intellectual abilities and tastes. Both were able linguists. Elizabeth was perhaps the more effective speaker. Though learned and sometimes impressive in his speeches, James was often too lengthy and verbose. A more successful writer than Elizabeth, James authored devotional treatises, poems, political treatises (among them a defense of the Divine Right of Kings and refutations of papal authority) and tracts on subjects ranging from demonology to the harmful effects of tobacco. Elizabeth is the better known of the two because of her longer reign, the overwhelming defeat of the Spanish Armada in 1588, Protestantism becoming almost universal in England under her watch, and the many modern biographies of her life, as well as the perpetual media frenzy surrounding her.

James was not called "the British Solomon," though, without reason. His love of learning was genuine and surely admirable by any standards. He presided over the age of Shakespeare's tragedies, and over such other notable literary giants as John Donne, Ben Jonson, George Herbert, and Francis Bacon. His

Gods goodneſſe.   Pſalmes.

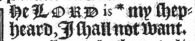

PSAL. XXIII.

Dauids confidence in Gods grace.

¶ A pſalme of Dauid.

*Eſa.40.11
Iere.23.5.
Ezech. 34.
Ioh.10.11.
23.
1.Pet.2.25.
†Heb. pa-
ſtures of ten-
der graſſe.*
†Heb. wa-
ters of quiet-
neſſe.

THE LORD is * my ſhep-
heard, I ſhall not want.

2 He maketh me to lie
downe in † greene pa-
ſtures: he leadeth mee be-
ſide the †ſtill waters.

3 He reſtoreth my ſoule: he leadeth
me in the pathes of righteouſnes, for
his names ſake.

*Pſal. 3.6.
& 118.6.

4 Yea though I walke through the
valley of the ſhadowe of death, * I will
feare no euill: for thou art with me, thy
rod and thy ſtaffe, they comfort me.

5 Thou prepareſt a table before me,
in the preſence of mine enemies: thou
†anointeſt my head with oyle, my cuppe
runneth ouer.

†Heb. ma-
keſt fat.

6 Surely goodnes and mercie ſhall
followe me all the daies of my life: and
I will dwell in the houſe of the LORD
†for euer.

†Heb. to
length of
dayes.

PSAL. XXIIII.

1 Gods Lordſhip in the world. 3 The citizens
of his ſpirituall kingdome. 7 An exhorta-
tion to receiue him.

¶ A pſalme of Dauid.

*Deut. 10.

THE earth is the LORDS,
and the fulneſſe thereof:

andt
10
LOI
Sela

1 Dau
eth
hel

triun
3 *
aſhai
tranſ
4
LO
5
me: †
on, c
6
tend
neſſc
7
you
to t
thy
8
the

Psalm 23 from the 1611 King James Bible

impact on English literature is considerable, not least because of his encouragement of and participation in the making of the jewel of our literature, the King James or Authorized Version of the Bible. That is James' crowning achievement. As for the claim attributed to King Henry IV of France that James was "the wisest fool in Christendom," it was a reckless exaggeration that had no basis in fact. James was no fool, as his Scottish and English subjects discovered, even if he was not always wise.

THE MILLENARY PETITION

After hearing of Elizabeth's death—as her closest of kin and legitimate heir to the English throne (he was related to the Tudors on both his father's and mother's side)—James soon began making preparations for the 400 mile journey from Edinburgh to London for the coronation ceremony. On Sunday, April 3, 1603, he attended divine service in St. Giles. Two days later he set forth from Edinburgh with a retinue of servants, nobles and courtiers. Along the way immense throngs lined the roads and cheered the new king. Church bells rang; mayors gave him the keys to their cities, and an ever increasing number of nobles and courtiers attached themselves to his train. There were stag hunts in parks, banquets, and other entertainments.[4]

Anticipating only suspicion and difficulties when arriving in England, James was pleasantly surprised at the exuberant reaction of the people. When he entered Berwick, the northernmost town in England on the east coast of the River Tweed, great crowds of people shouted "Welcome!" and "God save King James!" The acclamations continued for so long a time that the people had to be implored to be silent. In his first speech to Parliament, James recalled how, as he came down from Scotland, "the people of all sorts [rode] and ran, nay rather flew to meet him, their eyes flaming nothing but sparkles of affection, their mouths and tongues uttering nothing but sounds of joy, their hands, feet and all the rest of their members in their gestures discovering a passionate longing and earnestness to meet and embrace their new sovereign."[5]

The coronation occurred on the 25th of July, 1603, in Westminster Abbey, where every English king had been crowned since William the Conqueror was crowned there on December 25, 1066. James had postponed the coronation festivities until his wife, Anne of Denmark, arrived. Anne began the journey to London with her own retinue a few days after James departed. The people of England were deliriously happy to have a young king, an attractive wife and two young children, Henry age nine and Elizabeth age seven. Anne was expecting another child at the time of the coronation. A quiver full of children resulted from this union—seven in all—but only three would survive to adulthood. It had been almost a century since the people of England enjoyed such a sight. Indeed, the last time they had a young king with children was in the early days of Henry VIII. Edward VI died young with no wife or children. Mary Tudor married but was childless. Elizabeth reigned for 45 years but never married.

The King relished the cordial welcome in his new environment, but all was not rosy in merry old England. Numerous long-simmering and thorny issues awaited the new king. Before arriving in London, James would be made aware of some of these issues. The most urgent of these appeals was a controversial dispute in the Church of England which would linger long into the seventeenth century and beyond. While en route to London, the King was met by some of the leading bishops and theologians in the Church of England with Puritan sympathies. These Puritans were English ecclesiastical leaders who hoped to purify the Church of unscriptural beliefs and corrupt practices, especially those left over from the days of Roman Catholic domination. The delegation was led by John Reynolds, or Rainolds (1549–1607), President of Corpus Christi College, Oxford, regarded by many as one of the most learned men in England.[6]

The Puritans presented to the King the "Millenary Petition," the name of which implies that it was signed by a thousand men (it actually had only 753 signatures), mostly ministers of the Church of England.[7] Addressing some of the Puritans' long-standing grievances, it was hoped that this Petition might relieve them from their "common burden of human rites and ceremonies."[8] It asked for reforms in the English Church, for the correction of abuses that had intensified under Elizabeth's increasing preference for ritual and ceremony. It was only natural that the Puritans should think the new king would be sympathetic to their cause. James had repeatedly declared his loyalty to the Presbyterianism in which he had been educated. He had publicly acknowledged his gratitude that he belonged to "the purest Church in Christendom." He had given them ample reason to believe that his convictions would be compatible with theirs.

Some of the practices objected to in the Petition included the lack of discipline in the church, the sign of the cross in baptism, questions addressed to infants in baptism, excommunications for trifles, confirmation, the use of the cap and surplice, the reading in church of the Apocrypha, the use of the terms "priest" and "absolution," bowing at the name of Jesus, Sabbath-breaking and the keeping of other holy days, long church services, and "other practices considered high church or popish."[9] Also, ministers should not be recruited from "ignoramuses" but from more able and learned men. The practice of allowing non-resident clergymen should be abolished. They asked for an Act of Parliament to end the ambiguity surrounding clerical marriage. Interestingly, the Millenary Petition contained no mention of a new Bible translation, yet it was the beginning of the events that led to it.

Queen Elizabeth had objected to such a conference, but when it was proposed to King James, he delighted in the opportunity afforded him of showing off his learning to the bishops and Puritans. Originally planned for November, 1603,

164

because of an outbreak of the plague in London the conference had to be rescheduled for January, 1604. The famous Hampton Court Palace was appointed as the place where the conference would convene. Built by Cardinal Wolsey, this gigantic brick edifice of a thousand rooms was twelve miles southwest of London on the River Thames. Wolsey reveled in its opulence until Henry VIII wrested it from him, added to and embellished it and made it his own playground.

HAMPTON COURT CONFERENCE

King James received the Millenary Petition with a graciousness that delighted the Puritans but alarmed the English bishops. As a result, prior to the conference, Richard Bancroft, future Archbishop of Canterbury and the most outspoken critic of Puritanism, went to the King and persuaded him that if Puritans had their way, the English crown itself might be imperiled. The King met with other establishment clergy during the days before the conference and heard them brand the Puritans as treasonous and seditious persons and identify them with the Presbyterian ministers in Scotland, most of whom James detested. "I will tell you," James said to the bishops, "I have lived among this sort of men (Puritans) ever since I was ten years old, but I may say of myself, as Christ did of Himself, though I lived amongst them, yet since I had ability to judge, I was never of them."[10]

Puritan hopes, however, were buoyed by King James' willingness to consider their complaints, and especially since he had been king in a land where Calvinism was enthroned in the National Church. It seemed to them a propitious time to secure from the new king more toleration for their beliefs than they enjoyed during the later years of Elizabeth's reign; but those hopes were quickly dashed as the conference unfolded.

The three-day conference began at nine o'clock in the morning on Saturday, January 14, only days after the royal family enjoyed Christmas festivities in the palace. The conferees met in the King's Privy Chamber, a large reception hall of the palace on the east side of the Clock Court. The establishment clergy hardly knew what to expect from the new king: son of a Catholic queen, christened according to Catholic tradition, nurtured by Presbyterian divines in Scotland, and whose wife recently converted from Lutheranism to Catholicism.

On the first day of the conference King James admitted only the aged John Whitgift, Archbishop of Canterbury, once chaplain to Queen Elizabeth (a little over a month later Whitgift would be dead), and a handpicked selection of eight bishops, seven deans and two privy councilors. Outnumbered eighteen to four, the Puritans were not even admitted to the conference until the second day. Bancroft had won the day and the conference was heavily weighted in favor of the established Church. Like Constantine at the opening of the Council of Nicea, James delivered the opening address. For five hours he exposed the corruptions and deficiencies of the Church of England. This was not exactly what the bishops hoped to hear. In fact, Lancelot Andrewes later commented that "the King did wonderfully play the Puritan that day!" The bishops' fear that the King might be a closet Puritan were unfounded. The next day he lit into the Puritans.

The four moderate Puritans finally admitted to the conference on the second day—John Reynolds, Laurence Chaderton, Thomas Sparke, and John Knewstubs—were ridiculed by the King and bullied into silence. He addressed them as "dunces fit to be whipped," although they were among the most learned and highly respected men of the time. His denunciation of the Puritans enabled the bishops to breathe a sigh of relief.

Reynolds acted as spokesman for the Puritans and raised the question of church government. When he implied that it would be better for the bishops to govern jointly with a *presbyterie* of their brethren, the King exploded in anger. "If

166

you aim at a Scots Presbyterie," he shouted, "it agreeth as well with a monarchy as God and the devil! Then Jack, and Tom, and Will, and Dick shall meet, and at their pleasure censure me and my council and all our proceedings."[11] He then shouted what might be considered his defining summary of the whole matter: "No bishop, no King!"[12] Overruling almost all of the Puritans' objections, the King told them he would tolerate none of their nonconformity. He made it clear that the doctrine and polity of the state church was not up for evaluation and consideration. "I will make them conform themselves or I will harry them out of the land or else do worse."[13] True to his word, during the next seven years King James and Archbishop Bancroft, through deprivations, visitations, and the Canons of 1604, forced many Puritans out of England, and some of them migrated, first to Holland, then to the New World seeking more religious freedom.

The King was so enamored of his performance that on the day following the conference, he wrote to a friend in Scotland: "We have kept such a revel with the Puritans here as was never heard the like; I have peppered them as soundly as ye have done the *papists* there." But to Sir John Harington, one of Elizabeth's godsons and an apparent witness to the proceedings (also, incidentally, inventor of the flushing toilet—why it is nicknamed "John"), the King did more than preside. He was the principal opponent of the supporters of the Millenary Petition. "He talked much Latin," with "upbraiding rather than argument," Harrington commented. "If, as the bishops said, his Majesty spoke by power of inspiration, I wist not what they meant, [for] the Spirit was rather foul-mouthed."[14]

But all was not lost by the Puritans. This second day, January 16, 1604, proved to be one of the most momentous days in English history. A suggestion made on this day by Dr. John Reynolds met the King's enthusiastic approval. "May your majesty be pleased," said Reynolds, "that the Bible be newly translated [because] those that were allowed in the reigns of

Henry the Eighth and Edward the Sixth were corrupt and not answerable to the truth of the Original."[15] This suggestion appears to be an afterthought, not part of the agenda.

One of the principal complaints of the time was which Bible should be the standard text to use in both worship and private study. Three different versions were in circulation in the early seventeenth century, each with a loyal following, and each causing sharp dissent among religious parties in England. The two authorized versions of the Church of England—the Bishops' and the Great Bible—were preferred by the clergy, although the latter was losing ground to the newer Bishops' Bible. Some of the laity, however, still clung to the Great Bible. The Geneva Bible was the favorite of the masses of Englishmen as well as the Puritan leaders in the Church of England. The Geneva was a superior translation but not authorized by the state, and its Calvinistic notes offended the more traditional church leaders.

Flattered by the suggestion of a new translation, and ruminating over the legacy that might accrue to him as a result, James promptly expressed his approval. A lover of Scriptural quotation and disputation, the King had tried his hand in earlier days at translating the Psalms into meter. To have a hand in a translation that could well be the best of all English translations of the Bible was a prospect that fired his imagination.

Aware of the influence of the Geneva Bible on the King in his youthful days in Scotland, Reynolds may have secretly hoped he would declare the Geneva Bible the new Authorized Version, or a least a revised edition of it. But this was not to be. James made it clear he didn't like any of the previous English Bibles, especially the Geneva. "I profess," he said, "I could never yet see a Bible well translated in English; but I think that of all, that of Geneva is the worst."[16] The King's attack on the Geneva Bible no doubt came as a surprise to the Puritans. The King had been brought up on the Geneva Bible. The first Bible ever published in Scotland was the Bassandyne Bible in 1579, an edition of the

Geneva version, dedicated "To the Richt Excellent Richt heich and Mychtie Prince James the Sixt King of Scottis."[17]

In truth, his objection was not so much to the translation itself but to the marginal notes that seemed to contradict his cherished belief in the Divine Right of Kings. "For in the Geneva translation," he complained, "some notes are partial, untrue, seditious, and savoring of traitorous conceits," and he instanced Exodus 1:19 and 2 Chronicles 15:16.[18] The marginal note for Exodus 1:19 commends the Hebrew midwives for disobeying the Egyptian king's orders. The note for 2 Chronicles 15:16 states that King Asa's mother should have been executed, and not merely deposed, for her idolatry. "It is supposed that James' suspicious mind thought that this might react unfavorably upon the memory of his own mother, Mary Queen of Scots."[19] Such notes insinuating that disobedience to the King was lawful, James considered seditious. James would use his kingly power to keep the Geneva from becoming the new Authorized Version.

Though King James liked the idea of a new translation, his enthusiasm was not shared by all clerics present at the conference. After Reynolds made his plea for a new translation of the Bible, Richard Bancroft rose to his feet and lamented, "If every man's humour should be followed, there would be no end of translating."[20] But when he saw that the King agreed with Reynolds, Bancroft gradually warmed to the project and eventually gave his wholehearted allegiance to it. Indeed, he would be the driving force behind the new translation. Although the Puritans left the conference gaining few reforms they had hoped the King would favor, and no doubt somewhat dismayed, what they had gained by Reynolds' suggestion they could not have foreseen.

THE TRANSLATORS

It is not known with whom James made all the plans and arranged all the details. No doubt his primary source of information issued from Bishop Richard Bancroft. But about six months after the Hampton Court Conference, not only the general plan of procedure but the list of scholars who were to do the work had been fully prepared. On July 22, 1604, James wrote to Bancroft that he had "appointed certain learned men, to the number of four-and-fifty for the translating of the Bible." He also directed him to "move the bishops to inform themselves of all such learned men within their several dioceses, as, having especial skill in the Hebrew and Greek tongues, have taken pains in their private studies of the Scriptures for the clearing of any obscurities either in Hebrew or the Greek, or touching any difficulties or mistaking in the former English translations, which we have now commanded to be thoroughly viewed and amended; and thereupon to earnestly charge them signifying our pleasure therein, that they send such their observations to Mr. Lively, our Hebrew reader in Cambridge, or to Dr. Harding, our Hebrew reader in Oxford, or to Dr. Andrewes, Dean of Westminster, to be imparted to the rest of their several companies, that so our intended translation may have the help and furtherance of all our principal learned men within this our kingdom."[21] Bancroft was also told to provide for the compensation of the translators by means of Church preferment. In fact, many of the translators did receive high promotions in the Church, while Henry Savile, the only layman among them, was made a knight.

Though King James' letter mentions fifty-four translators, the list that has been preserved contains only forty-seven. The discrepancy is supposed to be accounted for by resignations and deaths between the time of appointment and the time when the translation work began. Most of the translators were middle-aged or older. Two would die before the translation work was finished: Edward Lively and John Reynolds. All were men, academically distinguished, belonged to the Church of England, and were expert in ancient or modern languages or both.

These foremost Bible scholars and linguists were selected to serve on six panels (or "companies")—two met at

Oxford University, two at Cambridge University, and two at Westminster Abbey. Each company was responsible for the translation of certain books of the Bible:

> The First Westminster Company translated Genesis through 2 Kings.
>
> The First Cambridge Company translated 1 Chronicles through the Song of Solomon.
>
> The First Oxford Company translated Isaiah through Malachi.
>
> The Second Cambridge Company translated the Apocrypha.
>
> The Second Oxford Company translated the Gospels, Acts, and Revelation.
>
> The Second Westminster Company translated Romans through Jude.

Gustavus Paine wrote a book about the King James translators and titled it, appropriately, *The Learned Men.* (see Appendix Four for entire list). It will be worthwhile to note some of the more esteemed of these "learned men."

Lancelot Andrewes, Dean of Westminster, presided over the First Westminster Company (Genesis through 2 Kings) that met in the Jerusalem Chamber of Westminster Abbey. Regarded as one of the foremost figures in the history of the English Church, Andrewes had begun the study of Greek at the age of six. Eventually, he would master fifteen languages, including Latin, Greek, Hebrew, Syriac, and Chaldee. His linguistic ability prompted someone to comment that, "had he been present at the tower of Babel, he could have served as interpreter general!"[22] Both Queen Elizabeth and King James thought highly of Andrewes. Not only was he an extremely accurate and painstaking scholar, he was a preacher of great power. Andrewes delivered the funeral oration at Elizabeth's funeral, and four months later spoke at the coronation of King James. In James' dying advice to his children, he admonished them to read the works of Andrewes.[23]

Hadrian Saravia at age 73 was the oldest of the translators, and a member of the First Westminster Company. He served as professor of divinity at the University of Leyden before moving to England in 1587. He was known for his expertise in Hebrew. **John Layfield** was not only fluent in Greek, his knowledge of ancient architecture was such that his advice was sought on passages having to do with the tabernacle and the temple as described in Exodus and 1 Kings. He was the only one of the translators to travel to the New World.

William Bedwell, a fellow of Trinity College, Cambridge, was renowned as "the father of Arabic studies in England." His knowledge of Near and Middle Eastern languages enabled him to compile a Persian dictionary and an Arabic lexicon. Universally recognized as one of the great linguists of the day, he was also knowledgeable in astronomy, mathematics, and geography.

John Overall, regius professor of divinity at Cambridge and the dean of St. Paul's Cathedral, was so fluent in Latin that he once admitted it was sometimes difficult for him to speak English at any length. Because most of the discussions at the translators' committee sessions were in Latin, this knowledge was to his advantage. Just before Overall joined the translator team, he married a young woman reputed to be "the greatest beauty of her time." It was not a match made in heaven. She proved to be a frivolous, unfaithful wife, having eloped one day with a local squire. Overall went after her, and the two seem to have eventually reconciled. Overall was not the only one whose life was affected by scandal. **Richard Thomson,** a Hebrew scholar and the rector of Upwell in Norfolk, was known as an urbane, worldly, cosmopolitan man who was known to favor "racy epigrams." He seldom went to bed sober, but in the mornings, so the story goes, "his mind was clear."

The First Cambridge Company (1 Chronicles through the Song of Solomon) was presided over by **Edward Lively,** regius professor of Hebrew at Cambridge, and known as the one most responsible for the growth of Hebrew studies in England. As the father of thirteen children, he always seemed to be in debt, never able to stay ahead of his bills. Only months after joining the Cambridge Company of translators, he died of "an ague and a squinsey," leaving his children orphans and destitute. His wife had preceded him in death some months before.

Laurence Chaderton was one of the four Puritans to attend the conference at Hampton Court. Chaderton became an outstanding linguist, expert in Hebrew, Latin, Greek, Spanish, and French. He was also known as one of the great preachers of his day. Chaderton proved to be the longest-lived of the translators, living through the reigns of four Tudors and two Stuarts into the English Civil War. Before he died at the age of 105, he was said to be able to read "without spectacles" a copy of the Greek New Testament "with very small type."

The First Oxford Company (Isaiah through Malachi) was presided over by **John Harding,** regius professor of Hebrew at Oxford. Though Harding was a highly qualified Hebrew scholar, he was overshadowed by **John Reynolds,** president of Corpus Christi College, Oxford. Not only was Reynolds the most notable member of the Company, he was the man who initiated the whole idea of the translation project. Friends described him as "a living library," "a third university," "a university unto himself;" and his "memory and diversity of reading" were said to be "near unto a miracle" and "an ever springing and never failing well." Known for his Puritan sympathies, Reynolds was regarded as the most capable spokesman for the Puritan cause. Unfortunately, Reynolds died in 1607 at the age of fifty-eight while the work of translation was still in progress.

Miles Smith, another member of the First Oxford Company, not only provided scholarly help in the translation process; he would be one of two chosen to edit the complete Bible text. Also, the great "Translators to the Reader" was written by him (see Appendix Three).

Thomas Ravis, known for his antipathy to the Puritans, presided over the Second Oxford Company (the Gospels, Acts, and Revelation). Like Reynolds, Ravis died in December 1609 before the work of translation was completed. But the most prominent man in this Company was **Sir Henry Savile,** one of the foremost classical scholars of his age. His travels often took him to Europe, where he collected manuscripts and rare books which he later bequeathed to the Bodleian Library. Interestingly, he was appointed Greek tutor to Queen Elizabeth.

Another person of note on the Second Oxford panel was **George Abbot,** a reputable Greek scholar and master of University College, Oxford. His Puritan sympathies would sometimes strain his relationship with the majority party in the English Church. Abbot, however, became a trusted adviser to the King. But an unforeseen event clouded his life and almost ruined his career. Once while hunting in a park with friends, he aimed at a deer, the arrow glanced off a tree and killed a gamekeeper. Although it was an accident, he became known as "a man of blood." It was a source of great distress to Abbot, and for the rest of his life he imposed on himself a monthly fast, besides feeling compelled to give a large sum of money to the victim's widow each year. After an inquiry on the accident, Abbot was exonerated by a special commission and also received a royal pardon. In 1611 he was appointed Archbishop of Canterbury.

William Barlow, dean of Chester and Bishop of Rochester, chaired the Second Westminster Company (Romans through Jude). Barlow was a member of the Hampton Court Conference and its historian. He was one of Elizabeth's favorite preachers. After his sermon on the plow, she is reported to have said, "Though his text was taken from the cart, his talk was good instruction for the court." He recorded his recollections of the conference in a brief tract entitled, *The Sum and Substance of the Conference, which, it pleased his Excellent Majesty to have with the Lords, Bishops, and other of his Clergy (at which the* *most of the Lords of the Council were present), in his Majesty's Privy-Chamber, at Hampton Court, January 14 1603.*

The Second Cambridge Company (The Apocrypha), consisted of seven members, and was chaired by **John Duport,** master of Jesus College, Cambridge. Duport was the son-in-law of Bishop Richard Cox of Ely, who had translated two of the New Testament books for the Bishops' Bible (1568). This Company had the distinction of having the youngest of all the translators, twenty-seven year old **Samuel Ward,** a chaplain to the King and master of Sidney Sussex College.

John Bois (also "Boys"), Fellow of St. John's College, Cambridge, was perhaps the most distinguished member of this company. Reported to have been an extraordinarily precocious child, he could read the Hebrew Bible at the age of six and write the Hebrew alphabet with elegance. By age 13 he was competent in New Testament and classical Greek. As an undergraduate at Cambridge he was famous for his work ethic: he studied from four o'clock in the morning till eight at night. He not only contributed to the duties of the Second Cambridge Company, completing his own portion of the Apocrypha ahead of schedule; he assisted another Company also, and was one of twelve who served on the exclusive General Committee of Review (two from each of the six companies met together daily for nine months at Stationer's Hall, London, as a revision committee). The committee's work might have remained a mystery had it not been for thirty-nine pages of notes of the proceedings made by Bois that were discovered in the Bodleian Library in 1958. These notes detail the committee's deliberations on Romans through Revelation, offering insight into how the group dealt with language and style.

Although **Thomas Bilson** was not one of the original translators, along with Miles Smith he took part in the work of final revision. Bilson provided the summary at the head of each chapter, the intention of which was to indicate the contents of the chapter. A fellow of New College, Oxford, he eventually

175

became Bishop of Winchester. As a High Churchman, Bilson had little sympathy for Puritan teachings and ideals. But he was said to be "as reverent and learned a Prelate as England every afforded, a deep and profound scholar." Bilson also wrote the brief Epistle Dedicatory to the King (see Appendix Two): "To the Most High and Mightie Prince, James by the grace of God King of Great Britaine, France and Ireland, Defender of the Faith, &c. The translators of the Bible, wish Grace, Mercie, and Peace, through Jesus Christ our Lord." Bilson praised James as the "principal Mover and Author of the work," and then dismissed any criticism of it in advance. "Since things of this quality have ever been subject to the censures of ill meaning and discontented persons, it may receive approbation and patronage from so learned and judicious a Prince as your Highness is, whose allowance and acceptance of our Labors, shall more honor and encourage us, then all the calumniations and hard interpretations of other men shall dismay us."

STRATEGY FOR THE NEW REVISION

It is to the credit of James that he devised a plan of translation vastly superior to what Archbishop of Canterbury, Matthew Parker, put forward for the Bishops' Bible. The King determined that this new translation would eliminate some of the deficiencies and weaknesses that he surmised were in all previous English translations of the Bible. "I wish some special pains were taken for an uniform translation," said the King; "which should be done by the best learned in both universities, then reviewed by the bishops, presented to the Privy Council, lastly ratified by Royal authority to be read in the whole Church and none other."[24]

With the approval and input of King James, Bishop of London **Richard Bancroft** drew up an elaborate set of guidelines for the translators to observe in order to ensure that partisan leanings were eliminated in the new version. They determined to minimize the risk of producing a Bible that might be perceived to favor Puritanism, Presbyterianism, or Roman Catholicism.

RICHARD BANCROFT'S TRANSLATION RULES

1. The ordinary Bible read in the Church, commonly called the *Bishops' Bible,* to be followed, and as little altered as the Truth of the original will permit.
2. The Names of the Prophets and the Holy Writers, with the other Names of the Text, to be retained, as nigh as may be, accordingly as they were vulgarly [commonly] used.
3. The Old Ecclesiastical Words to be kept, *viz.* the Word Church not to be translated Congregation &c.
4. When a Word hath diverse Significations [or meanings], that to be kept which hath been most commonly used by the most of the Ancient Fathers, being agreeable to the Propriety of the Place, and the Analogy of the Faith.
5. The Division of the Chapters to be altered, either not at all, or as little as may be, if necessity so require.
6. No Marginal Notes at all to be affixed, but only for the explanation of the *Hebrew* or *Greek* Words, which cannot without some circumlocution, so briefly and fitly be express'd in the Text.
7. Such Quotations of Places to be marginally set down as shall serve for the fit Reference of one Scripture to another.
8. Every particular Man of each Company, to take the same Chapter, or Chapters, and having translated or amended them severally by himself, where he thinketh good, all to meet together, confer what they have done, and agree for their Parts what shall stand.
9. As any one Company hath dispatched any one Book in this Manner they shall send it to the rest, to be considered of seriously and judiciously, for His Majesty is very careful in this Point.
10. If any Company, upon the Review of the Book so sent, doubt or differ upon any Place, to send them Word

thereof; note the Place, and withal send the Reasons, to which if they consent not, the Difference to be compounded at the general Meeting, which is to be of the chief Persons of each Company, at the end of the Work.

11. When any Place of Special Obscurity is doubted of, Letters to be directed, by Authority, to send to any Learned Man in the Land, for his Judgment of such a Place.

12. Letters to be sent from every Bishop to the rest of his Clergy, admonishing them of this Translation in hand; and to move and charge as many as being skillful in the Tongues; and having taken pains in that kind, to send his particular Observations to the Company, either at *Westminster* [Abbey], *Cambridge,* or *Oxford.*

13. The Directors in each Company, to be the Deans of *Westminster* and *Chester* for that Place; and the King's Professors in the *Hebrew* or *Greek* in either University.

14. These translations to be used when they agree better with the Text than the *Bishops' Bible: Tindoll's* [Tyndale's], *Matthew's, Coverdale's, Whitchurch's* [Great Bible], *Geneva.*

15. Besides the said Directors before mentioned, three or four of the most Ancient and Grave Divines, in either of the Universities, not employed in Translating, to be assigned by the Vice-Chancellor, upon Conference with the rest of the Heads, to be Overseers of the Translations as well *Hebrew* as *Greek,* for the better observation of the 4th Rule above specified.

According to Rule 1, it was not to be a new translation but a revision of the Bishops' Bible. The King had forty unbound folio copies of the Bishops' Bible, 1602 edition, sent to the translators, a strong message that they were to stick closely to that text.[25] But the translators did not allow themselves to be tethered to the Bishops' Bible. Earlier translations were to be used if it was deemed that they agreed better with the original text (Rule 14). The version that influenced the KJV more than any other was the Geneva Bible. This was the more extraordinary considering that the new translation was undertaken largely because of the King's antipathy to the Geneva.

Surprisingly, a number of translation entries in the KJV came directly from the Roman Catholic Rheims New Testament (A.D. 1582). The Douay Old Testament appeared too late to be used. In the First Epistle of John, for example, the following were all directly traceable to the Rheims: "Confess" is used where previous versions had "acknowledge" or "knowledge" (1:9). "Propitiation" is substituted for "reconciliation" or "atonement" (2:2). "Unction" is used instead of "ointment" (2:20). And in Romans "reprobate" is substituted for "lewd" (1:28). Some Latin words in the KJV have also come from the Rheims: "hymn" (Matt. 26:30); "decease" (Luke 9:31); "separated" (Rom. 1:1); "impenitent" (Rom. 2:5); "contemptible" (2 Cor. 10:10); and "sanctification" (1 Peter 1:2).

Rule 3 stipulates that old ecclesiastical words were to be reintroduced, such as "church" in place of "congregation," "charity" instead of "love." Tyndale's anti-ecclesiastical translations of these words were tabled. Rule 6 specifies that marginal notes that many leaders in the Church of England objected to in the Geneva Bible as well as in Tyndale's Bible were to be sparingly employed; and then only to clarify Hebrew and Greek words and to point out parallel passages in the text (Rule 7). Each panel was assigned particular books of the Bible to translate. Once each of the groups had made its translation, the work was to be reviewed by the other companies (Rules 8 & 9). This latter Rule was the only one to reference the King, and he is said to be "very careful" about this particular Rule. It is obvious that Bancroft, the author of the Rules, must have had long discussions with King James about what the Rules should contain. Each company had to supervise the work of every other company. Mutual supervision was felt to be absolutely necessary by the King. A "general meeting" consisting of the leaders of each company would then settle any differences if there were questions as to what the correct rendering should be (Rule 10). Nothing was left to chance, as is apparent from Rules 11 through 15.

John Selden, a contemporary of the translators, made an interesting observation on the methods adopted by the six companies:

> The Translators in King James' time took an excellent way. That part of the Bible was given to him who was most excellent in such a tongue (as the Apocrypha to Andrew Downes) and then they met together, and one read the translation, the rest holding in their hands some Bible, either of the learned tongues, or French, Spanish, Italian, &c. If they found any fault they spoke; if not, he read on."[26]

Unfortunately, little else is known of the methods actually adopted by the revisers. Dr. F. H. A. Scrivener notes, "Never was a great enterprise like the production of our Authorized Version carried out with less knowledge handed down to posterity of the laborers, their method and order of working."[27]

OTHER SOURCES UTILIZED BY THE TRANSLATORS

In addition to the earlier English Bibles, the translators had other sources at their disposal. They consulted the Masoretic Hebrew text of the Old Testament and the slightly modified Greek text of Erasmus' New Testament. None of the older Greek manuscripts, such as the Codex Sinaiticus, Alexandrinus, and Vaticanus, were available to the translators. Some had not been discovered, and the Codex Vaticanus was unavailable simply because the Roman Catholic authorities refused permission to all outsiders to review it until 1857.

In 1546, Robert Estienne (Stephanus) reprinted Erasmus' Greek New Testament. Between that date and 1551, he published four editions, making slight changes in each, some of which were based on the Complutensian Polyglot. In his fourth and final edition (1551), he added numbered verse divisions to his text. The first English Bible to adopt Estienne's versification method was the Geneva Bible (1560). Almost all English Bibles since have followed Estienne's lead. Theodore Beza, an associate of John Calvin and one of the foremost scholars of his day, published several editions of the Greek New Testament (1556–1598). "It was this series of successive revisions from Erasmus, to Estienne, to Beza, upon which the translators of the King James Bible primarily relied."[28] Also consulted were foreign Bibles, such as the German translations of Luther and Zwingli, the French translation of Olivetan, the Latin translations of Pagninus, Sebastian Munster, and Castalio, as well as the Latin Vulgate, the Chaldaic Targum, and the Syriac New Testament.

Because the translators recognized "this is the Word of God which we translate," they strove for accuracy, beauty, clarity, and dignity. Their linguistic ability, their reverence for the Scriptures, their commitment to faithfully communicating the meaning of the original language texts in understandable English, and their humility before the Holy Spirit as they undertook their task assured success.

The actual work of translating took the panels roughly three years; another three years were spent in reviewing the translations, and an additional nine months in preparing it for the press. Bishop of Winchester, Thomas Bilson, and Miles Smith of Brasenose College, Oxford, gave the whole Bible manuscript a final editing.

Just as Smith thought the work was at last completed, "In came my Lord of Canterbury [Richard Bancroft] to Stationers Hall," Smith complained, "demanding the final say." The High Church Archbishop gave it a final quick check-over, making at least fourteen changes, one of which proved to be quite controversial. Bancroft insisted that "the glorious word Bishoprick" be inserted in Acts 1:20, the same ecclesiastical word used in Tyndale's New Testament, the Great Bible, the Bishops' Bible, and the Catholic Rheims New Testament.

The Geneva Bible had "charge." Most of the KJV translators preferred "office," which word, incidentally, is inserted in the margin. *"Bishoprick"* was a much more acceptable term to High Church clerics because of its ecclesiastical linkage. Smith objected to the change, but Bancroft "is so potent," he wrote, "there is no contradicting him."[29] The finished product was what might be called a "politically correct" Bible, wherein all factions of the Church would be satisfied. It was truly an ecumenical version.

Published in London in 1611 by Robert Barker, the royal printer, the new Bible was a beautiful black-letter folio edition printed on the most expensive rag paper. Measuring approximately 16 by 10½ inches, the King James Bible was even larger than the Great Bible and similar in size and appearance to the Bishops' Bible. An elaborate engraved title page described the version as "The Holy Bible, Conteyning the Old Testament, and the New: *Newly Translated out of the Originall tongues: & with the former Translations diligently compared and revised, by his Majesties speciall Commandement. Appointed to be read in Churches.* ANNO DOM. 1611"

Two editions were published the first year, with numerous variations in the Biblical text. The first is known as "the great 'He' Bible," and the second as "the great 'She' Bible." The first printing renders the closing words of Ruth 3:15, "and he went into the city," while the next edition corrected it to read, "and she went into the city." The latter translation is most often found in modern English Bibles.

THE APOCRYPHA AND THE KJV

It comes as a surprise to many modern Christians to learn that the first edition KJV contained fourteen books that are not found in most modern English Bibles. These books, written between the dates of the Old Testament and the New Testament, are referred to as Apocrypha, a name ascribed to the books by Jerome (c. 345—420). The word "apocrypha" comes from the

Greek *apokrypto,* which means "to hide," or "conceal." The books were thought to contain "hidden" or "secret" truths. They are I and II Esdras, Tobit, Judith, the Rest of Esther, the Wisdom of Solomon, Ecclesiasticus or the Wisdom of Sirach, Baruch, the Song of the Three Children, Susanna, Bel and the Dragon, the Prayer of Manasseh, and I and II Maccabees. Not only were these books included in the 1611 KJV, they were inserted in all English Bibles predating the KJV.

The question many ask is, "Why are these books not in Bibles today?" Although some of these books are considered canonical by Roman Catholic and Eastern Orthodox churches, they are rejected by Jews and most non-Catholic groups. Jerome, a Catholic, did not intend to include any of the Apocryphal books when he translated the Old Testament from Hebrew into Latin (A.D. 391—to 405). While admitting that the [Catholic] Church reads the Book of Judith and Tobit and Maccabees, as well as Wisdom and Ecclesiasticus, he insists they are strictly uncanonical and should be used solely "for edifying the people, not for the corroboration of ecclesiastical doctrines."[30] He further explained that the additions to Esther, Daniel and Jeremiah had no place in the Hebrew Canon; and therefore had no right to be included in the Christian Bible as canonical Scriptures. At first Jerome resolved to translate only the canonical Scriptures, but at last he reluctantly yielded to the pressure of his friends and made a hasty translation of Tobit and Judith. He made it plain that it went against his better judgment to translate books which, in his view, lacked the authority of the Hebrew canon. These were the only books of the Apocrypha that he translated. The rest of the Apocryphal books were later added to the Vulgate from the Old Latin versions.

Origen (c. 185—254) explicitly describes the Old Testament canon as comprising only 22 books (because Jews combine several OT books, their 22 books equal the 39 in our modern Bibles). Athanasius (c. 296—373), chief theologian of Christian orthodoxy, differentiated "canonical books" from both "those that are read" by Christians only and the "Apocryphal books" rejected alike by Jews and Christians. One strong argument against the inclusion of these books in the canon of Bible is that the New Testament itself does not cite the Apocryphal books directly.

Even though Wycliffe's Bible (A.D. 1382) included the Apocrypha, the preface made it clear that these books were not to be regarded as inspired Scripture. Luther's German Bible in 1534 placed the books between the Testaments, demonstrating his belief that they were not to be thought of as equal in value to the canonical books. At the same time he described their value for devotional and historical purposes. Luther especially favored the Prayer of Manasseh. Myles Coverdale's English Bible (1535) was the first English Bible to follow Luther's example and segregate some of the Apocryphal books between the Testaments. The special title page of the Apocrypha section of Coverdale's Bible reads as follows: "The bokes and treatises which amonge the fathers of olde are not rekened to be of like authorite with the other bokes of the Byble, neither are they founde in the Canon of the Hebrue." The Great Bible of 1539 quotes with approval Jerome's judgment that they may be read for the edifying of the people, but not to confirm and strengthen the doctrine of the Church. Similarly, the Geneva Bible of 1560 states that they are to be read not for doctrine but for "knowledge of history" and "instruction of godly manners."

In the King James Version of 1611, no disclaimer is given to the Apocrypha such as the ones found in earlier English Bibles. They are simply headed, "Apocrypha." Indeed, they were regarded as so integral a part of the King James Version that one of the translators, George Abbot, after his appointment as Archbishop of Canterbury, issued a decree in 1615 stipulating that "no Bibles were to be bound up and sold without the Apocrypha on pain of a whole year's imprisonment."[31] The first English Bible in which the deliberate omission of the Apocryphal books is discussed "editorially" is the edition of the Geneva Version published at Amsterdam in 1640. Most Protestant English Bibles in the twenty-first century have omitted the disputed books or, in some few cases, have placed them after the Book of Revelation.

THE TRANSLATORS TO THE READER

The translators of the KJV felt that the work called for some explanation and defense. Myles Smith of Brasenose College, Oxford, was appointed to assume the important responsibility. Labeled "The Translators to the Reader," Smith's preface for many years stood at the beginning of the KJV. But for various reasons, perhaps its length and scholarly tone, rarely is it published in King James Bibles today. It is to be regretted that this preface or at least a condensed version of it is not to be found in modern King James Bibles. The preface provides excellent insight into the thinking and motives of the translators; uncovers the event that prompted the making of the translation; tells why the translators felt compelled to respond to anticipated criticisms from both Roman Catholics and Puritans; makes known why new versions of the Bible are sometimes necessary; divulges why the particular translation methods were employed; and reveals their conviction regarding Holy Scripture (see Appendix Three).

Modern King James Bibles have no explanation or introduction of any kind except for the somewhat fulsome dedication to King James, and that, too, is omitted in most Bibles (see Appendix Two).

NEW VERSION HAS ITS CRITICS

Like almost all versions when they first appear, the new Bible aroused suspicion and not a little disapproval. In fact, for a century-and-a-half the KJV was the object of severe criticism by certain clergymen and scholars. Hebrew scholar,

Hugh Broughton, piqued by his exclusion from the panel of translators, lashed out at the new translation:

> The late Bible . . . was sent me to censure, which bred in me a sadness that will grieve me while I breathe. It is so ill done. Tell his Majesty that I have rather be rent in pieces with wild horses, than any such translation by my consent should be urged upon poor churches.[33]

Broughton must have been particularly annoyed when the KJV translators rejected his advice to "translate with uniformity," meaning that the same English word, not its synonyms, must always be used when translating a Hebrew or Greek word. Miles Smith in "The Translators to the Reader" explained why Broughton's suggestion was tabled:

> We have not tied ourselves to a uniformity of phrasing or to an identity of words, as some peradventure would wish that we had done. . . . We thought [to translate with uniformity might] savor more of curiosity than wisdom, and that rather it would breed scorn in the atheist than bring profit to the godly reader. . . . We might also be charged (by scoffers) with some unequal dealing towards a great number of good English words.

John Selden complained that

> the Bible is translated into English words rather than into English phrase. The Hebraisms are kept, and the phrase of that language is kept: as for example, ("He uncovered her shame") which is well enough, so long as scholars have to do with it; but when it comes among the common people, lord, what gear [i.e. what rubbish] do they make of it![34]

In 1659, the Reverend Robert Gell, minister of the parish of St. Mary, Alder-Mary, in London, published an 800-page treatise denouncing the KJV, "discussing its faults in detail, counting among them a denial of Christ's authority."[34]

Not only did some scholars protest, many common people resented anyone tampering with or attempting to displace their cherished Bible, meaning the Geneva Bible. Indeed, a whole generation passed before the new King James Version exceeded the Geneva in popularity, and that was primarily due to an edict forbidding the printing of the Geneva Bible in England.

Although these criticisms were not altogether justified, they nonetheless demonstrate that the new version was not immediately welcomed with enthusiasm by all the recognized scholars of the day, nor was it considered a literary classic when it first appeared. Anticipating such criticism, Miles Smith in "The Translators to the Reader" wrote:

> Zeal to promote the common good, whether it be by devising any thing ourselves, or revising that which hath been labored by others, deserveth certainly much respect and esteem, but yet findeth but cold entertainment in the world. It is welcomed with suspicion instead of love, and with emulation [jealousy] instead of thanks; and if there be any hole left for cavil [criticism] to enter, (and cavil, if it does not find a hole, will make one) it is sure to be misconstrued and in danger to be condemned.

A COMPOSITE PRODUCTION

The KJV, like the one that preceded it (Bishops'), was a composite production, not an entirely new translation. While this could have diluted the quality of the new version, fortunately the translators were wise enough to incorporate most of the best features of those earlier translations, the end result being a Bible superior to all its predecessors. James Baikie makes the observation that "one of the most astonishing facts connected with the Version is the small amount of change which the scholars of King James found it necessary to make."[35] The early translators had done their work so well that drastic modification was unnecessary. Baikie adds, "Much of Tyndale and Coverdale remains unchanged in the Bible which we read today."[36]

Without detracting from the skill and reputation of the KJV translators—for there were superior linguistic and literary scholars among them—Tyndale is widely regarded as the real

187

genius behind the version. Tyndale's wish that the Bible should be understood by the "ploughboy" was fulfilled in the new version, owing to its spare and simple vocabulary of only eight thousand words. Time after time the reviewing committees decided that Tyndale's translations were the best. Some claim that at least eighty percent or more of the KJV came from the man who was tracked down by Henry VIII and Thomas More's agents seventy-five years earlier and burned at the stake.

In some cases, of course, the KJV translators made noteworthy and necessary changes from Tyndale. There is no denying that there was need for some fine tuning, some enrichment, some added resonance. One instance where the King James translators improved on Tyndale, at least from a stylistic standpoint, is in the use of the phrase, "three score and ten." Tyndale simply says "seventy." The decision of the translators to use this compound form would seem to reflect a desire to give their version a deliberately archaic flourish. Abraham Lincoln clearly responded to this aim in his famous Gettysburg Address: "Four score and seven years ago. . . ." Although not an actual quotation from the Bible (the word "fourscore" does appear 36 times in the KJV), it sounded a strong note of Biblical authority.

But some of the changes were not always for the good. Tyndale translates Hebrews 11:1, "Faith is a sure confidence of things which are hoped for, and a certainty of things which are not seen." The Great Bible (A.D. 1539) followed Tyndale to the letter. The KJV translators, however, revert to the more obscure rendering in the Catholic Rheims New Testament: "Now faith is the substance of things hoped for, the evidence of things not seen."

Perhaps the most frequently repeated set of words in the English language are these memorable Tyndale-King James lines: "Our Father, which art in heaven, Hallowed be thy name. . . ." A significant change from Tyndale is noticed in one of the petitions. Whereas the KJV adds, "And forgive us our debts, as we forgive our debtors," Tyndale gives us the more familiar refrain, "And forgive us our trespasses, as we forgive those who trespass against us."

English historian J. A. Froude (1818–1894) astutely observed,

> The peculiar genius which breathes through [the King James Version], the mingled tenderness and majesty, the Saxon simplicity, the preternatural grandeur, unequalled, unapproached in the attempted improvements of modern scholars—all are here, and bear the impress of one man, and that man [is] William Tyndale.[37]

Chapter Eight

THE INFLUENCE OF THE
EARLY ENGLISH BIBLES

It is trendy for the literati to praise the rhythmical and melodic language of the King James Bible, while at the same time denying and even ridiculing its message. Although offended by their blatant skepticism, believers can appreciate their recognition of the Bible's superior literary quality. Even outspoken atheist Richard Dawkins unabashedly heaps praise on the King James Bible. "The Authorized Version includes passages of outstanding literary merit in its own right, for example the Song of Songs and the sublime Ecclesiastes."[1] He even encourages the study of the Bible in public school classrooms. "But the main reason the English Bible needs to be part of our education is that it is a major source book for literary culture."[2] He then gives a long list of Biblical or Bible-inspired phrases and sentences that occur commonly in literary or conversational English. Surprisingly, Dawkins admits that "ignorance of the Bible is bound to impoverish one's appreciation of English literature."[3]

The Bible is more than literature, but it is literature; in fact, the best of literature. Whenever a list of "best books" is presented, the Bible usually ends up in the number one position. Our English speech and literature have been remarkably influenced by the Bible, especially the early English Bibles. There is little disagreement among literary experts that the King James Version is a masterpiece of English, and, along with the versions that preceded it, has exercised a significant and wholesome influence on the formation of the English language. As Luther's German version of the Bible helped to standardize the modern German language, the view of many linguistic experts is that the early English Bibles have done the same for our own language.[4]

Melvyn Bragg in his book, *12 Books that Changed the World,* claims the King James Bible "has informed the English Language more powerfully even than Shakespeare."[5] Bragg further states, "As the Reformation began to burn through Europe, William Tyndale started to preach in public and set out on a journey (translating the Bible from the original languages into English) which would, in my opinion, lead to an enrichment of the English language greater than that made by any other man."[6] David Daniell, former Professor of English at University College, London, boldly affirmed, "Without Tyndale, no Shakespeare."[7]

The rhythms, cadences, and imagery of the Bible crowd the words of British and American writers, from Shakespeare to many modern authors. Oxford professor Samuel Gardiner begins one of his essays with this quote: "In all study of English literature, if there be any one axiom which may be accepted without question, it is that the ultimate standard of English prose style is set by the King James Version of the Bible." Of course, this is the perspective of someone who lived in the 19th century, and not necessarily what all modern-day critics would acknowledge.

Years ago a writer remarked that prior to his time every student of English literature or of English speech, found three works or subjects referred to or quoted from more frequently than any others. These were the Bible, tales of Greek and Roman mythology, and *Aesop's Fables*. Of these three, the Bible furnishes the largest number of references.

William Shakespeare (1564–1616) quoted Scripture frequently in his writings. According to one authority, of the many books that influenced Shakespeare, the Bible and Ovid's Metamorphosis are the most important. There is no question that the Bible influenced him markedly, but it was the Geneva version and the Bishops' Bible that he quoted most often in his writings. The King James Version appeared only five years before his death; and only two of his works were written after the King James Bible appeared. The hundreds of Biblical references in Shakespeare's plays give ample evidence that he was well acquainted with Scripture. Not only is the range of his Biblical references impressive, but also the aptness with which he employs them. The late Dr. Naseeb Shaheen of the University of Memphis notes that Hamlet and Othello each have more than fifty Biblical references. No study of Shakespeare's plays is complete that ignores his use of Scripture.

John Milton (1608–1674) is regarded as one of England's greatest authors. According to one biographer, Milton always began the day with the reading of Scripture and kept his memory deeply charged with its phrases. His day began at 4 a.m., when he had the Hebrew Bible read to him, and then wrote until breakfast. His essays on the defense of liberty and the freedom of the press are shot through with Scripture quotations and arguments. His three great poems, "Paradise Lost," "Samson Agonistes," and "Paradise Regained," are Scriptural from first to last. Someone said, "Milton's mind was like a garden where the seeds of Scripture came to flower and fruit." He said, "There are no songs to be compared with the songs of Zion; no orations equal to those of the prophets; and no politics like those which the Scriptures teach. . . . In the very critical art of composition, it is so far above all kinds of lyrical poetry as to be incomparable."

It is often said that the greatest allegory in the English language is *Pilgrim's Progress*, by **John Bunyan** (1628–1688). For many years *Pilgrim's Progress* was the most widely read book in English literature after the Bible. It is still being printed after more then 300 years since it was first published. Its phrases, names, and subject matter are either directly or indirectly taken from the Bible. Thackeray took the motto of one of his best-known books from the Bible—but the title,

Vanity Fair, comes from *Pilgrim's Progress*. Charles Spurgeon, the famous 19th century English preacher, called it the most important book in his life other then Scripture. He is said to have read *Pilgrim's Progress* more than 100 times. Macaulay in his *History of England,* said of Bunyan that "he knew no language but the English as it was spoken by the common people; he had studied no great model of composition, with the exception of our noble translation of the Bible. But of that his knowledge was such that he might have been called a living concordance."

Samuel Johnson (1709–1850) was a poet, essayist, and lexicographer. After the Bible and Shakespeare, Johnson is possibly the best known and most frequently quoted figure in the whole range of English literature. His contribution to literature—most significantly his dictionary, the first major dictionary in our language—has had a most profound influence on the vitality of the English language of which we are the fortunate inheritors. Johnson was an inveterate reader of the Bible. It was said the one reason he did not always like to attend divine services was because he generally knew more about the Bible than the one doing the preaching. Johnson read the Bible every day and divided it into seven volumes for convenience. The essays he wrote for the Rambler were almost always moralistic in tone, and though not overtly Christian, they were the outcropping of his daily study of Scripture.

Samuel Taylor Coleridge (1772–1834) tells of many long and careful readings of the English Bible, so much so that he could say: "In the Bible there is more that finds me than I have experienced in all other books together; the words of the Bible find me at greater depths of my being." In the "Rime of the Ancient Mariner" much of the phraseology is Scriptural.

Jane Austen (1775–1817) displays features in her work of the influence of the Bible and of her upbringing in a clergyman's home. She was educated primarily by her father and had access to his large and eclectic library. The two big public texts that would have affected Austen almost from birth were the Bible and Thomas Cranmer's *Book of Common Prayer*. In her home the Bible would have been read aloud every day of her life. Although Austen almost never inserts references to the Bible in her novels, the moral and ethical sentiments of Scripture manage to creep through. Just as the Bible assails hypocrisy and cant, Austen in her own clever way often does the same through her characters.

John Kelman has written a whole book on the religion of **Robert Louis Stevenson** (1850–1894). Entitled *The Faith of Robert Louis Stevenson*, it tells of how he was raised by a nurse, Alison Cunningham ("Cummie"), whose library consisted chiefly of the Bible, *Pilgrim's Progress*, the shorter Catechism, and the *Life of Robert Murray McCheyne*. "She stored his hospitable mind," wrote Lord Guthrie, "with Bible stories and Bunyan, tales of Covenanters, and legends in prose and verse." This cultivated his latent seeds of poetry. Stevenson said that the 58th chapter of Isaiah was his favorite, because "it so repudiated cant and demanded a self-denying beneficence." He loved Bunyan's *Pilgrim's Progress*; but the Bible stood the highest of all books. Every great story or essay shows its influence. His *Dr. Jekyll and Mr. Hyde* is only his way of putting into modern speech Paul's distinction between the two natures in each of us. Over the shoulder of Stevenson you can see the great characters of Scripture urging him on to his best work.

Like Bunyan, **Abraham Lincoln** (1809–1865) educated himself largely by means of the Bible. This was especially true in the early years of his life. He completely mastered the Bible. Two other writers profoundly influenced him—Plutarch and Shakespeare—but their influence paled in comparison to that of the Bible. Lincoln could almost be said to be a man of one book. In his writings and speeches, the words and images of Scripture are everywhere apparent. Soon after the Battle of Gettysburg, a proposal was made to establish a soldier's cemetery near the battlefield, where Union dead could be reburied with dignity and honor. And on November 19, 1863, the dedication of the cemetery took place. On that occasion Lincoln gave what many consider the best summation in the nation's history of the meaning and price of freedom. It is generally referred to simply as "The Gettysburg Address," and is often called the greatest speech in American history.

The speech, which lasted only about two minutes, is powerful because Lincoln used the language of the sacred to describe a battlefield graveyard. At the beginning of his speech he used the familiar Biblical term, "fourscore," a term found 36 times in the Bible. He said, "Fourscore and seven years ago," instead of the wooden, "87 years ago." Lincoln was wise enough in his understanding of the power of words to use a familiar expression found in the Lord's Prayer—the word "hallow." Lincoln said, "But in a larger sense, we cannot dedicate, we cannot consecrate, we cannot hallow this ground." To "hallow" ground is to create a sacred space. Throughout his career, Lincoln appropriated the language of the Bible to create Biblical-sounding phrases. In his famous "House Divided" speech, he quoted directly from Mark 3:25. He was a masterful appropriator of the Bible's rhetorical power.

C. S. Lewis (1898–1963) was born in Belfast, Northern Ireland. A graduate of Oxford University, he would later become a fellow of Magdalen College for nearly 30 years. Afterwards he became the highly regarded first professor of Medieval and Renaissance Literature at Cambridge. As a teenager Lewis abandoned his faith, but his interest in fantasy and mythology— especially in relation to the words of George MacDonald— was part of what turned him from atheism to Christianity. A Scottish minister, poet, and novelist, MacDonald was especially known for his fairy tales and fantasy novels. Lewis wrote that he regarded MacDonald as "his Master." Lewis is thought by many to have been the foremost Christian apologist of his time. His books—*Mere Christianity, The Problem of Pain,* and *Miracles*—were all concerned to one degree or another, with refuting popular objections to Christianity and the Bible. His love and comprehension of Scripture are everywhere in evidence in his writings.

The Bible also has had a strong formative effect on many other great writers of English, such as John Donne, Daniel Defoe, Henry David Thoreau, Henry Melville, Nathaniel Hawthorne, Charlotte Bronte, Charles Dickens, Walt Whitman, Ralph Waldo Emerson, Thomas Hardy, D. H. Lawrence, Dorothy Sayers, G. K. Chesterton, William Faulkner, T. S. Eliot, John Updike, Annie Dillard, and the list could go on and on.

Historian John Green says,

"All the prose literature of England has grown up since the translation of the Scriptures [into English]. . . . When the Bible was ordered to be set up in [all] the churches [of England], Sunday after Sunday, day after day, as the crowd gathered around the Bible in the nave of St. Paul's, or the family group hung on its words in the devotional exercises at home, they were leavened with a new literature. . . . As a mere literary monument, the English version of the Bible remains the noblest example of the English tongue, while its perpetual use made it, from the instant of its appearance, the standard of our language. . . . The power of the book over the mass of Englishmen showed itself in a thousand superficial ways, and in none more conspicuously than in the influence it exerted on ordinary speech."[8]

Far greater than the Bible's effect on literature was and is the effect of the Bible on the character of people who have received and believed its transformative message. Tyndale nor the translators of the King James Version set out to create a literary classic. They felt their Divine calling was to make the Bible understandable to the average layperson in language befitting a Book of its significance. Miles Smith in the Preface to the KJV, underscores the avowed intent of the translators: "How shall people meditate on something they cannot understand? Indeed, without a translation in the *common language,* the unlearned are like children at Jacob's well without a bucket or something to draw water with."

As important as the erudite quality of the Bible is, it was not to preserve the superb literary excellence of the Bible that enabled John Wycliffe, William Tyndale and John Rogers to suffer shame and even willingly submit to martyrdom. Although John Wycliffe did not experience martyrdom, he was constantly harassed and threatened with punishment, and forty-four years after his death his bones were dug up and burned. Why did these men endure such cruel threats and even inhumane deaths? They were firmly convinced the book they were translating was the very Word of God, not some merely human production. Furthermore, they believed that *justification by faith alone*, without the appendage of human merit, was the Bible's clearly defined means of salvation; therefore, they would translate, regardless of the cost.

Not only was the message of the Bible necessary for a person's salvation, the translators believed it was essential to assist in one's journey toward spiritual maturity. A martyr in his early forties, William Tyndale gave the following rationale for translating the Bible into English: **"I perceived by experience how that it was impossible to establish the laypeople in any truth, except the Scripture were plainly laid before their eyes in their mother tongue, that they might see the process, order, and meaning of the text."**[9]

Appendix One:

GLOSSARY

Amanuensis—A scribal secretary employed to write what another dictates, or to copy what another has written.

Anathema/Anathematized—When used in the New Testament *anathema* means "accursed" or "the condition of being set apart for destruction." In the Roman Catholic Church, *anathematized* means the solemn ban of excommunication pronounced against a person considered a great offender and the consigning of that person to eternal damnation.

Apocrypha—Greek word meaning "secret" or "hidden." The Protestant designation for the fourteen or fifteen books that were included in the Septuagint (LXX), Latin Vulgate (OT) and all Catholic Bibles, but not in most Protestant English Bibles today. Almost all of these books were originally composed in Greek and are accepted as canonical by Eastern Orthodox and Roman Catholics. Rejected as canonical by Jews and Protestants, nevertheless they were included in all early English versions including the KJV, but were placed between the Testaments and regarded as worthy only for inspirational and historical purposes. They are known in Roman Catholicism as "Deuterocanonical books" (deuterocanonical means "second canon").

Aramaic—A Semitic language closely related to Hebrew, and traditionally the language of Syria. In OT times it became the *lingua franca* of most of the people from Mesopotamia to the Mediterranean coast, and continued to be so until the Arab conquests in the seventh and eighth centuries A.D. During the Babylonian Captivity in the sixth century B. C., Jews were forced to adopt Aramaic. When they eventually returned to their homeland, they brought the new language with them; consequently by the first century A.D., Aramaic was in general use in Israel. Some of the words of Jesus are in Aramaic (e.g., Mark 5:41; 7:34; 14:36; 15:34).

Authorized—Given or endowed with authority; legally or formally sanctioned. The KJV is often referred to as *The Authorized Version,* especially in England, but beyond the royal authority under which it was made, and the statement on the title page "Appointed to be read in churches," no formal authorization was ever given to it.

Autograph/Autographa—The original manuscript of an ancient document written in the hand of the original author or his amanuensis. No autograph of any Biblical book is extant. The nearest we have are the Dead Sea Scrolls (B.C. 100—A.D. 100) which contain portions of all OT books except Esther, and a small piece of papyrus codex (3.5x2.5 inches), containing verses from John's Gospel (18:31–33, 37–38) and dated from the first half of the second century.

Archbishop—The title given to a bishop who has jurisdiction over all other bishops of an ecclesiastical province.

Bible—Comes from the Greek word *Biblos,* which originally meant the inner bark of the papyrus plant. It came to refer first to the paper made from the bark and then to the scroll and the codex and eventually to the whole collection of thirty-nine books which make up the Old Testament and the twenty-seven books which make up the New Testament.

Bull (Papal)—The most solemn form of papal document, beginning with the name and title of the pope, dealing with an important subject, and having attached to it a leaden seal called a bulla. Many of these bulls were issued to prohibit the publication of supposedly heretical writings.

Bishopric—The see, diocese, or office of a bishop.

Canon—A Greek word meaning rule, norm, standard, measure. It was first used in relation to the Bible by Eusebius, and then from the fourth century by both Jews and Christians to designate books considered to be authentic Scripture. The Protestant New Testament canon and the Roman Catholic New Testament canon are identical, but Protestants follow the Old

200

Testament canon of the Hebrew Bible, while Roman Catholics endorse the Septuagint Old Testament canon that includes the Apocryphal books.

Cathedral—The official church of the bishop of a diocese. The Greek word *cathedra* means chair or throne; the bishop's "chair" symbolizes his teaching and governing authority, and is located in the principal church or "cathedral" of the local diocese of which he is the chief pastor.

Catholic—From the Latin *catholicus* meaning universal or general.

Celt/Celtic Church—A member of an Indo-European people who inhabited Britain at the time of the Roman occupation. The Celtic church is believed to have originated as early as the second century in parts of the British Isles, long before the Roman missions of Augustine of Canterbury (597). It managed to maintain its independence from the Roman Church until the Synod of Whitby (663/4).

Chapter division—The complete Bible of today is ordinarily divided into chapters and verses, but such divisions were not part of the original texts. They were developed at a much later date, primarily to make it easier for the Bible student to locate passages within a book. Although a great help for reference purposes, they do not always agree with the natural development of thought in the text. The introduction of the present system of chapter divisions is usually attributed to a Roman Catholic lecturer at the University of Paris, Stephen Langton, later Archbishop of Canterbury (d. 1228). His chapter divisions were introduced into the Vulgate, and afterwards into English Bibles.

Closed canon—An exclusive list of authoritative works; a *canon* that is not open for additions or deletions. Most Protestants believe the thirty-nine Old Testament books and twenty-seven New Testament books are not to be augmented, hence the Bible is considered a closed canon.

Codex (pl. Codices)—The forerunner of the format we call a "book." A replacement for the scroll, it did not come into use until around A.D. 100, and was formed by taking one or more sheets of papyrus or vellum and sewing them together at the spine. For the first time it was possible to have the whole Bible together, which was not possible with scrolls. The Bible on one scroll would have been far too bulky.

Colophon—An inscription at the end of a book or manuscript, used especially in the 15th and 16th centuries, giving the title or subject of the work, its author, the name of the printer or publisher, and the date and place of publication.

Council of Trent—A theological council (1545–1563) of the Roman Catholic Church to respond to the challenges that emerged from the teachings of Martin Luther and other Protestant Reformers. The Council, which spanned the office of five popes, defined and regulated doctrines and practices of the Roman Church which the Reformers had attacked. The Council confirmed transubstantiation, that the substance of bread and wine is changed into the body and blood of Christ; tradition was said to be equally authoritative with Scripture; the correct interpretation of the Bible was the exclusive prerogative of the Catholic Church; only the Vulgate was to be used in public readings and doctrinal commentaries; and the fourteen books considered *Apocryphal* by Protestants were acknowledged as canonical—equal in authority with all thirty-nine books in the Jewish canon.

Covenant—A solemn agreement between human beings or between God and a human being involving mutual commitments or guarantees. In the Old Testament or Covenant, God revealed His law through Moses and prepared His people for salvation through the prophets. In the New Testament or Covenant, Christ established a new and eternal covenant through His own sacrificial death and resurrection.

Criticism (Textual)—(See *Textual Criticism*)

Diocese—A fully organized ecclesiastical jurisdiction in the Roman Catholic and other churches under the pastoral direction of a bishop.

Divine Right of Kings—A theory widely held in the Middle Ages that royal authority was divinely ordained. This theory, as practiced by the Stuarts (James I, Charles I & II, etc.) in seventeenth century England, was founded on the belief that the king possessed an absolute grant of authority from God Himself, hence disobedience to the king was disobedience to God.

Eastern Orthodox Church—is also known as the Orthodox, Greek, or Greco-Russian Church. The final breech between Greek Catholics and Roman Catholics came in A.D. 1054.

Folio—A book made of full-sized leaves or sheets, each folded once to form four pages (about 12 x 15 inches), or a book of the largest size.

Friar—Term applied in the Catholic Church to members of mendicant orders (members of religious orders without property rights who worked or begged for their support) to distinguish them from members of monastic orders.

Glosses—Notes in the margins of the Bible intended to clarify, improve, or explain.

Gothic Type—A heavy-faced type that originated in Germany, sometimes called "Old English" or "Black Letter," and resembling early European handlettering (calligraphy). All early English Bibles, with the exception of the Geneva Bible, were printed in Gothic Type.

Hebrew Language—The language of virtually all of the Old Testament. One of the Semitic languages, similar to Babylonian, Assyrian, Chaldean and Phoenician. An alphabetic script consisting of 22 letters, written from right to left and only in consonantal form until the Masoretes added vowel points (A.D. 600–900).

Heresy/Heretic—From the Greek *hairesis,* meaning a set of principles or school of thought. Now used to mean an opinion, doctrine, or particular interpretation of Scripture which conflicts with the generally accepted teaching of the main body of Christians. A heretic is a person who holds such an opinion or doctrine.

High Churchman—was a member of the Church of England who emphasized its historical continuity as a branch of the Catholic Church and upheld "high" conceptions of the divine basis of authority in Church and State, of the rights of monarchy and episcopacy, and the nature of the sacraments. Lancelot Andrewes, one of the King James translators, was a notable High Churchman.

Humanism—As used in reference to Renaissance leaders, it refers to a confidence in human nature, coupled with a belief in the power of education. This confidence in human nature was tempered by skepticism, particularly in theological matters. For many humanists, the church was regarded as having simply a civic function to fulfill. Not all humanists, however, were religious skeptics. Many, such as Erasmus, were not critical of the Bible but of those who deviated from its teachings.

Indulgence—An official relaxation of law that shortens or cancels one's sufferings due to sin, and it usually has reference to the sufferings in purgatory. During the Middle Ages, letters of indulgence bearing the name of the pope not only relieved those in the land of the living from the temporal consequences of their sins but released the souls of their dead loved ones from purgatory, and all for a simple monetary transaction.

Inspiration—Literally "God-breathed" (from 2 Tim. 3:16). The process by which the Holy Spirit of God enabled the human authors and editors of Scripture to record His very words without sacrificing their individual styles, with the result that their writings are designated the Word of God.

Inquisition—A tribunal in the Roman Catholic Church for dealing with heretics, authorized by Gregory IX in 1231 to search them out, hear and judge them, sentence them to various forms of punishment, and in some cases to hand them over to civil authorities for punishment. The institution was responsible for many excesses, especially in the second half of the thirteenth century. In Spain, persecution of supposed heretics was particularly virulent and continued until early in the nineteenth century.

Koine Greek—Greek *he koine dialektos,* "the common dialect." The "common" vernacular or marketplace Greek of the Greco-Roman world during the first Christian centuries, distinct from the more beautiful but difficult classical Greek of Homer and Plato. The New Testament was originally written in language much like Koine Greek, mostly by authors for whom it was a second language. The choice of this "common" Greek as the target language to spread the new faith suggests that God intends His Word to be in the everyday language of people, not in an urbane or abstruse style suitable only for the scholarly elite, nor in an antiquated style—comprehensible, but no longer the current language of the general population.

Laypeople—those non-ordained members within the church who hold unofficial roles of service or leadership. Laypeople have been closely linked to the church's mission and service from earliest times. In some cases, laypeople are entrusted with the ministry of preaching.

Lexicon—In Biblical studies, the common designation for a dictionary of Hebrew, Greek or Latin words.

Literal translation—a "word-for-word" translation from one language to another as opposed to an idiomatic, thought-for-thought translation or paraphrase.

LXX—Roman numeral symbol for the Septuagint, meaning "seventy," and referring to the seventy or so scribes at

Alexandria, Egypt, alleged to have translated the Hebrew Bible into Greek in about B.C. 250–150.

Manuscript—A handwritten copy of an ancient text in the language in which it was written.

Martyr—A Greek word, meaning "witness," that came to mean one who voluntarily suffered death for the Christian faith.

Masoretes—Jewish scribes known as Masoretes (transmitters) who helped preserve the Old Testament text. Over a period of centuries (sixth through the tenth) they faithfully copied the books of the Old Testament. Among the best known aspects of their work was the introduction into the text of vowel points and accents. Previously the Hebrew language had only consonants. These features were intended to show how words should be pronounced at a time when Hebrew had ceased to be a living language. The official Hebrew text still used today by both Christian and Jewish translators is "The Masoretic Text."

Minuscule—A professional writing style in a free-flowing hand, characterized by small, connected letters, something like cursive script. It was developed around the ninth century. The term is used to refer to those manuscripts written in such a style. See also *uncial.*

Monastery—The dwelling place of monks belonging to certain religious orders in the Catholic Church. The male monastic leaders have such titles as abbot and prior; females, abbess and prioress. In most cases, an abbey is the same as a monastery.

Monk—A member of a monastic order in the Catholic Church who binds himself by religious profession to attachment to a monastery, the contemplative life and the work of his community.

New Testament—Tertullian was the first Christian theologian to write in Latin. Writing around the year A.D. 200, he coined the Latin term *Novum Testamentum,* meaning "New Testament," which we still use.

Nonconformists—Originally the term was used in the 17th century of those in the Church of England who refused to conform to the discipline and practice (esp. the ceremonies) of the established Church. The word is now applied generally to Presbyterians, Baptists, Methodists, Congregationalists, etc.; all who are not in communion with the Church of England.

Octavo—A small book of about 6 x 9 inches, determined by printing on sheets folded to form eight leaves or sixteen pages.

Old Latin—An early translation of the Greek Bible into Latin. Produced as early as the second century of our era, this work may be a collection of independent translations and should be distinguished from the Vulgate, a Latin version made directly from the Hebrew and Greek.[1]

Paper—Thin, flat material made from pulped wood, cloth, or fiber, and used for a writing surface in Europe since the fourteenth century.

Papyrus (pl. papyri)—A primitive kind of ancient paper or writing material made from strips of papyrus reed placed in a crisscross fashion and pounded to make a flat writing surface. The papyrus plant grew in the marshes of Egypt. We get our word "paper" from the papyrus plant.

Parchment—Also called vellum; ancient flat writing material prepared from the skin of goats, sheep or other animals, the hair of which has been removed and the skin rubbed smooth. The most complete extant manuscripts of the New Testament were written on vellum.

Pardoner—A Catholic Church official charged with the granting of indulgences in the Middle Ages, in return for offerings made to the Church.

Parish—A church served by a pastor (priest) in a certain geographical area of a Catholic diocese.

Penance—A sacrament in the Roman Catholic Church that signifies a reentry into God's grace whenever the sinner had lapsed from his state at baptism. "The acts of the penitent—contrition, the confession of sins, and satisfaction or reparation—together with the prayer of absolution by the priest, constitute the essential elements of the Sacrament of Penance."[2]

Pentateuch—The first five books of the Old Testament: Genesis, Exodus, Leviticus, Numbers, and Deuteronomy.

Pope—The alleged successor of St. Peter as Bishop of Rome and Supreme Pontiff of the Roman Catholic Church. "The pope exercises a primacy of authority as Vicar of Christ and shepherd of the whole Church; he receives the divine assistance promised by Christ to the Church when he defines infallibly a doctrine of faith or morals."[3]

Pseudepigrapha—(Literally, "false writings"). A collection of some sixty-five documents written between 25 B.C.– A.D. 200 by Jews and Christians but were never included in the Old Testament canon or the Apocrypha. This collection includes various types of literature, some of it attributed to Biblical characters, such as Enoch, Ezra, Baruch, Elijah, Abraham, Isaac, and Jacob, but in reality these names are pseudonyms.

Puritan/Puritanism—A movement for further reformation in the Church of England that began in the reign of Elizabeth I (1558–1603). The purpose of the movement was to purge ("purify") the Church of England of the last vestiges of Roman Catholicism and bring it more into line with the Scriptures. At the request of almost 1000 Puritan clergy, a meeting was called by King James I at Hampton Court in 1604 to deal with certain abuses that these concerned Puritans enumerated in the Millenary Petition presented to the new king on his way to the coronation. Out of this conference came a new translation of the Bible (A.V. 1611), the result of a suggestion by one of the Puritan clergy (John Reynolds) that a new translation was needed in England.

Quarto—Literally "one quarter." It refers to manuscripts or books having four leaves (eight pages) to the sheet, that is 9½ by 12 inches (scale of American Library Association).

Receptor language—The language being translated into.

Rector—In the late Middle Ages in England, a clergyman (ecclesiastic) who had the charge of a parish with full possession of all its rights, tithes, etc.

Reformation—The period, mostly in the sixteenth century, when attempts to reform the Church in Europe resulted in the separation of the Protestant Churches from the Roman Catholic Church.

Relics—According to Roman Catholics, the material remains of a saint and any other objects which may have had contact with that saint. Only those relics authorized by a cardinal or bishop are to be venerated by the faithful.

Religious Order—In the Roman Church an institute "entered freely in response to the call of Christ to perfection, and characterized by the profession of the evangelical counsels of poverty, chastity, and obedience."[4] Examples are Franciscans, Dominicans, Jesuits, Benedictines, etc.

Renaissance—The revival of learning which took place in Europe in the fifteenth and sixteenth centuries.

Scribes—Scholars whose vocation was to make written copies of earlier manuscripts.

Scroll—Long continuous roll made of either papyrus or parchment and wound on a pair of rods. The beginning of a scroll was on the right rather than the left (since the Hebrews wrote from right to left). The word *book* in the Authorized Version means "scroll."

Semitic—In linguistics, a language family that encompasses the following groups: Canaanite (Ugaritic, Hebrew, Phoenician, Moabite), Aramaic (Palestinian Aramaic, Syriac, Mandean), Akkadian (Babylonian, Assyrian), and "South" Semitic (Arabic, Ethiopic, South Arabian).[5]

Septuagint—A pre-Christian Greek translation of the Hebrew Scriptures made by Jewish scholars, and later adopted by Greek-speaking Christians. Jews were scattered over the Middle East and elsewhere, and Greek, not Hebrew, became the commonly used language. The Septuagint (from *septuaginta,* the Latin word for seventy, LXX) was undertaken by the Greek-speaking Jews in Alexandria, Egypt, from the third to the second century B.C. The early Christians, who often used Greek as their common language of communication, accepted the Old Testament as sacred, and they knew it in the Septuagint version. A large number of the Old Testament quotations in the New Testament are taken from the Septuagint, not the Hebrew original. The Septuagint thus became the "authorized version" of the early Gentile churches. To this day it is the official version of the Old Testament used in the Eastern Orthodox Church.

Simony—The practice of buying or selling ecclesiastical offices.

Target language—The language into which a particular text is to be translated.

Textual criticism—The process by which scholars establish the text of Scripture as near to the original as possible. Since we no longer have any original manuscripts or "autographs," scholars must sort and evaluate the extant copies and make decisions about which reading among the *variants* is most likely the correct one (Erasmus used this process when analyzing the eight or nine Greek manuscripts at his disposal to produce what later became known as the *Textus Receptus*). Because at times the word "criticism" means "finding fault with," it is important to note that when it is used in the sense explained above, it means "evaluation," the analysis of something with the intent of determining its value.

Textus Receptus—Latin for "received text," or "the text received by all." The Greek text that underlies all early English Bibles, from Tyndale to the Authorized Version of 1611. The term is most often used to refer to Erasmus' Greek text of

1535 (a revision of the first text produced by Erasmus in 1516) and Stephanus' third edition Greek text of 1550. It was named the Received Text in the introduction of the Elzevir's second edition Greek New Testament (1633).

Torah—The English transliteration of the Hebrew word for "law." It is most commonly used with reference to the first five books of the Old Testament (Pentateuch).

Translation—The rendering of a word, phrase, or version from one language into another, the intent of which is to give the words in the target language a meaning equivalent to that of the original.

Transmission—The process by which the Biblical manuscripts have been copied and recopied down through the ages; it deals with the history of the text from the autographs to the present printed Hebrew and Greek Testaments.

Transubstantiation—"Transubstantiation indicates that through the consecration of the bread and the wine [elements used in the Mass] there occurs the change of the entire substance of the bread into the substance of the Body of Christ, and of the entire substance of the wine into the Blood of Christ—even though the appearances or 'species' of bread and wine remain."[6]

Unicial manuscript—Unicial literally means, "inch high." It refers to a manuscript written in formally printed large letters similar in size to capital letters; common until about the eighth century.

Vellum—Also called parchment; a fine quality writing material in ancient times, usually prepared from calf, lamb, or goatskin. "It took the hides of 4500 animals to make the vellum for just 50 Bibles. Add to that the cost for the preparation of the parchment and the scribal fee, and producing a Bible was a very expensive operation which only the wealthy could afford."[7]

Verbal inspiration—Suggests that the very words of the Bible as originally given were vested with divine authority and not merely the thoughts or ideas.

Vernacular—The common language of the people.

Verse divisions—Sometime in the early 1200's Stephen Langton, Archbishop of Canterbury, divided each book of the Bible into chapters. More than three hundred years later a French printer, Robert Stephanus (Estienne), took the process a step further and divided each chapter into verses. Stephanus, a Protestant convert and associate of Reformation leader, John Calvin in Geneva, believed that Bible study would be enhanced if each chapter was divided into numbered verses. He accomplished this, according to his son, while traveling on horseback from Paris to southern France. Stephanus published at Geneva in 1551 a Greek and Latin edition of the New Testament, the first ever with chapters divided into separate verses. The first complete Bible divided into verses was Stephanus' Latin Vulgate issued at Geneva in 1555. The verse divisions devised by Stephanus were widely and rapidly adopted. The first English Bible to adopt verse divisions was the Geneva Bible in 1560. Every English edition since has copied Langton's chapter and Stephanus' versification model.

THE EPISTLE DEDICATORY

(The Dedication of the 1611 KJV to King James)

TO THE MOST HIGH AND MIGHTY PRINCE JAMES by the Grace of God KING OF GREAT BRITAIN, FRANCE, AND IRELAND. DEFENDER OF THE FAITH, &c. *The translators of the Bible wish Grace, Mercy, and Peace through* JESUS CHRIST *our* Lord

GREAT and manifold were the blessings, most dread Sovereign, which Almighty God, the Father of all mercies, bestowed upon us the people of *England*, when first He sent Your Majesty's Royal Person to rule and reign over us. For whereas it was the expectation of many, who wished not well unto our *Zion*, that upon the setting of that bright Occidental Star, Queen *Elizabeth* of most happy memory, some thick and palpable clouds of darkness would so have overshadowed this Land, that men should have been in doubt which way they were to walk; and that it should hardly be known who was to direct the unsettled State; the appearance of Your Majesty, as of the *Sun* in his strength, instantly dispelled those supposed and surmised mists, and gave unto all that were well affected exceeding cause of comfort; especially when we beheld the Government established in Your Highness, and Your hopeful Seed, by an undoubted Title, and this also accompanied with peace and tranquility at home and abroad.

But among all our joys, there was no one that more filled our hearts than the blessed continuance of the preaching of God's sacred Word among us; which is that inestimable treasure which excelleth all the riches of the earth; because the fruit thereof extendeth itself, not only to the time spent in this transitory world, but directeth and disposeth men unto that eternal happiness which is above in heaven.

Then not to suffer this to fall to the ground, but rather to take it up, and to continue it in that state, wherein the famous Predecessor of Your Highness did leave it: nay, to go forward with the confidence and resolution of a Man in maintaining the truth of Christ, and propagating it far and near, is that which hath so bound and firmly knit the hearts of all Your Majesty's loyal and religious people unto You, that Your very name is precious among them: their eye doth behold You with comfort, and they bless You in their hearts, as that sanctified Person who, under God, is the immediate Author of their true happiness. And this their contentment doth not diminish or decay, but every day increaseth and taketh strength when they observe that the zeal of Your Majesty toward the house of God doth not slack or go backward, but is more and more kindled, manifesting itself abroad in the farthest parts of *Christendom*, by writing in defense of the Truth, (which hath given such a blow unto that man of sin, as will not be healed), and every day at home, by religious and learned discourse, by frequenting the house of God, by hearing the Word preached, by cherishing the Teachers thereof, by caring for the Church, as a most tender and loving nursing Father.

There are infinite arguments of this right Christian and religious affection in Your Majesty; but none is more forcible to declare it to others than the vehement and perpetuated desire of accomplishing and publishing of this work, which now with all humility we present unto Your Majesty. For when Your Highness had once out of deep judgment apprehended how convenient it was, that out of the Original Sacred Tongues, together with comparing of the labors, both in our own and other foreign Languages, of many worthy men who went before us, there should be one more exact Translation of the holy Scriptures into the *English Tongue*; Your Majesty did never desist to urge and to excite those to whom it was commended, that the work might be hastened, and that the business might be expedited in so decent a manner, as a matter of such importance might justly require.

And now at last, by the mercy of God and the continuance of our labors, it being brought unto such a conclusion, as that we have great hopes that the Church of *England* shall reap good fruit thereby; we hold it our duty to offer it to Your Majesty, not only as to our King and Sovereign, but as to the principal Mover and Author of the work: humbly craving of Your most Sacred Majesty, that since things of this quality have ever been subject to the censures of ill meaning and discontented persons, it may receive approbation and patronage from so learned and judicious a Prince as Your Highness is, whose allowance and acceptance of our labors shall more honor and encourage us than all the calumniations and hard interpretations of other men shall dismay us. So that if, on the one side, we shall be traduced by Popish Persons at home or abroad who therefore will malign us, because we are poor instruments to make God's holy Truth to be yet more and more known unto the people, whom they desire still to keep in ignorance and darkness; or if, on the other side, we shall be maligned by self conceited Brethren who run their own ways and give liking unto nothing but what is framed by themselves and hammered on their [own] anvil; we may rest secure, supported within by the truth and innocency of a good conscience, having walked the ways of simplicity and integrity as before the Lord; and sustained without by the powerful protection of Your Majesty's grace and favor, which will ever give countenance to honest and Christian endeavors against bitter censures and uncharitable imputations.

The Lord of heaven and earth bless Your Majesty with many and happy days, that, as His heavenly hand hath enriched Your Highness with many singular and extraordinary graces, so You may be the wonder of the world in this latter age for happiness and true felicity, to the honor of that great GOD, and the good of His church, through Jesus Christ our Lord and only Savior.

Appendix Three:

THE TRANSLATORS TO THE READER

(Author's note: Some of the words, punctuation, and spelling have been updated, and in some cases changes of expression have been made for the sake of clarification).

THE BEST THINGS HAVE BEEN FALSELY ACCUSED

Zeal to promote the common good, whether by devising anything ourselves, or revising what has been accomplished by others, certainly deserves much respect and admiration, yet finds only a cold reception in the world. It is welcomed with suspicion instead of love, and with jealousy instead of thanks. And if there is any hole left for criticism to enter (and criticism, if it does not find a hole, will make one), it is sure to be misconstrued and in danger of being condemned. This will easily be admitted by all who know history or have any experience. For was any thing ever projected that savored in any way of newness or improvement that did not endure many a storm of contradiction or opposition? A man would think that civility, wholesome laws, learning and eloquence, synods, and Church support (not to mention other things of this kind) should be as safe as a sanctuary and out of range, as they say, of any man that would lift up the heel, or dog that would move his tongue against them. For by civility we are distinguished from brute beasts who merely follow their sensual appetites. By wholesome laws we are bridled and restrained from outrageous behavior and doing injury to others, whether by fraud or by violence. By education we are enabled to inform and reform others by the light and awareness that we ourselves have attained unto. Further, when we are brought together to talk face to face at synods, we more quickly settle our differences than by writings, which can be endless. And finally, that the Church should be sufficiently provided for is so agreeable to good reason and conscience that those mothers are held to be less cruel who kill their babies as soon as they are born, than those nursing fathers and mothers (spiritual leaders whoever and wherever they may be) who withhold sustenance from those who hang upon their breasts (and upon whose breasts they indeed do hang to receive the spiritual and pure milk of the Word). Thus it is apparent that these things we speak of are basic necessities, and therefore none can speak against them without being absurd, or treat them with contempt without hint of wickedness.

Yet for all that, scholars know that certain worthy men have been brought to untimely death for no other fault than attempting to produce good order and discipline in their countrymen. And in some countries it was made a capital crime to propose that a new law abrogate on old law, even though the old law was most pernicious. And certain leaders who would be considered pillars of the State and models of virtue and prudence, could not be brought for a long time to adopt approved standards of good letters and refined speech; shying away from them as from rocks or containers of poison. And fourthly, he was no babe but a mature scholar who said, in passion perhaps (and in writing so as to remain in posterity), that he had not seen any good come from any synod or meeting of the Clergy, but rather the contrary. And finally, with regard to Church support and allowances that are provided for the ambassadors and messengers of the great King of kings, there is a story (or fable as it is called by a superstitious reader) that at such time as the professors and teachers of Christianity in the Church of Rome (then a true Church), were liberally endowed, a voice was heard from heaven, saying, "Now is poison poured down into the Church," etc. Thus not only as often as we speak, as one says, but also as often as we do anything of note or consequence, we subject ourselves to everyone's censure, and happy is he who is least subjected to idle gossip, for it is impossible to completely escape the snare of it. If anyone imagines that this is true only of unimportant people, and that princes are privileged and by their high estate exempt from criticism, he is deceived. "The sword devours one as well as another," it says in Samuel (II Samuel 11:25). As the great commander charged his soldiers in a certain battle to strike at no part of the enemy but at the face; and as the king of Syria commanded his chief captains "to fight neither with small nor great, save only against the king of Israel" (I Kings 22:31), so it is too true, that envy strikes most spitefully at the fairest and highest in authority. David was a worthy prince, and no man could compare to him for his early deeds; and yet when he brought back the ark of God in solemn triumph, as worthy an act as he ever performed, he was scorned and scoffed at by his own wife (II Samuel 6:16). Solomon was greater than David, not in virtue but in power. And by his power and wisdom he built a temple to the Lord that was the glory of the land of Israel, and the wonder of the whole world. But was his magnificence admired by all? We doubt it. Otherwise why, after his death, do they blame him and then appeal to his son to ease their burden? "Make," they say, "the hard service of your father and his heavy yoke lighter" (I Kings 12:4). Most likely Solomon had burdened them with heavy taxes and troubled them with forced labor; consequently they reacted foolishly, wishing in their heart the temple had never been built. It is a hard thing to please everyone, even when we please God best, and seek to approve ourselves to everyone's conscience.

THE HIGHEST PERSONAGES HAVE BEEN SLANDERED

If we will descend to later times, we shall find many similar examples of this kind, or rather unkind treatment. The first Roman Emperor [Julius Caesar] never did a more pleasing deed for the learned, nor more profitable to posterity, for the accurate recording of events, than when he corrected the Calendar, basing it on the solar year. Yet for this, he was maligned for novelty and arrogance, and brought him only disrepute. Also the first Christian Emperor, Constantine (at least the first to openly profess the faith himself and allow others to do the same), by strengthening the empire at great expense and providing for the Church as he did, got for his effort the name Pupillus, meaning a wasteful Prince that needed a guardian or overseer. So Theodosius, the best Christian Emperor, for the love that he had for peace, thereby to enrich both himself and his subjects, and because he did not go to war until he was forced into it, was judged to be a weakling. The truth is, he excelled in feats of chivalry and demonstrated as much when he was provoked, but he was condemned for giving himself to ease and pleasure. Justinian, the most learned Emperor of former times—at least the greatest politician—dispensed with superfluous laws, systematizing them with some order and method. But what thanks did he receive for this action? He was stigmatized by some as an Epitomist, that is one who destroyed worthy volumes to bring his abridgments into demand. This is the way excellent Princes have been treated in former times. Their good deeds have been misjudged and maligned. Nor is there any likelihood that envy and malignity died and were buried with the ancients. No, no! The reproof of Moses applies to most ages: "You are risen up in your fathers' place, a new generation of sinful men" (Numbers 32:14). The wise man said, "What has been done is what will be done, and there is no new thing under the sun" (Ecclesiastes 1:9). And St. Stephen adds, "As your fathers did, so do you" (Acts 7:51).

HIS MAJESTY'S INSISTENCE, DESPITE SLANDER, FOR A SURVEY OF ENGLISH TRANSLATIONS

And now more to the purpose. His Majesty that now reigns (and long may he reign and his offspring after him), according to the singular wisdom given to him by God and the rare learning and experience he has attained to, knew full well that whoever attempts any thing for the public, especially if it pertains to religion or with making the Word of God accessible and understandable, sets himself on a stage to be frowned upon by every evil eye; indeed, he casts himself headlong on a row of pikes to be gored by every sharp tongue. For he who meddles with men's religion in any way meddles with their customs, no, with their inalienable rights. And though they find no satisfaction in what they have, they cannot bear to have it altered. Nevertheless, his royal heart was not daunted or discouraged by this or that opinion, but stood as resolute as an immovable statue, or like an anvil that cannot easily be beaten into plates. He knew who had chosen him to be a soldier, or rather a captain (II Timothy 2:4), and being assured that the course which he intended was for the glory of God and the building up of His Church, he would not allow it to be broken off by anyone's speeches or actions. It certainly belongs to kings, yes, especially to them, to be concerned for religion, to know it correctly, to profess it zealously, and to promote it to the best of their ability. This is their glory before all nations that mean well, and it will bring to them a far more excellent weight of glory in the day of the Lord Jesus. For the Scripture does not say in vain, "Those who honor me I will honor" (I Samuel 2:30). Nor was it an empty word that Eusebius delivered long ago when he said that piety towards God was the weapon, and the only weapon, that both preserved Constantine's person, and avenged him of his enemies.

THE PRAISE OF HOLY SCRIPTURE

But now what is piety without truth? What truth, what saving truth is there without the Word of God? What Word of God is there that we may be sure of without the Scriptures? We are commanded to search the Scriptures (John 5:39; Isaiah 8:20). Those who search and study them are commended (Acts 17:11 and 8:28, 29). Those who are unskillful in them or slow to believe them are reproved (Matthew 22:29; Luke 24:25). They can make us wise unto salvation (II Timothy 3:15). If we are ignorant, they will instruct us; if out of the way, they will bring us home; if out of order, they will reform us; if sorrowful, they will comfort us; if dull, they will quicken us; if cold, they will inflame us. A supernatural voice once said to St. Augustine, *"Tolle, lege; Tolle, lege,"* "Take up and read, take up and read the Scriptures." Again St. Augustine says, "Whatever is in the Scriptures, believe me, is high and divine. There is verily truth and a doctrine most fit for the refreshing and renewing of men's minds, and truly so tempered, that everyone may draw from it that which is sufficient for him, if he comes to draw with a devout and pious mind, as true religion requires." And St. Jerome adds: "Love the Scriptures, and wisdom will love you." St. Cyril in writing against Julian says, "Even boys that are brought up in the Scriptures become very religious," etc. But why should we mention these three or four uses of Scripture, when whatever is to be believed or practiced or hoped for is contained in them? Why should we mention these three or four quotations of the Fathers, since whoever is worthy the name of a Father, from the time of Christ on down has likewise written not only of the riches, but also of the perfection of the Scriptures?

"I adore the fullness of the Scripture," says Tertullian writing against Hermogenes. And again to Apelles, a heretic of the same kind, he says: "I do not accept what you conclude from your own store of knowledge apart from Scripture." So also Saint Justin Martyr before him says, "We must by all means remember that it is not lawful or possible to learn any thing of God or of true piety, except from the Prophets, who teach us by divine inspiration." Similarly, Saint Basil says, "It is an unmistakable falling away from the faith, and a fault of presumption, either to reject any of those things that are written, or to bring in any of those things that are not written." We will omit similar statements by St. Cyril, Bishop of Jerusalem in the fourth of his *Catechetical Lectures,* or St. Jerome against Helvidius, St. Augustine in his third book against the letters of Petilian, and in quite a few other places in his works. Also we hesitate to descend to later Fathers, lest we should weary the reader. If the Scriptures then are acknowledged to be so complete and so perfect, how can we excuse ourselves of negligence if we do not study them from curiosity, if we are not content with them?

Men talk much about the Eiresion garland, how many sweet and good things it had hanging on it; of the Philosopher's stone that turns copper into gold; of Cornucopia, filled with all kinds of food; of the herb Panaces that was good for all diseases; of the drug Catholicon that works for all purgatives; of Vulcan's armor, that was a protection against all thrusts and blows, etc. Well, that which they falsely or vainly attributed to these things for physical benefits, we may justly and with full confidence ascribe to the Scriptures for spiritual good. It is not only an armor, but also a whole armory of weapons, both offensive and defensive, by which we may save ourselves and put the enemy to flight. It is not an herb, but a tree, or rather a whole paradise of trees of life, which bring forth fruit every month, and the fruit of it is for food and the leaves for medicine (Revelation 22:2). It is not a pot of *Manna* or a cruse of oil, which were for a symbol or for a meal or two; but rather a shower of heavenly bread sufficient for a whole army, regardless of its size, and a whole cellar full of oil vessels. It is enough to provide for all our necessities and discharge all our debts. In a word, it is a pantry full of wholesome food instead of moldy traditions; a drug store (St. Basil calls it) of antidotes against poisonous heresies; a complete body of profitable laws against rebellious spirits; a treasury of costliest jewels against worthless rituals; finally, a fountain of purest water springing up to everlasting life. And why should we be surprised? The original is from heaven, not from earth. The author is God, not man. The composer is the Holy Spirit, not the Apostles or Prophets. The penmen were such as were sanctified from the womb and endued with a principal portion of God's Spirit. The contents consist of truth, piety, purity, uprightness. The form is

God's word, God's testimony, God's oracles, the word of truth, the word of salvation, etc. The effects are a clear understanding, a stable confidence, repentance from dead works, a new life, holiness, peace, and joy in the Holy Spirit. Finally, the end and reward of its study is fellowship with the saints, participation of the heavenly nature, the promise of an inheritance immortal, undefiled, and that never shall fade away. Happy is the person who delights in the Scripture, and thrice happy the one who meditates on it day and night.

TRANSLATION IS NECESSARY

But how shall people meditate on something they cannot understand? How shall they understand something that is kept hidden in an unknown language? As Paul says, "Unless I know the meaning of the language, I will be a foreigner to the one who is speaking, and the one speaking will be a foreigner to me" (I Corinthians 14:11). The Apostle makes no exception for any language; whether Hebrew the most ancient, or Greek the most copious, or Latin the finest. Nature prompts us to admit that we are plainly deaf in those languages we do not understand, and we turn a deaf ear to them. The Scythinan considered the Athenian, whom he did not understand, barbarous. So the Roman did the Syrian and the Jew. Even St. Jerome himself called the Hebrew language barbarous, very likely because it was unfamiliar to so many. The Emperor of Constantinople called the Latin language barbarous, although Pope Nicolas strongly objected. And the Jews, long before Christ, called all other nations *Lognazzim*— "speakers of strange languages" (Psalm 114:1), which is little better than barbarous. As one complained that in the Roman Senate someone was always calling for an interpreter; so, lest the Church be driven to the same predicament, it is necessary to have translations already prepared. It is a translation that opens the window to let in the light; that breaks the shell that we may eat the kernel; that pulls aside the curtain that we may look into the most holy place; that removes the cover of the well that we may get to the water, even as Jacob rolled away the stone from the mouth of the well so the flocks of Laban could be watered (Genesis 29:10). Indeed, without a translation in the common language, the unlearned are like children at Jacob's well (which was deep) without a bucket or something to draw water with; or as the person mentioned by Isaiah, who, when given a sealed book and told, "Read this," was compelled to answer, "I cannot, because it is sealed" (Isaiah 29:11).

THE TRANSLATION OF THE OLD TESTAMENT FROM HEBREW INTO GREEK

At a time when God was known exclusively in Jacob and His name praised only in Israel and in no other place; while the dew lay only on Gideon's fleece and all the ground around it was dry (Judges 6:37), the one language of Hebrew was sufficient, because all the people spoke the language of Canaan or Hebrew. But when the fullness of time drew near that the Sun of righteousness, the Son of God, should come into the world, whom God ordained to be a reconciliation through faith in His blood, not of the Jew only, but also of the Greek, yes, of all those who were scattered abroad; it pleased the Lord to stir up the spirit of a Greek Prince (a Greek by descent and language) even Ptolemy Philadelphus, king of Egypt, to commission the translation of the book of God out of Hebrew into Greek.

This is the Septuagint, as it is commonly called, the translation of the seventy interpreters who prepared the way for our Savior among the Gentiles by a written form of preaching, just as Saint John the Baptist did among the Jews by vocal preaching. The Greeks, because of their love of learning, were not willing to allow valuable books to lie molding in kings' libraries, but enlisted many of their servants who were proficient scribes, to copy them out so the books could be widely circulated among the people. Again, the Greek language was

225

well known and familiar to most inhabitants in Asia by reason of the conquests the Greeks had made (under Alexander), and also by the colonies which they established. For the same reasons also the Greek language was well understood in many places of Europe, and even in Africa as well. Therefore the Word of God in Greek became like a candle set on a candlestick which gives light to all that are in the house; or like a proclamation sounded forth in the marketplace, which most people immediately take knowledge of. Therefore Greek was best suited to contain the Scriptures, both for the first preachers of the Gospel to appeal to as a witness, and also for the learners of those times to search and use for reference. It is certain that this translation was not always sound or perfect and needed to be corrected in many places. And who was better qualified for this work than the Apostles and their colleagues?

Yet it seemed good to the Holy Spirit and to the apostles to take what they found (for the most part it was true and sufficient), rather than to make a new translation in the new world and in the beginning stage of the Church. To do so would have exposed them to many objections and quibblings. They would have been perceived as producing a translation to serve their own purpose, hence appearing to bear witness only to themselves. Their witness therefore would be disregarded. We may suppose this to be the reason why the translation of the Seventy (the Septuagint) was accepted as being authoritative.

Notwithstanding, although it was commended generally, yet it did not fully satisfy the scholars, especially the Jews. For not long after the time of Christ, Aquila produced a new translation, and after him Theodotion, and after him Symmachus. Then there was a fifth and sixth edition, the authors of which are unknown. With the Septuagint, these made up the Hexapla, an esteemed and useful work complied by Origen. Nevertheless, the edition of the Septuagint received the most credibility, and therefore not only was placed in the central position by Origen, because of its worth and excellency compared to the others, as Epiphanius admits, but also was used by the Greek Fathers as the basis for their commentaries. Indeed, Epiphanius attributes so much to it that he regards the authors not only as interpreters, but in some respects as prophets. And Justinian the Emperor, who required his Jewish subjects to use the Translation of the Seventy, gave as his reason that the authors were enlightened with the gift of prophecy. Yet for all that, as the Egyptians are said by the Prophet to be men and not God, and their horses flesh and not spirit, so it is evident, and St. Jerome affirms as much, that the Seventy were interpreters, not prophets. As learned men, they did many things well, but yet as men they stumbled and fell: one through oversight, another through ignorance. Sometimes they were known to add to the original, and sometimes to take from it, which made the Apostles leave them many times when they left the Hebrew. (Their consuming passion was) to deliver the sense according to the truth of the Word as the Spirit gave them utterance. This will suffice as regards the Greek translations of the Old Testament.

TRANSLATION FROM HEBREW AND GREEK INTO LATIN

There were also within a few hundred years after Christ many translations made into the Latin tongue. This tongue was also a very fit medium to convey the law and the Gospel, because in those times very many countries of the West, and of the South, East, and North, spoke or understood Latin, since they had become Roman provinces. But now the Latin translations were too numerous to all be good, for as St. Augustine said, they were without number. Again, they were not out of the Hebrew fountain (we speak of the Latin translations of the Old Testament) but out of the Greek stream; therefore the Greek being not altogether clear, the Latin derived from it must needs be muddy. This moved St. Jerome, a most learned Father and without controversy the best linguist of his age or of any that went before him, to undertake the translating of the Old Testament out of the very fountains themselves (Hebrew and Greek). This he performed with that evidence of great learning, judgment, industry, and faithfulness that he has forever bound the Church unto him in a debt of special remembrance and thankfulness.

THE TRANSLATING OF THE SCRIPTURES INTO THE VERNACULAR LANGUAGES

Even before the faith of Christ was generally embraced in the Roman Empire, the Church was supplied with Greek and Latin translations (for scholars know that even in Saint Jerome's time, the Consul of Rome and his wife were both pagan, as was the majority of the Senate). Yet in spite of this, godly scholars were not content to have the Scriptures in the language which they themselves understood, Greek and Latin, just as the good lepers were not content to eat well themselves, but informed their neighbors about the supply of food God had sent, that they also might provide for themselves. Therefore scholars provided translations into the common language of their countrymen for the benefit and edifying of the unlearned who hungered and thirsted after righteousness and who also had souls to be saved. Hence most nations, shortly after their conversion, heard Christ speaking to them in their mother tongue, not by the voice of their minister only, but also by the written word translated. If anyone doubts this, numerous examples exist, if further proof is required.

First, Saint Jerome says, "The Scriptures translated in previous years *in the languages of many nations* show that the things added (by Lucian or Hesychius) are false." The same Jerome elsewhere affirms that he had made a translation from the Septuagint for his countrymen of Dalmatia. Erasmus understands these words to mean that St. Jerome translated the Scriptures into the Dalmation language. Also Sisto da Siena and Alfonso de Castro (to mention only two), men not to be opposed by those of Rome, candidly confess as much. St. Chrysostom who lived in St. Jerome's time, agrees with him: "The doctrine of St. John did not vanish away as the philosopher's did, but the Syrians, Egyptians, Indians, Persians, Ethiopians, and many other nations, being barbarous people, translated it into their (mother) tongue, and have learned to be true Christians." To this may be added the words of Theodoret, who is next to him both for antiquity and for learning. His words are these: "Every country that is under the sun is full of these words (of the Apostles and Prophets). And the Scriptures in the Hebrew language are translated not only into the language of the Greeks, but also of the Romans, Egyptians, Persians, Indians, Armenians, Scythians, Sauromatians, and, briefly, into all the languages that any nation uses." In like manner Ulfilas is reported by Paulus Diaconus and Isidore, and before them by Sozomen, to have translated the Scriptures into the Gothic language. John, Bishop of Seville, is said by Vasseus to have translated them into Arabic about A.D. 717. Bede is said by Cistertiensis to have turned a great part of them into Saxon. Einhard is said by Trithemius to have abridged the French Psalter, as Bede had done the Hebrew, about the year 800. King Alfred is said by the same Cistertiensis to have translated the Psalter into Saxon. Methodius is said by Aventinus to have translated the Scriptures into Sclavonian and printed at Ingolstadt about A.D. 900. Waldo, Bishop of Freising, is said by Beatus Rhenanus to have commissioned about that time a metrical translation of the Gospels into German, which is still extant in the library of Corbinian. Valdes is said by many to have translated them himself, or to have had them translated into French about the year 1160. Charles V, called "The Wise," is said to have commissioned them to be translated into French about two hundred years after Valdes, many copies of which are yet extant, as Beroaldus confirms.

Even in the days of our King Richard II, John Trevisa translated them into English, and many hand-written English

Bibles, very likely translated in that same period, are still to be seen today. The Syrian translation of the New Testament by Widminstadius is in most scholars' libraries, and many have copies of the Psalter in Arabic by Augustinus Nebiensis. Postel affirms that in his travels he saw the Gospels in the Ethiopian language; and Ambrose Thesius alleges he saw an Indian Psalter which he believes was published by Potken in Syrian characters. So that to have the Scriptures in the mother tongue is not a quaint idea lately concocted, either by Lord Cromwell in England, or by the Lord Radevil in Poland, *or* by the Lord Ungnadius in the Emperor's dominion, but has been thought about and put into practice long ago, even from the earliest days of the conversion of any nation, no doubt because it was believed to be most useful in causing faith to grow more quickly in men's hearts, and enabling them to say with the words of the Psalm, "As we have heard, so we have seen" (Psalm 48:8).

THE UNWILLINGNESS OF OUR CHIEF ADVERSARIES FOR THE SCRIPTURES TO BE DIVULGED IN THE MOTHER TONGUE

Now the Church of Rome would seem at last to show a motherly affection towards her children by allowing them to have the Scriptures in their mother tongue (Rheims/Douay Version). But indeed it is a gift not deserving to be called a gift. It is a useless gift. They must first get a license in writing before they may read it, and to get permission, they must prove to their Confessor that they are, if not frozen in the dregs, at least soured with the leaven of their superstition. Nevertheless, it seemed too much to Clement VIII that there should be any license granted to have the Scriptures in the common language, and therefore he overruled and frustrated the grant of Pius IV. They are so afraid of the light of the Scriptures that they will not trust the people with it, even though it is translated by their own loyal men and licensed by their own Bishops and Inquisitors.

So unwilling are they to communicate the Scriptures to the people's understanding in any way, that they are not ashamed to admit that we forced them to translate it into English against their wills. This seems to argue a bad cause, or a bad conscience, or both. We are sure that it is not the one with good gold who is afraid to bring it to the touchstone, but the one who has the counterfeit. Neither is it the true man who shuns the light, but the criminal, lest his deeds should be reproved. Nor is it the plain-dealing merchant that is unwilling to have the weights or measures examined, but the one who uses deceit. But we will overlook this fault and return to the matter of translation.

THE OBJECTIONS OF BOTH OUR BROTHERS AND OUR ADVERSARIES AGAINST THIS WORK

Many men's mouths have been open for a good while now, and even yet are not stopped, about the translation so long in progress (Authorized Version), or rather the scrutinizing of translations made previously, and they ask what may be the reason or necessity of the effort. "Has the church been deceived," so they say, "all this while? Has her unleavened bread been mixed with leaven, her silver with dross, her wine with water, her milk with lime? St. Irenaeus warns, 'It is quite wrong to mix lime with God's milk.' We hoped that we had been in the right way, that we had had the oracles of God delivered to us, and that though all the world had reason to be offended and to complain, yet we had none. Has the nurse held out the breast with nothing but wind in it? Has the bread delivered by the Fathers of the Church proved (in Seneca's words) to be stones? If this is not handling the Word of God deceitfully," as some of our brethren say, "what is?" Also the adversaries of Judah and Jerusalem, like Sanballat in Nehemiah, mocked, as we hear, both the work and workers, saying, "What are these weak Jews doing? Will they make the stone whole again out of the burnt dust heaps? Even if they build, a fox could go up and break down their stone wall."

In like manner our adversaries ask, "Was their translation good before? Why do they correct it now? If it was not good, why was it made available to the people? Indeed, why did the Catholics (meaning Popish Romanists) always risk harm to themselves for refusing to go to hear it? No. If it must be translated into English, Catholics are best qualified to do it. They have the scholarship, they know when a thing is done well, and they know when to quit."

We will answer them both briefly. To the former, being brethren, we say with St. Jerome, "Do we condemn the ancient versions? Not at all, but learning from the endeavors of those who were before us, we do the best we can in the house of God." It was as if he said, "Being provoked by the example of the scholars who lived before my time, I have considered it my duty to examine whether my talent in the knowledge of linguistics may be useful in some way to God's Church. Otherwise I should seem to have learned those languages in vain, and appear to give more glory to human scholars (however ancient) than they deserved." This is what St. Jerome is thought to have said.

A SATISFACTION TO OUR BRETHREN [THE PURITANS]

And we would repeat St. Jerome's words and say that we are far from condemning the work of any who travailed before us in this way, either here or abroad, either in King Henry's time or King Edward's (if there was any translation or correction of a translation in his time), or Queen Elizabeth's of ever renowned memory. We acknowledge that they were raised up by God for the building and equipping of His Church, and that they deserve to be held by us and posterity in everlasting remembrance. The judgment of Aristotle is worthy and well known: "If Timotheus had not been, we would not have had much sweet music; but if Phrynis (Timotheus' master) had not been, we would not have had Timotheus." Therefore blessed be those, and most honored be their name, who break the ice and take the first steps toward helping to advance the saving of souls. Now what can be more useful for this purpose than to deliver God's book to God's people in a language they can understand? There is no profit in a hidden treasure of a fountain that is sealed, as Ptolemy Philadelphus wrote to the Rabbis or masters of the Jews (according to Epiphanius). And as St. Augustine says, "A man would rather be with his dog than with a stranger (whose language is strange to him)." Yet for all that, as nothing is begun and perfected at the same time and the later thoughts are believed to be the wiser, so, being helped by their labors (the early Bible translators) and building on the foundation they laid, if we endeavor to improve on what they did so well, we are sure that no one has reason to dislike us. And we are persuaded that if they were alive, they would thank us. The vintage of Abiezer was good, yet the gleanings from Ephraim's vineyard were even better (Judges 8:2). Joash, the king of Israel, did not satisfy himself till he had struck the ground three times, and yet he offended the prophet (Elisha) for not striking it more. Aquila, of whom we spoke before, translated the Bible as carefully and as skillfully as he could, and yet he thought it necessary to go over it again; and then, as Saint Jerome attests, it got a reputation among the Jews for accuracy.

How many books of profane learning have been gone over again and again by the same translators or by others? There are at least six or seven different translations extant of Aristotle's *Ethics*. Now if all this effort is bestowed on the gourd, which provides us with little shade and which today flourishes but tomorrow is cut down, what may we bestow, no, what must we bestow on the vine, the fruit which makes glad the conscience of man, and the stem which abides forever? And this is the Word of God that we translate. "What is the chaff (compared) to wheat?" says the Lord (Jeremiah 23:28). Or as Tertullian says, if a glass trinket is so treasured by us, how much more should

233

we value the true pearl? Therefore no one's eye should be evil because his Majesty's is good; neither should any be sorrowful that we have a Prince who seeks the increase of the spiritual wealth of Israel. Let the Sanballats and Tobiahs do so, for which action they justly deserve reproof. But let us rather bless God from the bottom of our heart for arousing him (King James I) a religious concern to have the (former) translations of the Bible maturely considered and examined. For in this way it so happens that whatever is sound already, and all is substantially sound in our Protestant versions; in fact, the worst of ours is far better than the (Roman Catholic's) authentic Vulgate, the same will shine more brightly than gold that has been rubbed and polished. Also, if any thing is doubtful or superfluous, or not in agreement with the original, it may be corrected and the truth set in its place. And what can the King command to be done that will bring him more true honor than this? And how can those who have been commissioned to this work better approve themselves to the King, show their obedience to God and their love to his saints, more, than by yielding their service and all that is within them for the accomplishing of this work? But besides all this, they (the Puritans) were the principal proponents behind it, and therefore ought least to quarrel about it. For the very historical truth is that it was the petitions of the Puritans when the new king (King James I) was on his way to be crowned in London, that initiated the conference at Hampton Court to hear their complaints. When by force of reason they could not make a case on any other grounds, they had recourse at the last to the plea that they could not with good conscience subscribe to the Communion book, since the Bible used in it was, as they said, a most corrupted translation. And although this was judged to be a very poor and empty ploy, yet his Majesty began to reflect on the good that might ensue from a new translation, and presently commissioned this translation which is now presented to you. This much we have said to satisfy our scrupulous brethren.

AN ANSWER TO THE ACCUSATIONS OF OUR ADVERSARIES

Now to our adversaries we answer: we do not deny, rather we affirm and declare that the very meanest translation of the Bible in English set forth by men of our profession (for we have seen no Catholic version of the whole English Bible as yet) contains the Word of God, no, is the Word of God. The King's speech which he delivers in Parliament when translated into French, Dutch, Italian, and Latin, is still the King's speech, though it is not interpreted by every translator with equal skill, nor perhaps with as suitable phrasing or the same clarity. For it is widely known that things are identified by their primary characteristics. A non-Christian man once said, "When the beauties in a poem are more numerous (than its faults), I shall not take offence at a few blots." A man may be counted a virtuous man though he has made many slips in his life, else no one could be considered virtuous, for "in many things we all offend" (James 3:2). Also a man may be considered handsome and lovable though he has some warts on his hand; yes, and freckles as well as scars on his face. There is no reason therefore why the Word translated should be denied to be the Word or forbidden to be circulated, notwithstanding that some imperfections and blemishes may be noted in the setting forth of it. For has there ever been anything perfect under the sun, where Apostles or apostolic men, that is, men endued with an extraordinary measure of God's Spirit, and privileged with the privilege of infallibility, were not involved? The Romanists therefore in refusing to hear and daring to burn the Word when it was translated, did no less than "insult the Spirit of grace" (Hebrews 10:29), from whom originally it proceeded, and whose sense and meaning, as well as man's weakness would enable, it expressed.

Consider an example or two. Plutarch wrote that after Rome had been burned by the Gauls, they soon began rebuilding it. But doing it in haste, they did not build the streets nor proportion the houses in the most attractive way. Was Cataline therefore an honest man or a good patriot when he sought to destroy Rome? Or was Nero a good Prince who indeed set it on fire? So from the story of Ezra and the prophecy of Haggai it may be supposed that the temple built by Zerubbabel after the return from Babylon was by no means to be compared to the former built by Solomon, for those who remembered the former wept when they considered the latter. Notwithstanding, was this latter temple abhorred and forsaken by the Jews or profaned by the Greeks?

In like manner we are to think of translations. The translation of the Septuagint departs from the original in many places, neither does it come near it for clarity, gravity, and majesty; yet which of the Apostles condemned it? Condemn it? No, they used it, as is apparent, and as St. Jerome and most learned men confess. They would not have done so, nor by their example of using it so honor and commend it to the Church, if it had been unworthy the appellation and name of the Word of God.

And then they urged as their second defense for vilifying and abusing English Bibles, or some parts of it which they had seen, that heretics indeed were the authors of the translations. They call us heretics by the same right that they call themselves Catholics, both being wrong. We marvel what divinity taught them so. We are sure Tertullian was of another mind: "Do we try men's faith by their person, or should we try their persons by their faith?" Also St. Augustine was of another mind, for when he came upon certain rules for better understanding the Word made by Tyconius, a Donatist, he was not ashamed to make use of them; in fact, he even inserted them into his own book, commending them so far as they were worthy to be commended *(De Doctrina Christiana, book* 3). In short, Origen and the whole church of God for some hundred years were of another mind. They were so far from treading under foot, much less from burning the translation of Aquila, a proselyte, one that had turned to Judaism, of Symmachus and Theodotion, both Ebionites, considered most vile heretics, that they joined them together with the Hebrew original and the translation of the Septuagint (as has been noted before by Epiphanius), and set them forth openly to be considered and perused by all. But we weary the unlearned who need not know so much, and trouble the learned, who know it already.

Yet before we end, we must answer a third criticism and objection of theirs against us for altering and amending our translations so often, for which they deal harshly and strangely with us. For whoever was considered at fault for going over that which he had done and amending it where necessary? St. Augustine was not afraid to exhort St. Jerome to a Palinodia or recantation. The same St. Augustine was not ashamed to retract, we might say, revoke, many things he had written, and even glories that he sees his own infirmities. If we will be children of the truth, we must consider what it says and trample on our own interests, yes and upon other people's too, if either be in any way a hindrance to it. So much for the cause. Now to the accusers we say that of all men they ought to be most silent in this case. For what varieties (of editions) do they have and what alterations have they made, not only of their service books, portesses, and breviaries, but also of their Latin translation? The service book supposed to have been made by St. Ambrose *(Officium Ambrosianum)* was for a great while in special use and demand; but Pope Adrian, calling a council with the aid of Charles the Emperor, abolished it. Indeed, he burned it and commanded the service book of Saint Gregory to be used universally. Well, once the *Officium Gregorianum* becomes the standard text, does it continue without change or altering? No. The very Roman service was in two forms; the new form and the old—the one used in one Church, the other in another—as the Romanist Pamelius notes in his preface to *Micrologus*. The same Pamelius cites Radulphus de Rivo to the effect that about the year of our

Lord 1277 Pope Nocolas III removed out of the churches of Rome the more ancient books of service and brought into use the missals of the Friars Minorites, and commanded them to be observed there, insomuch that about a hundred years after, when Radulphus happened to be in Rome, he found all the books to be of the new edition. Neither was this chopping and changing in the more ancient times only, but also of late. Pius Quintus himself confessed that almost every bishopric had a peculiar kind of service, unlike that which others had. This moved him to abolish all the other breviaries, though ancient, privileged, and published by Bishops in their Dioceses, and to establish and ratify only that which he himself set forth in the year 1568.

Now when the Father of their Church, who gladly would heal the sore of the daughter of his people softly and slightly, and make the best of it, finds so much fault with them for their differences and disagreements, we hope the children have no great cause to boast of their uniformity. But the difference that appears between our translations and our frequent corrections of them is the thing that we are especially charged with. Let us see therefore whether they are without fault in this respect (if indeed it is to be considered a fault to correct), and whether they are fit to throw stones at us. "They that are less sound themselves ought not to point out the infirmities of others" (Horace). If we should tell them that Valla, Stapulensis, Erasmus, and Vives found fault with their Vulgate version, and consequently wished the same to be amended or a new one to be made, it is quite possible they would answer that we produced their enemies for witnesses against them. Although they were no more enemies than St. Paul was to the Galatians for telling them the truth; and it were to be wished that they had dared to tell it to them plainer and oftener. But what will they say to the fact that Pope Leo X allowed Erasmus' translation of the New Testament by his apostolic letter and bull, even though it was so much different from the Vulgate? That Leo exhorted

Pagnini to translate the whole Bible, and bore whatever expenses were necessary for the work? Surely, as the apostle reasoned with the Hebrews (7:11; 8:7), that "if the former Law and Testament had been sufficient, there had been no need of the latter;" so we may say, that if the old Vulgate had been at all points adequate, all the labor and expense involved in preparing a new version was unnecessary. If they say it was one Pope's private opinion and that he consulted only himself, then we can go further with them and demonstrate that more of their chief men, even their own Council of Trent champions, Paiva and Vega, and their own Inquisitors, Hieronymus ab Oleastro, and their own Bishop Isidorus Clarius, and their Cardinal Thomas a Vio Cajetan, either make new translations themselves or follow new ones of other men's making, or note the defects in the Vulgate, without fearing to dissent from it, or to disagree with it. And do they call this a uniform text and a uniform judgment about the text, with so many of their worthies disclaiming the now accepted opinion? No.

We will now come to the heart of the matter. Does not their Paris edition differ from the Louvaine edition, and Hentenius' edition from both of them, and yet all of them were allowed by ecclesiastical authority? Does not Sixtus Quintus confess that certain Catholics (he means certain of his own side) were so eager to translate the Scriptures into Latin that Satan, taking occasion by them, though they thought of no such matter, did strive as he could, out of so uncertain and manifold a variety of translations, to confuse them, that nothing might seem to be left certain and firm in them? And did not the same Sixtus ordain by an inviolable decree, with the counsel and consent of his Cardinals, that the Latin edition of the Old and New Testaments, which the Council of Trent declared to be authentic, is the same without controversy which he then published, being diligently corrected and printed in the Vatican printing house? This is what Sixtus states in the Preface of his Bible. And yet Clement VIII, his immediate successor, published another edition of the Bible, containing in it numerous differences from that of Sixtus, and many of them weighty and substantial; and yet this edition is considered by all means to be authentic. This indecisiveness is clearly an example of not having the faith of our glorious Lord Jesus Christ with yea and nay. Again, what is sweet harmony and consent if this is it? Therefore, as Demaratus of Corinth advised the great King Philip of Macedon before he talked of the dissensions among the Greeks, that he should settle his domestic broils (for at that time his queen and his son and heir were in a deadly feud with him). So while our adversaries make so many different versions themselves and complain so much about the worth and authority of them, they cannot with any display of fairness challenge us for changing and correcting.

THE PURPOSE OF THE TRANSLATORS, THEIR METHODS AND PRINCIPLES

But is it high time to leave our adversaries and to show briefly what we proposed for ourselves, and what course we followed in our perusal and survey of the Bible. Truly, good Christian reader, we never thought from the beginning that we should need to make a new translation, nor yet to make of a bad one a good one (for then the accusation of Sixtus was true in a sense, that our people had been fed with gall of dragons instead of wine, with whey instead of milk), but to make a good one better, or out of many good ones one principal good one, not justly to be objected to. That has been our endeavor, our mark. For this purpose many were chosen who were greater in other men's eyes than in their own, and that sought the truth rather than their own praise. Again, they came or were thought to come to the work, (as one says) not as students, but *exercitati,* that is accomplished scholars. For the chief overseer and supervisor under his Majesty, to whom not only we but also our whole Church was much indebted, knew by his wisdom, what Nazianzen taught so long ago, that it is a preposterous order to teach first and learn after, that to learn and practice at the same time is neither commendable for the workman nor safe for the work. Therefore only those were chosen who could say modestly with Saint Jerome, "While beginning as a young man I have with much toil and effort partially acquired the Hebrew language, the Latin I have known almost from the cradle." St. Jerome makes no mention of the Greek language in which he excelled, because he did not translate the Old Testament from the Greek (Septuagint), but from the Hebrew.

And on what basis did these translators assemble? In dependence on their own knowledge, their sharpness of wit, their depth of judgment, or as it were in the arm of the flesh? By no means. They trusted in Him who has the key of David (Revelation 3:7), who opens and no man shuts. They prayed to the Lord, the Father of our Lord (Jesus Christ) in the same manner that St. Augustine did: "O let your Scriptures be my pure delight; do not let me be deceived in them, neither let me deceive by them." In this confidence and with this devotion they assembled together; not so many that one might hinder another; and yet many, lest anything by chance might escape them. If you ask what they had before them, truly it was the Hebrew text of the Old Testament and the Greek of the New. These are the two golden pipes or rather conduits, through which the olive branches empty themselves into the gold (Zechariah 4:12). Saint Augustine calls them "precedent," or "original tongues;" Saint Jerome, "fountains." The same Jerome affirms, and Gratian has not failed to put it into his decree, that "as the credibility of the old books (he means the Old Testament) is to be tested by the Hebrew volumes; so the New is to be tested by the Greek language" (he means by the original Greek).

If truth is to be tested against these languages, then where should a translation be made from but out of them? These languages therefore (that is, Scriptures in these languages) we set before us to translate, being the languages in which

God was pleased to speak to His Church by His Prophets and Apostles. Neither did we run over the work with the speed of a galloping horse like the Septuagint translators, if it is true what is reported of them that they finished it in 72 days. Neither were we barred or hindered from going over it again, having done it once, like St. Jerome, if that be true which he himself reported, that he could no sooner write any thing, but presently it was caught from him and published before he could correct it. Neither, to be brief, were we the first to undertake the task of translating the Scriptures in English, and consequently destitute of former helps, as was Origen, who was the first to write commentaries on the Scriptures, and not surprisingly overshot himself many times.

None of these things moved us. The work was not crammed into 72 days, but has cost the workmen, as light as it seems, the pains of twice seven times 72 days and more. Matters of such weight and consequence are to be pursued with prudence: for in a matter of great importance a man does not fear being blamed for taking whatever time is necessary. Neither did we hesitate to consult the translators or commentators: Chaldee, Hebrew, Syrian, Greek, or Latin; no, nor the Spanish, French, Italian, or Dutch. Neither did we disdain to revise that which we had done and to bring back to the anvil that which we had hammered. But having and using the great helps as were needful, and fearing no reproach for slowness, nor coveting praise for speed, we have at length, through the good hand of the Lord upon us, brought the work to the state that you now see.

REASONS FOR ALTERNATIVE READINGS IN THE MARGIN

Some perhaps would have no alternative readings in the margin, lest that show of uncertainty might undermine the authority of the Scriptures, leaving no basis for deciding controversies. But we do not hold their judgment to be sound on this point. For, as St. Chrysostom says, "everything that is necessary is obvious," and St. Augustine adds, "those things that are plainly set down in the Scriptures include everything that concerns faith, hope, and love." Yet for all that, it cannot be disguised that partly to exercise and whet our intellect, partly to keep the curious from loathing them for their plainness, partly also to stir up our devotion to crave the assistance of God's Spirit by prayer, and lastly, that we might actively seek help from our brethren by conference, and never scorn those that are not in all respects as educated as they should be (being ignorant in many things ourselves), but in matters of less importance. Consequently fearfulness would better suit us than confidence, and if we must resolve, resolve to be modest. As St. Augustine says, "It is better to be reserved about those things which are not revealed, than to strive about those things that are uncertain."

There are many words in the Scriptures that are never found there only once ("having neither brother nor neighbor," as the Jews say), so that we cannot be helped by similar passages or words. Again, there are many rare names of certain birds, animals, and precious stones, concerning which the Jews themselves are so divided among themselves for judgment, that they may seem to have defined this or that, more because they wanted to say something, than because they were sure of what they said, as St. Jerome says of the Septuagint. Now in such a case is not a marginal note helpful to admonish the reader to seek further rather than conclude or dogmatize upon this or that without admitting additional debate? For as it is incredulous to doubt those things that are obvious, so it is presumptuous to be definite about such things as the Spirit of God has left questionable (even in the judgment of the judicious).

Therefore as St. Augustine says, "Variety of translations is profitable for the finding out of the sense of the Scriptures;" so we are persuaded that alternative readings in the margin, where the text is not so clear, must be helpful; indeed is necessary. We know that Sixtus V expressly forbids any alternative readings in the margin of their Vulgate edition (and though it is not altogether the same thing to what we have in mind, yet it looks that way), yet we think that not all of his own side favor him in this opinion. They who are wise would rather have their judgments at liberty where there are differences of readings than to be captive to one choice, when it may be the other choice is best. If they were sure that their high priest (the Pope) had all laws shut up in his breast, as Paul II bragged, and that he was as free from error by special privilege as the dictators of Rome who were made by law inviolable, then his word would be an oracle and his opinion a decision. But the eyes of the world are now open, God be thanked, and have been a great while. They find that he is subject to the same affections and infirmities that others are, that his skin is penetrable, and therefore they will grant and embrace only so much as he proves, not as much as he claims.

REASONS WE DID NOT INSIST ON UNIFORMITY OF PHRASING OR IDENTITY OF WORDS

Another thing we think necessary for you to know, gentle reader, is that we have not tied ourselves to a uniformity of phrasing or an identity of words, as some perhaps wish we had done, because they note that some scholars elsewhere have been very precise in this manner. Truly, if the word expressed the same sense in both places (for there are some words that are not of the same meaning everywhere) we were especially careful, and made it a matter of conscience according to our duty, not to vary from the sense of that which we had translated before. Our intention was to express the same idea in the same particular word; for example, if we translate the Hebrew or Greek word once as *purpose,* never to call it *intent;* or *journeying,* never *traveling; think,* never *suppose; pain,* never *ache; joy,* never *gladness,* etc. Thus to moderate the matter, we thought it might smack of curiosity rather than wisdom, and would breed scorn in the atheist rather than bring profit to the godly reader. For has the kingdom of God become words and syllables? Why should we be in bondage to them, if we could be free? Why should we use one word exclusively, when we could use another one that is just as suitable? One godly Church Father in primitive times was greatly disturbed and rebuked a bishop sharply after hearing him explain the phrase, "Take up your bed and walk" (Mark 2:9). Instead of citing the Greek text correctly, which has the word *krabbaton* for "bed," he used the word *skimpus,* although there is little or no difference in their meaning. Another one reports that he was much abused for turning *cucurbita* ("gourd," the reading the people were accustomed to) into *hedera* ("vine"). Now if this were to happen today over such frivolous matters, we might justly fear harsh censure if we should make verbal and unnecessary changes. We might also be accused by scoffers of partiality towards a great number of good English words. It is written of a certain great philosopher that he is reputed to have said that those logs were happy that were made images to be worshipped; while their fellow logs, just as good as they, lay for kindling beside the fire. So if we should say, as it were, to certain words, "Stand up higher, have a place in the Bible always;" and to others of equal quality, "Get out of here, be banished for ever," we might perhaps be accused by the words of St. James, "Are you not partial in yourselves, and are become judges of evil thoughts" (James 2:4). In addition, being overly exact in the use of words was always considered the next step to frivolity, and so was it to be too particular about names too. Also we cannot follow a better model for verbal expression than God Himself. He uses different words in Holy Scripture when referring to the same thing; so we, if we will not be superstitious, may exercise the same liberty in our English versions of the Hebrew and Greek, based on the resources He has given us.

Finally, we have on the one side avoided the strictness of the Puritans, who leave the old ecclesiastical words and replace them with others, as when they use *washing* for *baptism,* and *congregation* instead of *church*. Also on the other side we have shunned the obscurity of the Papists, in their *Azimes, tunike, rational, holocausts, proepuce, pasche,* and a number of similar words, in which their late translation (Rheims New Testament) is full. The purpose is to darken the sense, that since they are forced to translate the Bible, yet by the use of obscure language it may be kept from being understood. But we desire that the Scripture may speak like itself, as it does in the language of Hebrew, that it may be understood even by the uneducated.

Many other things we might warn you of, gentle reader, if we had not already exceeded the limits of a preface. It remains that we commend you to God and to the Spirit of His grace which is able to build further than we can ask or think. He removes the scales from our eyes, the veil from our hearts, opening our minds that we may understand His Word, enlarging our hearts, yes correcting our affections, so that we may love it above gold and silver, yes that we may love it to the end. You are brought unto fountains of living water which you did not dig. Do not cast dirt into them like the Philistines, neither prefer broken pits to them like the wicked Jews. Others have labored, and you may enter into their labors. Do not receive such great things in vain. Do not despise such a great salvation! Do not be like swine to tread under foot such precious things, nor yet like dogs to tear and abuse holy things. Do not say to our Savior like the Gergesites, "Depart out of our coasts;" nor yet like Esau, sell your birthright for a mess of pottage. If light has come into the world, do not love darkness more than light. If food, if clothing be offered, do not go naked, do not starve yourselves. Remember the advice of Nazianzen, "It is a grievous or dangerous thing to neglect a great market (with its opportunities to make money) and then seek to make money afterwards." Also the encouragement of St. Chrysostom, "It is altogether impossible that anyone who is serious and watchful should ever be neglected."

Finally, remember the admonition and threat of St. Augustine, "Those who despise God's will inviting them, shall feel God's will taking vengeance of them." It is a fearful thing to fall into the hands of the living God, but it is a blessed thing and will bring us to everlasting blessedness in the end, if, when God speaks to us, we listen and heed; when He sets His Word before us, we read it; when He stretches out His hand and calls, we answer, "Here I am; here we are to do Your will, O God." The Lord work a care and conscience in us to know Him and serve Him, that we may be acknowledged of Him at the appearing of our Lord Jesus Christ, to whom with the Holy Spirit, be all praise and thanksgiving. Amen.

THE KING JAMES TRANSLATORS
(BY COMPANY AND ASSIGNMENT)

FIRST WESTMINSTER COMPANY
(Genesis through 2 Kings)

Lancelot Andrewes: Dean of Westminster; Bishop of Chichester (1605).

William Bedwell: Rector of St. Ethelburga's, London.

Francis Burleigh: Fellow of Chelsea College, London.

Richard Clarke: Fellow of Christ's College, Cambridge; Vicar of Munster on the Isle of Thanet, Kent.

Geoffrey King: Fellow of King's College, Cambridge; Regius Professor of Hebrew, Cambridge (1607).

John Layfield: Fellow of Trinity College, Cambridge; Rector of St. Clement Danes, London.

John Overall: Dean of St. Paul's.

Hadrian a Saravia: Prebendary of Westminster, Canterbury and Worcester; Vicar of Lewisham, Kent.

Richard Thomson: Fellow of Clare College, Cambridge.

Robert Tighe: Archdeacon of Middlesex; Vicar of All Hallows, Barking, London.

FIRST CAMBRIDGE COMPANY
(1 Chronicles through the Song of Solomon)

Edward Lively: Regius Professor of Hebrew, Cambridge.

Roger Andrewes: Rector of St. Martin's, Ongar, Essex.

Andrew Bing: Fellow of Peterhouse; Regius Professor of Hebrew (1608).

Laurence Chaderton: Master of Emmanuel College, Cambridge.

Francis Dillingham: Fellow of Christ's College, Cambridge.

Thomas Harrison: Fellow of Trinity College, Cambridge.

John Richardson: Rector of Upwell, Norfolk; Regius Professor of Divinity, Cambridge (1607).

Robert Spalding: Fellow of St. John's College, Cambridge; Regius Professor of Hebrew (1605).

FIRST OXFORD COMPANY
(Isaiah through Malachi)

John Harding: Regius Professor of Hebrew, Oxford; President of Magdalen College (1607).

Richard Brett: Rector of Quainton, Buckinghamshire; Fellow of Lincoln College, Oxford.

Richard Fairclough: Rector of Bucknell, Oxfordshire; Fellow of New College, Oxford.

Thomas Holland: Rector of Exeter College, Oxford.

Richard Kilbye: Rector of Lincoln College, Oxford; Regius Professor of Hebrew 1610).

John Reynolds: President of Corpus Christi College, Oxford.

Miles Smith: Prebendary of Hereford and Exeter Cathedrals.

William Thorne: Rector of Tallard Royal, Wiltshire.

SECOND CAMBRIDGE COMPANY
(The Apocrypha)

John Duport: Master of Jesus College, Cambridge; Prebendary of Ely Cathedral.

John Bois: Fellow of St. John's College, Cambridge; Rector of Boxworth, Cambridgeshire.

William Branthwaite: Fellow of Emmanuel College, Cambridge.

Andrew Downes: Fellow of St. John's College, Cambridge; Regius Professor of Greek.

Jeremiah Radcliffe: Fellow of Trinity College, Cambridge; Vicar of Orwell, Cambridgeshire.

Robert Ward: Fellow of King's College, Cambridge.

Samuel Ward: Master of Sidney Sussex College, Cambridge.

SECOND OXFORD COMPANY
(the Gospels, Acts, and Revelation)

Thomas Ravis: Dean of Christ's Church College, Oxford; Bishop of Gloucester (1605); Bishop of London (1607).

George Abbot: Dean of Winchester Cathedral; Bishop of Lichfield and Coventry (1609); Bishop of London (1610); Archbishop of Canterbury (1611).

John Aglionby: Principal of St. Edmund Hall.

Richard Edes: Dean of Worcester.

John Harmer: Fellow of New College, Oxford.

Leonard Hutten: Canon of Christ Church, Oxford.

James Montague: Dean of Worcester, succeeding Edes; Bishop of Bath and Wells (1608).

John Perin: Regius Professor of Greek, Oxford.

Ralph Ravens: Rector of Great Easton, Essex; Fellow of St. John's College, Oxford.

Sir Henry Savile: Warden of Merton College, Oxford; Provost of Eton.

Giles Thomson: Fellow of All Soul's College, Oxford; Dean of Windsor.

SECOND WESTMINSTER COMPANY
(Romans through Jude)

William Barlow: Dean of Chester; Bishop of Rochester (1605).

William Dakins: Professor of Divinity, Gresham College, London.

Roger Fenton: Fellow of Pembroke College, Cambridge.

Ralph Hutchinson: President of St. John's College, Oxford.

Michael Rabbett: Fellow of Trinity College, Cambridge.

Thomas Sanderson: Rector of All Hallows, London.

John Spencer: President of Corpus Christi College, Oxford (1607).

Appendix Five:

FAMILIAR BIBLICAL PHRASES AND IMAGES

(Editor's note: Not all of these familiar phrases and images were original to the KJV. Most of them were copied from earlier translators. However, the KJV acted as a kind of conduit through which they became popular. Tyndale was the number one influence.)

LET THERE BE LIGHT (Genesis 1:3):
  "And God said, *Let there be light*: and there was light."

FORBIDDEN FRUIT (Genesis 3:2–3):
  "And the woman said unto the serpent, We may eat of the fruit of the trees of the garden; but of the fruit of the tree which is in the midst of the garden, God hath said, *You shall not eat of it, neither shall you touch it, lest you die.*"

AM I MY BROTHER'S KEEPER? (Genesis 4:9):
  "And the Lord said unto Cain, Where is Abel, your brother? And he said, I know not: *am I my brother's keeper?*"

EAST OF EDEN (Genesis 4:16):
  "And Cain . . . dwelt in the Land of Nod, on the *east of Eden.*"

AS OLD AS METHUSELAH (Genesis 5:27):
  "And all the days of Methuselah were *nine hundred sixty and nine years.*"

COAT OF MANY COLORS (Genesis 37:3):
  "Israel . . . made [Joseph] *a coat of many colors.*"

THE FAT OF THE LAND (Genesis 45:18):
  "I will give you the good of the land of Egypt, and you shall eat *the fat of the land.*"

LET MY PEOPLE GO (Exodus 5:1):
"Thus saith the Lord God of Israel, *Let my people go.*"

HARD-HEARTED (Exodus 7:3):
"And I will *harden* Pharaoh's *heart.*"

EYE FOR EYE (Exodus 21:23–24):
"And if any mischief follows, then you shall give life for life, *eye for eye.*"

THE APPLE OF HIS EYE (Deuteronomy 32:10):
"He kept him as "*the apple of his eye.*"

EARS TINGLE (1 Samuel 3:11):
"And the Lord said to Samuel, Behold, I will do a thing in Israel, at which both the *ears* of everyone that hears it shall *tingle.*"

HOW ARE THE MIGHTY FALLEN (2 Samuel 1:19):
"Your glory, O Israel, is slain upon your high places: *how are the mighty fallen.*"

TAKE ROOT (2 Kings 19:30):
"The remnant that is escaped of the house of Judah shall yet again *take root* downward."

OLD AS THE HILLS (Job 15:7):
"Are you the first man that was born? Or *were you made before the hills*?"

THE SKIN OF MY TEETH (Job 19:20):
"I am escaped by *the skin of my teeth.*"

THE ROOT OF THE MATTER (Job 19:28):
"Why do we persecute him, seeing *the root of the matter* is found in me?"

OUT OF THE MOUTHS OF BABES (Psalm 8:2):
"*Out of the mouth of babes* . . . you have ordained strength."

THE VALLEY OF THE SHADOW OF DEATH (Psalm 23:4):
"Yea, though I walk through *the valley of the shadow of death*."

MY CUP RUNNETH OVER (Psalm 23:5):
"Thou anointest my head with oil; *my cup runneth over*."

GO FROM STRENGTH TO STRENGTH (Psalm 84:7):
"They *go from strength to strength*."

AT THEIR WITS END (Psalm 107:27):
"They stagger like a drunken man, and are *at their wit's end*."

VANITY OF VANITIES (Ecclesiastes 1:2):
"*Vanity of vanities*; all is vanity."

TO EVERY THING THERE IS A SEASON (Ecclesiastes 3:1):
"*To every thing there is a season*, and a time to every purpose under the heaven."

FLY IN THE OINTMENT (Ecclesiastes 10:1)
"*Dead flies cause the ointment* . . . to send forth a stinking savor."

BEAT SWORDS INTO PLOWSHARES (Isaiah 2:4):
"And they shall *beat their swords into plowshares*."

WOE IS ME (Isaiah 6:5):
"Then said I, *woe is me*."

DROP IN A BUCKET (Isaiah 40:15):
"Behold, the nations are like a *drop of a bucket*."

LIKE A LAMB TO THE SLAUGHTER (Isaiah 53:7):
"He is brought as *a lamb to the slaughter*."

NO REST FOR THE WICKED (Isaiah 57:20):
"The *wicked* are like the troubled sea, when it cannot *rest*."

RISE AND SHINE (Isaiah 60:1):
"*Arise, shine*; for your light is come."

HOLIER THAN THOU (Isaiah 65:5):
"Stand by thyself, come not near me; for I am *holier than thou*."

BALM IN GILEAD (Jeremiah 8:22):
"Is there no *balm in Gilead*; is there no physician there?"

CAN A LEOPARD CHANGE ITS SPOTS? (Jeremiah 13:23):
"Can the Ethiopian *change* his skin, or *the leopard his spots*?"

SOUR GRAPES (Ezekiel 18:2):
"The fathers have eaten *sour grapes*, and the children's teeth are set on edge."

FEET OF CLAY (Daniel 2:33):
"His legs of iron, his *feet . . . of clay*."

WRITING ON THE WALL (Daniel 5:5):
"In the same hour came forth fingers of a man's hand, and *wrote over against the candlestick upon the plaster of the wall* of the king's palace."

REAP THE WHIRLWIND (Hosea 8:7):
"For they have sown the wind, and they shall *reap the whirlwind*."

PLOWSHARES INTO SWORDS (Joel 3:10):
"Beat your *plowshares into swords*, and your pruning hooks into spears."

SALT OF THE EARTH (Matthew 5:13):
"You are *the salt of the earth*."

A CITY SET ON A HILL (Matthew 5:14):
"*A city set on a hill* cannot be hid."

A HOUSE DIVIDED AGAINST ITSELF CANNOT STAND (Matthew 12:25):
"Every city or *house divided against itself shall not stand*."

THE BLIND LEADING THE BLIND (Matthew 15:14):
"If *the blind lead the blind*, both shall fall into the ditch."

SIGNS OF THE TIMES (Matthew 16:3):
"You can discern the face of the sky; but can you discern *the signs of the times*?"

THE KEYS OF THE KINGDOM (Matthew 16:19):
"I will give unto thee *the keys of the kingdom* of heaven."

MANY ARE CALLED BUT FEW ARE CHOSEN (Matthew 22:14):
"For *many are called but few are chosen*."

THE SPIRIT IS WILLING BUT THE FLESH IS WEAK (Matthew 26:41):
"Watch and pray, that you enter not into temptation; *the spirit indeed is willing, but the flesh is weak*."

BLOOD MONEY (Matthew 27:6):
"It is not lawful to put them into the treasury, because it is *blood money*."

GET BEHIND ME SATAN (Mark 8:33):
"Jesus rebuked Peter, saying, *Get behind me, Satan*."

PHYSICIAN, HEAL THYSELF (Luke 4:23):
"You shall surely say to me this proverb, *Physician, heal thyself*."

EAT, DRINK, AND BE MERRY (Luke 12:19):
"Soul, thou hast much goods laid up for many years; take thine ease, *Eat, drink, and be merry.*"

THE FATTED CALF (Luke 15:23):
"Bring hither *the fatted calf*, and kill it; and let us eat and be merry."

CAST THE FIRST STONE (John 8:7):
"He that is without sin among you, let him *cast the first stone.*"

GIVE UP THE GHOST (Acts 12:23):
"And immediately an angel of the Lord smote him…and he *gave up the ghost.*"

A MAN AFTER HIS OWN HEART (Acts 13:22):
"I have found David . . . *a man after my own heart.*"

TURNED THE WORLD UPSIDE DOWN (Acts 17:6):
"These that have *turned the world upside down.*"

THE POWERS THAT BE (Romans 13:1):
"There is no power but of God; *the powers that be* are ordained of God."

ALL THINGS TO ALL MEN (1 Corinthians 9:22):
"I am made *all things to all men*, that I might by all means save some."

SUFFER FOOLS GLADLY (2 Corinthians 11:19):
"For you *suffer fools gladly*, seeing you yourselves are wise."

THORN IN THE FLESH (2 Corinthians 12:7):
"Lest I should be exalted . . . there was given to me a *thorn in the flesh.*"

FALL FROM GRACE (Galatians 5:4):
"[If you desire to be] justified by the law, you are *fallen from grace.*"

REAP WHAT YOU SOW (Galatians 6:7):
"Whatsoever a man *soweth*, that shall he also *reap.*"

EVERY WIND OF DOCTRINE (Ephesians 4:14):
"That we henceforth be no more children, tossed to and fro, and carried about with *every wind of doctrine.*"

THE LOVE OF MONEY (1 Timothy 6:10):
"*The love of money* is the root of all evil."

FIGHT THE GOOD FIGHT (1 Timothy 6:12):
"*Fight the good fight* of faith, lay hold on eternal life."

ENTERTAINING ANGELS UNAWARE (Hebrews 13:2):
"Be not forgetful to entertain strangers; for thereby some have *entertained angels unawares.*"

THE QUICK AND THE DEAD (1 Peter 4:5):
"[You] shall give an account to him that is ready to judge *the quick and the dead.*"

COVER A MULTITUDE OF SINS (1 Peter 4:8):
"Love shall *cover a multitude of sins.*"

ALPHA AND OMEGA (Revelation 1:8):
"I am *Alpha and Omega*, the beginning and the ending, saith the Lord."

Appendix Six:

COMPARATIVE TRANSLATIONS
(John 1:1–5)

ANGLO SAXON BIBLE—A.D. 995: On fruman waes word, and daet word waes mid Gode, and Gode waes daet word. Daet waes on fruman mid Gode. Ealle ping waeron geworhte purh hyne, and nan ping naes geworht butan him. Daet waes lif de on him geworht waes, and daet life waes manna leoht; And daet leoht lyht on pystrum, and pystro daet ne genamon.

WYCLIFFE BIBLE—1382: In the bigynnynge was the word and the word was at god, and god was the word, this was in the bigynnynge at god, alle thingis weren made bi hym: and withouten hym was made no thing. That thing that was made in him was liif, and the liif was the lizt of men, and the lizt schyneth in derknessis; and derknessis comprehendiden not it.

TYNDALE BIBLE—1534: In the beginnynge was the worde, and the worde was with God: and the worde was God. The same was in the beginnynge with God. All thinges were made by it, and with out it, was made nothinge, that was made. In it was lyfe, and the lyfe was the light of men, and the light shyneth in the darcknes, but the darcknes comprehended it not.

COVERDALE BIBLE—1535: In the begynnynge was the worde, and the worde was with God, and God was the worde. The same was in the begynnynge with God. All thinges were made by the same, and without the same was made nothinge that was made. In him was the life, and the life was the light of men: and the light shyneth in the darknesse, and the darknesse comprehended it not.

MATTHEW'S BIBLE—1537: In the beginnynge was the worde and the worde was with God: and the worde was God. The same was in the beginnynge wyth God. All thinges were made by it and wythout it was made nothynge that was made.

261

In it was lyfe and the lyfe was the lyght of men, and the lyght shyneth in the darknes but the darknes comprehended it not.

GREAT BIBLE—1539: In the begynnynge was the worde, and the worde was with God: and God was the worde. The same was in the begynnynge with God. All thynges were made by it, and without it, was made nothynge that was made. In it was lyfe, and the lyfe was the light of men, and the light shyneth in darcknes, and the darcknes comprehended it not.

GENEVA BIBLE—1560: In the beginning was the Worde, and the Worde was with God and that Worde was God. 2 The same was in the beginning with God. 3 All things were made by it, and without it was made nothing that was made. 4 In it was lif, and the lif was the light of men. 5 And the light shineth in the darkenes, and the darkenes comprehended it not.

BISHOPS' BIBLE—1568: In the beginning was the Word, and the Word was with God, and God was that Word. 2 The same was in the beginning with God. 3 All things were made by it and without it, was made nothing that was made. 4 In it was life, and the life was the light of men. 5 And the light shineth in the darkenesse, and the darkenesse comprehendeth it not.

RHEIMS BIBLE—1582: In the beginning was the WORD, and the WORD was with God, and God was the WORD. 2 This was in the beginning with God. 3 Al things were made by him: and without him was made nothing. That which was made, 4 in him was life, and the life was the light of men: 5 and the light shineth in darkenesse, and the darkenesse did not comprehend it.

KING JAMES BIBLE—1611: In the beginning was the Word, and the Word was with God, and the Word was God. 2 The same was in the beginning with God. 3 All things were made by him; and without him was not any thing made that was made. 4 In him was life; and the life was the light of men. 5 And the light shineth in darknesse; and the darknesse comprehended it not.

AMERICAN STANDARD VERSION—1901: In the beginning was the Word, and the Word was with God, and the Word was God. 2 The same was in the beginning with God. 3 All things were made through him; and without him was not anything made that hath been made. 4 In him was life; and the life was the light of men. 5 And the light shineth in the darkness, and the darkness apprehended it not.

REVISED STANDARD VERSION—1946: In the beginning was the Word, and the Word was with God, and the Word was God. 2 He was in the beginning with God; 3 all things were made through him, and without him was not anything made that was made. 4 In him was life, and the life was the light of men. 5 The light shines in the darkness, and the darkness has not overcome it.

NEW WORLD TRANSLATION (Jehovah's Witness)— 1961: In [the] beginning the Word was, and the Word was with God, and the Word was a god. 2 This one was in [the] beginning with God. 3 All things came into existence through him, and apart from him not even one thing came into existence. What has come into existence 4 by means of him was life, and the life was the light of men. 5 And the light is shining in the darkness, but the darkness has not overpowered it.

NEW INTERNATIONAL VERSION—1978: In the beginning was the Word, and the Word was with God, and the Word was God. 2 He was with God in the beginning. 3 Through him all things were made; without him nothing was made that has been made. 4 In him was life, and that life was the light of men. 5 The light shines in the darkness, but the darkness has not understood it.

NEW KING JAMES VERSION—1982: In the beginning was the Word, and the Word was with God, and the Word was God. 2 He was in the beginning with God. 3 All things were made through Him, and without Him nothing was made that was made. 4 In Him was life, and the life was the light of men. 5 And the light shines in the darkness, and the darkness did not comprehend it.

NEW LIVING TRANSLATION—1996: In the beginning the Word already existed. He was with God, and he was God. 2 He was in the beginning with God. 3 He created everything there is. Nothing exists that he didn't make. 4 Life itself was in him, and this life gives light to everyone. 5 The light shines through the darkness, and the darkness can never extinguish it.

ENGLISH STANDARD VERSION—2001: In the beginning was the Word, and the Word was with God, and the Word was God. 2 He was in the beginning with God. 3 All things were made through him, and without him was not any thing made that was made. 4 In him was life, and the life was the light of men. 5 The light shines in the darkness, and the darkness has not overcome it.

THE NET BIBLE—2001: In the beginning was the Word, and the Word was with God, and the Word was fully God. 2 The Word was with God in the beginning. 3 All things were created by him, and apart from him not one thing was created that has been created. 4 In him was life and the life was the light of mankind. 5 And the light shines on in the darkness, but the darkness has not mastered it.

THE HOLMAN CHRISTIAN STANDARD BIBLE—2004: In the beginning was the Word, and the Word was with God, and the Word was God. 2 He was with God in the beginning. 3 All things were created through Him, and apart from Him not one thing was created that has been created. 4 In Him was life, and that life was the light of men. 5 That light shines in the darkness, yet the darkness did not overcome it.

Appendix Seven:

ENGLISH BIBLE TIMELINE

(A Chronology of Representative English Translations from Wycliffe to the Present)

Date	Translation
1382	Wycliffe's Bible
1526	Tyndale's New Testament
1530	Tyndale's Pentateuch and Jonah
1535	Coverdale's Bible
1537	Matthew's Bible
1539	Taverner's Bible
1539	Great Bible
1560	Geneva Bible (NT 1557)
1568	Bishops' Bible
1609/1610	Rheims/Douay Bible (NT 1582)
1611	King James Version
1616	King James Version ("first considerable revision" according to Scrivener)
1629	King James Version (revision; 1st edition printed at Cambridge)
1638	King James Version ("The authentic corrected *Cambridge Bible"*)
1750	Richard Challoner's first revision of Rheims Bible (NT 1749)
1755	John Wesley's New Testament (a revision of the KJV)
1762	King James version (Cambridge *Standard* edition corrected by D.F.S. Paris)

1769   King James Version (Oxford *Standard* edition corrected by Dr. Benjamin Blayney)

1772   Richard Challoner's fifth (and last) revision of Rheims New Testament

1808   The Holy Bible by Charles Thomson (the first English translation of the Septuagint into English and the first English New Testament translated and published in America)

1833   Holy Bible (Noah Webster's revision of the KJV)

1850   American Bible Society's first *Standard* corrected edition of the KJV

1850   American Bible Union [Baptist] revision of the KJV New Testament ("immersion version")

1863   Robert Young's Literal Translation of the Holy Bible

1876   The Holy Bible . . . Translated Literally from the Original Tongues, By Julia E. Smith (the first woman to translate the whole Bible)

1885   The English Revised Version (New Testament 1881)

1901   The American Standard Version (revision of The English Revised Version)

1901   The Twentieth Century New Testament

1903   Fenton's Holy Bible in Modern English (New Testament 1895)

1903   Richard Weymouth's The New Testament in Modern Speech

1917   Jewish Publication Society's The Holy Scriptures According to the Masoretic Text

1923   Edgar Goodspeed's The New Testament, An American Translation

1924   Helen Barrett Montgomery's The Centenary Translation of the New Testament

1925   James Moffatt's The Holy Bible: A New Translation (NT 1913; OT 1924)

1926   Concordant Version (based on the principle that every word in the original should have its own English equivalent)

1927   Complete Bible, An American Translation (Goodspeed's NT; J.P. Smith's OT)

1937   Charles B. Williams' The New Testament: A Translation in the Language of the People

1941   Confraternity New Testament (Old Testament published 1948–1959)

1949   Ronald Knox's The New Testament in English (OT 1948/1950)

1952   S.H. Hooke's The Basic Bible (NT 1941)

1952   The Revised Standard Version (NT 1946)

1955   Charles Kingsley Williams' New Testament in Plain English

1958   Hugh J. Schonfield's Authentic New Testament/ Original New Testament

1959   J.B. Phillips' The New Testament in Modern English

1960   Watchtower's (Jehovah's Witness) New World Translation of the Holy Scriptures (NT 1950)

1962/1969 Jewish Publication Society's New Jewish Version (NJV)

1965   The Amplified Bible (NT 1958)

1966   The Jerusalem Bible

1968/1969 William Barclay's The New Testament: A New Translation

1970   The New English Bible (NT 1961)

1970   The New American Bible (first American Catholic Bible to be translated from the original languages)

1971   The Living Bible (NT 1966)

1971   New American Standard Bible (NT 1963)

1976   Today's English Version/Good News for Modern Man (NT 1966)

1978   New International Version (NT 1973)

1982   The New King James Version (NT 1979)

1986   The New Jerusalem Bible

1989   The Revised English Bible with Apocrypha

1990   The New Revised Standard Version

1991   New Century Version/The Everyday Bible

1993   Holy Bible, New Life Version

1994   The Message (OT in progress)

1995   Contemporary English Version (NT 1991)

1995   God's Word

1995   An Inclusive Version

1995   New American Standard Bible (updated edition)

1995   The Schocken Bible, The Five Books of Moses (vol. I)

1996   New Living Translation (revision of the Living Bible)

1998   Complete Jewish Bible (Messianic Jewish Resources International)

2001   The English Standard Version (based on the Revision Standard Version)

2001   The NET Bible (first appeared on Internet before being printed)

2001   Today's New International Version (TNIT)

2003   The Message

2004   The Holman Christian Standard Bible (NT 2000)

Endnotes

Introduction

1 H.G.G. Herlots, *How Our Bible Came to Us: Its Texts and Versions* (New York: Oxford University Press, 1954), 11.

2 Henri Daniel-Rops, *What is the Bible?* (New York: Hawthorn Books, 1958), 8.

3 "The Bible and the Presidents," February 1992; available from Grace in Focus, http://www.faithalone.org/news/index.html#1992; (31 March 2003).

4 Daniel-Rops, 8–9.

5 "New Scripture Translations Are a Profound Blessing to Remote Peoples of the World," *News from the American Bible Society,* Spring, 2003.

6 "Incredible Growth in Scripture Translation." American Bible Society, www.biblesociety.org/index2htm., (23 July 2003).

Chapter 1

1 Robert McCrum, *The Story of English* (New York: Viking Penguin Inc., 1986), 19.

2 Ibid., 19.

3 Professor Lechler, *John Wycliffe and His English Precursors* (London: The Religious Tract Society, 1904), 7.

4 Ibid., 68–69.

5 John H. McWhorter, *The Power of Babel: A Natural History of Language* (New York: Harper Collins Publishers, rep. 2003), 96.

6 Ibid.

7 *The American Heritage Dictionary of the English Language* (Boston: American Heritage Publishing Co., 1970), XVI.

8 Ibid.

9 McWhorter, 96.

10 Ibid., 95.

[11] McCrum, 84.

[12] Ernest Weekley, *The English Language* (New York: Jonathan Cape and Harrison Smith, 1929), 39.

[13] Trudy Tynan, "Edition of Collegiate Dictionary Unveiled," *The Cincinnati Enquirer*, 30 June 2003.

[14] John McClintock and James Strong, *Cyclopaedia of Biblical, Theological, and Ecclesiastical Literature*, vol. 3, reprinted (Grand Rapids: Baker Book House, 1981), 197.

[15] Ibid., 197.

[16] Ibid., 197.

[17] Bruce M. Metzger, *The Bible in Translation* (Grand Rapids: Baker Book House, 2001), 55.

[18] William Canton, *The Bible and the Anglo-Saxon People* (London: J.M. Dent & Sons, Ltd., 1914), 4–5.

[19] *The Oxford Dictionary of the Christian Church* (Oxford: University Press, 1997), 348.

[20] *Cyclopaedia of Biblical, Theological, and Ecclesiastical Literature*, vol. 3, 198.

Chapter 2

[1] A. Parmelee, *A Guidebook to the Bible* (London: Hodder & Stouton, 1963), 257.

[2] Ibid., 257.

[3] Ibid., 257–258; *Cyclopaedia of Biblical, Theological, and Ecclesiastical Literature*, vol. 3, 830.

[4] J. N. D. Kelley, *Jerome, His Life, Writing, and Controversies* [1975] (Peabody: Hendrickson Publishers, 1998 [1975], 86.

[5] J. N. D. Kelly, 159.

[6] Cyril Gaul, ed., *Rome and the Study of Scripture: A Collection of Papal Enactments on the Study of Holy Scripture Together with the Decision of the Biblical Commission* (St. Meinrad, Indiana: Abbey Press, 1942), 74.

7 Kelly, 162.

8 Ibid., 163.

9 Ibid., 168.

10 Parmalee, 259.

11 Ibid., 260.

12 Sir Frederic Kenyon, *The Story of the Bible: A Popular Account of How It Came to Us* [1936] (Grand Rapids: W.B. Eerdmans Pub. Co., 1967), 51.

13 Robert L. Sumner, *Bible Translations* (Ingleside, Texas: Biblical Evangelism Press, 1979), 26–27.

Chapter 3

1 J. Paterson Smyth, *How We Got Our Bible* (New York: Harper & Row, Publishers, 1912), 61.

2 Ibid., 63.

3 A squire was the chief landed proprietor in a district. A manor was the lord's residence in such a district.

4 Melvin M. Cammack, *John Wycliffe and the English Bible* (New York: American Tract Society, 1938), 4.

5 The Black Death is known today as the Bubonic Plague.

6 "The Black Death: Bubonic Plague," www.byu.edu/ipt/projects/middleages/LifeTimes/Plague.html, N. pag.

7 Barbara W. Tuchman, *A Distant Mirror: The Calamitous 14th Century* (New York: Alfred A. Knopf, 1978), 92–93.

8 Ibid., 93.

9 "The Black Death in England 1348–1350," www.britainexpress.com/History/medieval/black-death.htm, 1.

10 Tuchman, 95.

11 W. Kenneth Connolly, *The Indestructible Book* (Grand Rapids: Baker Book House Co., 1996), 69.

12 Tuchman, 25.

[13] Eamon Duffy, *Saints & Sinners: A History of the Popes,* (New Haven: Yale University Press, rep. with corrections, 1997), 121.

[14] Peter De Rosa, *Vicars of Christ: The Dark Side of the Papacy* (New York: Crown Publishers, Inc., 1988), 75.

[15] Ibid.; Robert L. Sumner, "The Biblical Evangelist," vol. 34, No.3 (2003), 10.

[16] An "antipope" is a person set up as the Bishop of Rome in opposition to the person already holding the see or held to be lawfully elected to it. There have been about 35 antipopes in the history of the Roman Catholic Church. *The Oxford Dictionary of the Christian Church,* 79.

[17] Brian Moynahan, *The Faith, A History of Christianity* (New York: Doubleday, 2002), 301.

[18] R.E.L. Masters, *Patterns of Incest* (New York: The Julian Press, Inc., 1963), 33.

[19] De Rosa, 105.

[20] John Faunce, *Lucrezia Borgia* (New York: Crown Publishers, 2003), dj.

[21] Masters, 33.

[22] George Faludy, *Erasmus* (New York: Stein and Day Publishers, 1970), 163.

[23] Tuchman, 27.

[24] Moynahan, 296.

[25] In the later Middle Ages the right to share in an indulgence was hawked around Europe by the "Pardoners," whose dubious sales techniques resulted in a source of great profit to the ecclesiastical authorities.

[26] Tuchman, 30.

[27] Will Durant, *The Story of Civilization: The Reformation,* vol. 6 (New York: Simon and Schuster, 1957), 18.

[28] Ibid., 18.

[29] Smyth, 61.

30 Tuchman, 30–31.

31 Durant, vol. 6, 19–20.

32 Ibid., 20.

33 Ibid., 20.

34 Tuchman, 28.

35 Supposedly bones and artifacts related to Biblical figures and saints.

36 Faludy, 164.

37 De Rosa, 60.

38 Eamon Duffy, *Saints and Sinners* (New Haven: Yale University Press, 1997), 115.

39 Connolly, 73.

40 Laura H. Wild, *The Romance of the English Bible: A History of the Translation of the Bible into English from Wycliffe to the Present Day* (Garden City, NY: Doubleday, Doran & Company, Inc., 1929), 37–38.

41 Ibid., 38.

42 John Fines, *Who's Who in the Middle Ages* (New York: Barnes and Noble, 1970), 205.

43 Benson Bobrick, *Wide as the Waters* (New York: Simon & Schuster, 2001), 56.

44 Wild, 40.

45 Charles Gulston, *Our English Bible: No Greater Heritage, The Drama of the Birth of the English Bible* (Grand Rapids: William B. Eerdmans Publishing Co., 1961), 106.

46 David S. Schaff, *John Huss: His Life, Teachings and Death, After Five Hundred Years* (New York: Charles Scribners' Sons, 1915), 49.

47 Ibid., 49–50.

48 Ibid, 50. Earlier in the 14th century these men had taken a similar stand on the pope's relation to the church and state that Wycliffe took.

[49] Mary M. Trammell & William G. Dawley, *The Reforming Power of the Scriptures* (Boston: The Christian Science Publishing Society, 1996), 120.

[50] Ibid., 120.

[51] Ibid., 120–121.

[52] Bobrick, 48.

[53] Ibid., 49.

[54] John Eadie, *The English Bible,* vol. 1 (London: Macmillan and Co., 1876), 81.

[55] Smyth, 63–64.

[56] Connolly, 78.

[57] Ibid., 78.

[58] It seems to have derived from the Dutch word "lollen," to mumble, and was applied in English to religious eccentrics and wandering vagabonds.

[59] Moynahan, 295.

[60] Durant, vol. 6, 116.

[61] Charles L. Wallis, *The Treasure Chest* (New York: Harper & Row Publishers, 1965), 37.

[62] Durant, vol. 6, 116.

[63] Connolly, 79.

[64] Moynahan, 306.

[65] Ibid., 306.

[66] Christopher Allmand, *Henry V* (Berkeley: The University of California Press, 1992), 303.

[67] Durant, vol. 6, 116–117.

[68] G.M. Trevelyan, *England* in *the Age of Wycliffe, 1368–1520* [1899] (New York: Harper & Row, 1963), 336–338.

[69] Bobrick, 73.

[70] Connolly, 78.

71 John Foxe, *Acts and Monuments of Matters Happening in the Church* (London: John Day, 1563), N. pag.

72 Trammel & Dawley, 126–127.

73 Price, 225.

74 Durant, 361.

75 Robert Maynard Hutchins, ed., *John Milton,* in *Great Books of the Western World* (Chicago: Encyclopedia Britannica, Inc., 1952) 405.

Chapter 4

1 Tim Wood, *The Renaissance* (New York: Viking, 1993), 4.

2 Ibid., 5.

3 Ibid., 6.

4 Richard L. DeMolen, *The Meaning of the Renaissance and Reformation* (Boston: Houghton Mifflin, 1974), 72.

5 Ibid., 7.

6 J.D. Douglas, *New International Dictionary of the Christian Church,* 2nd ed. (Grand Rapids: Zondervan Publishing House, 1978), 836.

7 R.J. Schoeck, *Erasmus of Europe: The Prince of Humanists 1501–1536* (Edinburgh: Edinburgh University Press, 1993), 183.

8 Ibid.

9 Historians mark this event as the beginning of the Byzantine Empire, even though this officially took place under the Roman Empire.

10 Moynahan, 264.

11 Ibid.

12 Martin Davies, *The Gutenberg Bible* (San Francisco: Pomegranate Artbooks, nd), 6.

13 Jaroslav Pelican, *The Reformation of the Bible: The Bible of the Reformation* (New Haven: Yale University Press, 1996), 91.

[14] Geddes MacGregor, *The Bible in the Making* (Philadelphia: J.B. Lippincott Company, 1959), 15.

[15] Ibid., 15.

[16] McCrum, 93.

[17] Christopher Hill, *The English Bible and the Seventeenth-Century Revolution* (London: The Penguin Press, 1993), 9.

[18] Ibid., 9–10.

[19] Ibid., 10.

[20] William R. Estep, *Renaissance and Reformation* (Grand Rapids: William B. Eerdmans Publishing Company, 1986), 79.

[21] Durant, vol. 6, 273.

[22] Estep, 92.

[23] The credit for printing the first Greek New Testament belongs to Cardinal Ximenes de Cisneros, Archbishop of Toledo, Spain. The fifth volume of his famous Polyglot Bible (called the Complutensian Polyglot) containing the New Testament text in both Greek and Latin, was printed at Alcala in Spain in 1514. However, Pope Leo X withheld permission for publication, and owing to various other delays, it was not published until 1522. By that time it had lost the honor of being the first printed Greek Testament to be published.

[24] For the second edition of 1519 Erasmus yielded to pressure and changed the much-criticized title *Instrumentum* to *Testamentum*.

[25] Durant, 285.

[26] V.H. Green, *Luther and the Reformation* (New York: Capricorn Books, 1964), 9.

[27] Faludy, 188.

[28] Richard Friedenthal, *Luther, His Life and Times* (New York: Harcourt Brace Jovanovich, Inc., 1970), 453.

[29] Shoeck, 187.

[30] Roland H. Bainton, *Erasmus of Christendom* (New York: Charles Scribners' Sons, 1969), 158.

[31] Richard Tarnas, *The Passion of the Western Mind* (New York: Ballantine Books, 1993), 233.

[32] Ibid., 233.

[33] Bainton, *Erasmus of Christendom*, 154.

[34] Ibid., 234.

[35] Ibid., 456.

[36] Some sources add the expression, "Here I stand. I cannot do otherwise."

[37] Tarnas, 239.

[38] S.L. Greenslade, *The Cambridge History of the Bible: The West from the Reformation to the Present Day,* vol. 3 (Cambridge: Cambridge University Press, 1963), 94.

[39] Brian Lunn, *Martin Luther* (London: Ivor Nicholson and Watson Limited, 1934), 178–179. Sally Stepanek, *Martin Luther* (New York: Chelsea House, 1986), 96. Barclay M. Newman, *Creating and Crafting the Contemporary English Version: A New Approach to Bible Translation* (New York: American Bible Society, 1996), 3–4.

[40] Greenslade, ed., 94.

[41] Heinrich Bornkamm, *Luther in Mid-Career* (Philadelphia: The Fortress Press, 1983), 1.

[42] Margaret A. Currie, *The Letters of Martin Luther* (London: MacMillan and Co., Limited, 1908), 78.

[43] O.M. Norlie, *The Translated Bible* (Philadelphia: The United Lutheran Publication House, 1934), 83.

[44] Ibid., 90.

[45] Roland H. Bainton, *Here I Stand: A Life of Martin Luther* (New York: Abingdon Press, 1960), 327.

[46] Ibid., 327.

[47] Lunn, 169.

[48] Ibid., 93.

[49] Bainton, 327.

[50] Edith Simon, *Luther Alive: Martin Luther and the Making of the Reformation* (New York: Doubleday & Company, Inc., 1968), 289.

[51] Friedenthal, 311.

[52] Norlie, 93–94.

[53] Friedenthal, 311.

[54] Ibid., 311.

[55] Norlie, 97.

[56] Henry Zecher, "The Bible Translation That Rocked the World," http.//www.christianitytoday.com/holidays/nbw/features/34h035.html (15 January 2003).

[57] Eric W. Gritsch, *A History of Lutheranism* (Philadelphia: The Fortress Press, 2002), 32.

[58] "Zecher," 1.

[59] Norlie, 102.

[60] Zecher, 1.

[61] Norlie, 191.

[62] Durant, 523.

[63] Ibid.

[64] From the papers of the family of Sir Thomas Tresham. The quotation is taken from Paul F.M. Zahl, *Five Women of the English Reformation* (Grand Rapids: William B. Eerdmans Publishing Company, 2001), 13.

[65] From John Foxe's *Acts and Monuments* (1837–41 edition), vol. 5, p. 175, as quoted in Zahl, 14.

[66] Zahl, 15.

[67] Patricia Crawford, *Women & Religion in England 1500–1720* (Reprinted, London: Routledge, 1996), 28.

[68] Bobrick, 139.

[69] Joanna Denny, *Anne Boleyn: A New Life of England's Tragic Queen* (London: Piatkus, Ltd., 2004), 127.

Chapter 5

¹ Philip Hughes, *A Popular History of the Reformation* (Garden City: Hanover House, 1957), 165–166.

² Peter Ackroyd, *The Life of Thomas More* (New York; London: Doubleday, 1998), 277.

³ North Nibley, Stinchcombe, and Slimbridge.

⁴ John Foxe, *Foxe's Book of Martyrs,* William Byron Forbush, ed. (Philadelphia: The John C. Winston Company, 1926 [1563]), 176–177.

⁵ David Daniell, *Let There Be Light: William Tyndale and the Making of the English Bible* (London: The British Library, 1994), 6–7.

⁶ John Foxe, William Byron Forbush, ed., 177.

⁷ David Daniell, *Tyndale's Old Testament* ["W.T. to the Reader"] (New Haven: Yale University Press, 1992), 4.

⁸ William Dallmann, *William Tyndale* (St. Louis: Concordia Publishing House, nd), 12.

⁹ Alister E. McGrath, *In the Beginning* (New York: Doubleday, 2001), 69.

¹⁰ Bobrick, 90.

¹¹ Christopher Wordsworth, *Ecclesiastical Biography: or Lives of Eminent Men,* vol. 2 (London: F. S. & J. Rivington, 1810), 236.

¹² Ibid., 237.

¹³ Daniell, ed., *Tyndale's Old Testament*, 4.

¹⁴ Ibid., 4.

¹⁵ William Tyndale; David Daniell, ed. *The Obedience of a Christian Man* (London: Penguin Press, 2000), 24.

¹⁶ Daniell, ed., *Tyndale's Old Testament*, 4–5.

¹⁷ Ibid., 4.

¹⁸ Ibid., 5.

[19] Brian Moynahan, *If God Spare My Life*: William Tyndale, *The English Bible* and *Sir Thomas More—A Story of Martyrdom and Betrayal* (London: Little, Brown, 2002).

[20] Ibid.

[21] Laura H. Wild, *The Romance of the English Bible: A History of the Translation of the Bible into English from Wycliffe to the Present Day* (Garden City: Double, Doran & Company, Inc., 1929), 102.

[22] John Richard Green, *History of the English People,* vol. 2 (New York: Lovell, Coryell & Company, nd), 124.

[23] Ibid., 124.

[24] Bobrick, 98.

[25] A person whose function or duty was the distribution of alms on behalf of the king.

[26] James Baikie, *The English Bible & Its Story: Its Growth, Its Translators & Their Adventure* (London: Seeley, Service & Co. Limited, 1928), 170–171.

[27] McGrath, 83.

[28] "Love," not "charity," was kept by all translations up to and including the first edition of the Bishops' Bible, but later editions substituted "charity," as did the KJV, having been influenced by the Catholic Rheims New Testament.

[29] Moynahan, 105.

[30] J.F. Mozley, *William Tyndale* (London: Society for Promoting Christian Knowledge, 1937), 115.

[31] Located on the grounds of St. Paul's Cathedral, St. Paul's Cross (or St. Paul's Preaching Cross) was the setting of some of the most dramatic scenes in the history of England. It was the traditional spot for the announcement of general proclamations, civil as well as religious in nature. Here papal bulls were promulgated, the pronouncements of dire excommunications were heard, public confessions and recantations of heresy were voiced, and heretical books were burned (including Tyndale's Testaments).

[32] See Ackroyd, 308–310; Moynahan, *If God Spare My Life,* 103–104, 167–169, 246–248.

[33] Bobrick, 112.

[34] Mozley, 147.

[35] Ibid., 147–148.

[36] The story appeared in Hall's *Chronicle* of 1548. In the summer of 1529 Cuthbert Tunstall was on the Continent negotiating the treaty of Cambrai, as Hall explains in some detail. [David Daniell, *William Tyndale: A Biography],* 196.

[37] Moynahan, *If God Spare My Life*, 177.

[38] A.G. Dickens, *The English Reformation* (London: B.T. Batsford LTD, 1964), 70.

[39] See Chapter 4.

[40] Mozley, 333–335; Moynahan, *If God Spare My Life,* 330–331.

[41] Moynahan, 331.

[42] Ibid., 331.

[43] Daniell, *William Tyndale*, 383.

Chapter 6

[1] Bobrick, 143.

[2] Ibid., 143.

[3] Using the pseudonym, Thomas Matthew, Rogers produced the second complete English Bible in 1537.

[4] "The word 'corrector' implies not only that he was a proof-reader, but also an editor and translator." [Paul Arblaster, Gergely Juhasz, & Guido Latre, eds, *Tyndale's Testament (Turnhout, Belgium: Brepols Publishers, 2002),* 143].

[5] Valerie R. Hotchkiss & Charles C. Ryrie, eds., *Formatting the Word of God* (Dallas, Bridwell Library, 1998), 69.

[6] Bobrick, 144.

[7] Ibid., 145.

[8] Arblaster, Juhasz, Latre, 39.

[9] F.F. Bruce, *The English Bible: A History of Translations* (London: Lutterworth Press, 1961), 55–56.

[10] Bobrick, 146.

[11] Bruce, 64.

[12] Hotchkiss & Ryrie, 69.

[13] H. Josiah Penniman, *A Book About the English Bible* (New York: the MacMillan Company, 1920), 361.

[14] Eadie, vol. 1, 311–312.

[15] Trammell & Dawley, 152.

[16] Bobrick, 148.

[17] Trammell & Dawley, 153.

[18] Hotchkiss & Ryrie, 75.

[19] Eadie, vol. 1, 345.

[20] Pope, 212.

[21] Baikie, 221.

[22] Alfred W. Pollard, *Records of the English Bible: The Documents Relating to the Translation and Publication of the Bible in English, 1525–1611* (London: Oxford University Press, 1911), 24.

[23] Brook Foss Westcott, and William Aldis Wright, A *General View of the History of the English Bible,* 3d rev. ed. (London: the Macmillan Company, 1916), 207.

[24] Bruce, 70.

[25] A.W. Pollard, 227.

[26] Hotchkiss & Ryrie, 77.

[27] F.F. Bruce, 68.

[28] Westcott, 79–80.

[29] Ibid., 80.

[30] Also known as the Cranmer Bible, the result of a preface written by Thomas Cranmer for the second edition in 1540.

[31] H. Wheeler Robinson, ed., *The Bible in its Ancient and English Versions* (Oxford: The University Press, 1940), 178.

[32] Ibid., 178–179.

[33] Ibid., 179–180.

[34] Ibid., 180.

[35] Ibid., 180.

[36] Ibid., 180.

[37] Trammell & Dawley, 159.

[38] It was not called *The Geneva Bible* by the translators. The title page simply stated, "THE BIBLE AND HOLY SCRIPTVRES CONTEYNED IN THE OLDE AND NEWE TESTAMENT." Because the place of translation and printing (Geneva) was referenced on the title page, *The Geneva Bible* gradually became its nickname.

[39] J.R. Green, *A Short History of the English People,* vol. 3 (New York: Harper & Brothers, 1898), 933–938.

[40] F.G. Kenyon & H.F.D. Sparks, "English Versions," *Hasting's Dictionary of the Bible* (New York: Charles Scribners' Sons, rev. ed., 1963), 256.

[41] Pollard, 297.

[42] Although some Catholics suffered persecution during Elizabeth's reign, in no way could her reign be compared to Mary's in the extent of cruelty imposed.

[43] Hugh Pope, *English Versions of the Bible* (St. Louis: B. Herder Book Co., 1952), 250; James G. Carleton, *The Part of Rheims in the Making of the English Bible* (Oxford: The Clarendon Press, 1902), 16–17.

[44] In 1667 Louis XIV of France seized Douay, which henceforth was known as Douai. Consequently, the version is now often called the Douai Bible. Metzger, 68.

[45] Carleton, 18.

[46] Ibid., 18.

[47] Pope, 258.

[48] Ibid., 264.

[49] Ibid., 264.

Chapter 7

[1] David Harris Willson, *King James VI and I* (London: Jonathan Cape, 1959), 22.

[2] Ibid., 24.

[3] Ibid., 24–25.

[4] Bobrick, 201.

[5] Willson, 170–171.

[6] Gustavus S. Paine, *The Learned Men* (New York: Thomas Y. Crowell Company, 1959), 3.

[7] Walter Farquhar Hook, *Lives of the Archbishops of Canterbury,* vol. 10 (London: Richard Bentley & Son, 1875), 200.

[8] McGrath, 150.

[9] Paine, 2; Hook, vol. 10, 200.

[10] Willson, 202.

[11] Baikie, 258.

[12] Willson, 207.

[13] Ibid., 207.

[14] Ibid., 208.

[15] Baikie, 262.

[16] Pope, 308–309.

[17] Baikie, 263.

[18] Robinson, 309.

[19] F. F. Bruce, 97.

[20] Robinson, 309.

21 William Muir, *Our Grand Old Bible: Being the Story of the Authorized Version of the English Bible, Told for the Tercentenary Celebration* (London: Morgan and Scott LD, 1911), 87.

22 Metzger, 72.

23 W. J. Heaton, *The Puritan Bible,* vol. 3 (London: Francis Griffiths, 1913), 274.

24 John Stevens Kerr, Charles Houser, ed., *Ancient Texts Alive Today: The Story of the English Bible* (New York: American Bible Society, 1999), 114.

25 Ward S. Allen & Edward C. Jacobs, *The Coming of the King James Gospels: A Collation of the Translators' Work-in-Progress* (Fayetteville: The University of Arkansas Press, 1995), 5.

26 Samuel Harvey Reynolds, ed., *The Table Talk of John Selden* (Oxford: The Clarendon Press, 1892), 9.

27 F. H. A. Scrivener, *The Authorized Edition of the English Bible: Its Subsequent Reprints and Modern Representatives* (Cambridge: The University Press, 1884), 9.

28 William R. Kimball, *The Book of Books* (Joplin: College Press Publishing Co., 1986), 211.

29 Bobrick, 248.

30 Kelly, 160–161.

31 Edgar J. Goodspeed, *The Story of the Apocrypha* (Chicago: The University of Chicago Press, 1939), 6.

32 Robinson, 209.

33 Seldon, 10.

34 Errol F. Rhodes and Liana Lupas, eds, *The Translators to the Reader: The Original Preface of the King James Version of 1611 Revisited* (New York: American Bible Society, 1997), 1–2.

35 Baikie, 294.

36 Ibid., 294.

37 T. Harwood Pattison, *The History of the English Bible* (Philadelphia: American Baptist Publication Society, 1894), 182.

Chapter 8

[1] Richard Dawkins, *The God Delusion* (Boston: Houghton Mifflin Company, 2006), 383.

[2] Ibid., 383.

[3] Ibid., 385.

[4] Muir, 188.

[5] Melvyn Bragg, *12 Books That Changed the World* (London: Hodder & Stoughton, 2006), 265.

[6] Ibid., 272.

[7] David Daniell, *The Bible in English* (New Haven: Yale University Press, 2003), 158.

[8] John R. Green, vol. 2, 12–13.

[9] Daniell, ed., *Tyndale's Old Testament,* 4.

APPENDIXES

Appendix One

[1] Karen H. Jobes & Moises Silva, *Invitation to the Septuagint* (Grand Rapids: Baker Book House, 2000), 326.

[2] *Catechism of the Catholic Church,* 2nd ed. (Rome: Libreria Editrice Vaticana, 1997), 892.

[3] Ibid., 894.

[4] Ibid., 872.

[5] Karen H. Jobes & Moises Silva, 326.

[6] *Catechism of the Catholic Church,* 2nd ed., 1997, 902.

[7] Alec Gilmore, *A Dictionary of the English Bible and its Origins* (London: Fitzroy Dearborn Publishers, 2000), 176.

Bibliography

Ackroyd, Peter. *The Life of Thomas More.* New York & London: Doubleday, 1998.

Allen, Ward S. & Edward C. Jacobs. *The Coming of the King James Gospels, A Collation of the Translators' Work-in-Progress.* Fayetteville: The University of Arkansas Press, 1995.

Allmand, Christopher. *Henry V.* Berkeley: The University of California Press, 1992.

The American Heritage Dictionary of the English Language. Boston: American Heritage Publishing Co., 1970.

Arblaster, Paul; Gergely Juhasz; & Guido Latre, eds. *Tyndale's Testament.* Turnhout, Belgium: Brepols Publishers, 2002.

Archer, Gleason L. *Encyclopedia of Bible Difficulties.* Grand Rapids: Zondervan Publishing House, 1982.

Armitage, Thomas. *A History of the Baptists,* 2 vols. New York: Bryan Taylor & Co., 1890.

Bacon, Francis. *The Essays or Counsels, Civil and Moral.* Reprinted. Mount Vernon, NY: The Peter Pauper Press, nd.

Baikie, James. *The English Bible & Its Story: Its Growth, Its Translators & Their Adventure.* London: Seeley, Service & Co. Limited, 1928.

Bainton, Roland H. *Erasmus of Christendom.* New York: Charles Scribners' Sons, 1969.

_____. *Here I Stand: A Life of Martin Luther.* New York: Abingdon Press, 1950.

Barackman, Floyd H. *Practical Christian Theology: Examining the Great Doctrines of the Faith.* 3rd ed. Grand Rapids: Kregel Publications, 1998.

Bartlett, John, Justin Kaplan, eds. *Familiar Quotations.* Boston, Toronto, London: Little, Brown and Company, 1992.

Beal, Timothy. *Biblical Literacy: The Essential Bible Stories Everyone Needs to Know.* New York: Harper Collins, 2009.

Beegle, Dewey M. *God's Word Into English.* New York: Harper & Brothers, 1960.

Bobrick, Benson. *Wide as the Waters.* New York: Simon & Schuster, 2001.

Bornkamm, Heinrich. *Luther in Mid-Career.* Philadelphia: Fortress Press, 1983.

Bragg, Melvyn. *12 Books That Changed the World.* London: Hodder & Stoughton, 2006.

Bruce, F.F. *The English Bible: A History of Translations.* London: Lutterworth Press, 1961.

Butterworth, Charles C. *The Literary Lineage of the King James Bible, 1340–1611,* Reprinted. New York: Octagon Books, 1971.

Cammack, Melvin M. *John Wycliffe and the English Bible.* New York: American Tract Society, 1938.

Canton, William. *The Bible and the Anglo-Saxon People.* London: J. M. Dent & Sons, Ltd., 1914.

Carleton, James G. *The Part of Rheims in the Making of the English Bible.* Oxford: The Clarendon Press, 1902.

Catechism of the Catholic Church. 2nd ed. Rome: Libreria Editrice Vaticana, 1997.

Cathcart, William. *The Baptist Encyclopedia.* 2 vols. Philadelphia: L. H. Everts, 1881.

Connolly, W. Kenneth. *The Indestructible Book.* Grand Rapids: Baker Book House Co., 1996.

Crawford, Patricia. *Women & Religion in England 1500–1720.* Reprinted. London: Routledge, 1996.

Cross, F.L., E.A. Livingstone, eds. *The Oxford Dictionary of the Christian Church.* Reprinted. Oxford: University Press, 1997.

Currie, Margaret A. *The Letters of Martin Luther.* London: Macmillan and Co., Limited, 1908.

Dabney, Robert L. *Discussions: Evangelical and Theological.* 3 vols. Reprinted. London: Banner of Truth Trust, 1967.

Dagg, John. *Manuel of Theology.* Rep. New York: Arno Press, 1980.

Dallmann, William. *William Tyndale.* St. Louis: Concordia Publishing House, nd.

Daniel-Rops, Henri. *What is the Bible?* New York: Hawthorn Books, 1958.

Daniell, David. *Let There Be Light: William Tyndale and the Making of the English Bible.* London: The British Library, 1994.

_____. *Tyndale: A Biography.* New Haven & London: Yale University Press, 1994.

_____. *Tyndale's Old Testament ["W. T. to the Reader"].* New Haven & London: Yale University Press, 1992.

_____. *The Bible in English.* New Haven & London: Yale University Press, 2003.

Davies, Martin. *The Gutenberg Bible.* San Francisco: Pomegranate Artbooks, nd.

Dawkins, Richard. *The God Delusion.* Boston: Houghton Mifflin Company, 2006.

DeMolen, Richard L. *The Meaning of the Renaissance and Reformation.* Boston: Houghton Mifflin, 1974.

Denny, Joanna. *Anne Boleyn: A New Life of England's Tragic Queen.* London: Piatkus Books, Ltd., 2004.

De Rosa, Peter. *Vicars of Christ: The Dark Side of the Papacy.* New York: Crown Publishers, Inc., 1988.

Dickens, A. G. *The English Reformation.* London: B.T. Batsford, Ltd., 1964.

Douglas, J.D. *New International Dictionary of the Christian Church.* 2nd ed. Grand Rapids: Zondervan Publishing House, 1978.

Duffy, Eamon. *Saints and Sinners.* New Haven: Yale University Press, 1997.

Durant, Will. *The Story of Civilization,* 11 vols. New York: Simon and Schuster, 1957.

Eadie, John. *The English Bible,* 2 vols. London: Macmillan and Co., 1876.

Ericson, Millard. *Christian Theology.* Revised. Grand Rapids: Baker Books, 2000.

Estep, William R. *Renaissance and Reformation.* Grand Rapids: William B. Eerdmans Publishing Company, 1986.

Faludy, George. *Erasmus.* New York: Stein and Day Publishers, 1970.

Faunce, John. *Lucrezia Borgia.* New York: Crown Publishers, 2003.

Fines, John. *Who's Who in the Middle Ages.* New York: Barnes & Noble, 1970.

Foxe, John. *Acts and Monuments of Matters Happening in the Church.* London: John Day, 1563.

_____. *Foxe's Book of Martyrs.* William Byron Forbush, ed. Reprinted, Philadelphia: The John C. Winston Company, 1926.

Friedenthal, Richard. *Luther: His Life and Times.* New York: Harcourt Brace Jovanovich, Inc., 1970.

Froude, J.A. *Life and Letters of Erasmus: Lectures Delivered at Oxford, 1893–94.* New York: Charles Scribners Sons, 1894.

Fuller, Andrew. *Andrew Fuller's Works,* 3 vols. Reprinted, Harrisonburg, Virginia: Sprinkle Publications, 1988.

Gaul, Cyril, ed. *Rome and the Study of Scripture: A Collection of Papal Enactments on the Study of Holy Scripture Together with the Decision of the Biblical Commission.* St. Meinrad, Indiana: Abbey Press, 1943.

Gillming, Norma, ed. *The Best of Noel Smith.* Springfield, Missouri: n.p., 1985.

Gilmore, Alec. *A Dictionary of the English Bible and its Origins.* London: Fitzroy Dearborn Publishers, 2000.

Goodspeed, Edgar J. *The Story of the Apocrypha.* Chicago: The University of Chicago Press, 1939.

Graves, J.R. *Seven Dispensations.* Memphis: Baptist Book House, 1883.

Green, John Richard. *A Short History of the English People.* 4 vols. New York: Harper & Brothers, 1898.

Green, V.H. *Luther and the Reformation.* New York: Capricorn Books, 1964.

Greenslade, S.L. *The Cambridge History of the Bible.* 3 vols. Cambridge: The University Press, 1976.

Gritsch, Eric W. *A History of Lutheranism.* Philadelphia: The Fortress Press, 2002.

Gulston, Charles. *Our English Bible: No Greater Heritage, The Drama of the Birth of the English Bible.* Grand Rapids: William B. Eerdmans Publishing Co., 1961.

Henry, Matthew. *Commentary on the Whole Bible.* 5 vols. Reprinted. Old Tappan, N. J.: Fleming H. Revell Company, nd.

Herklots, H.G.G. *How Our Bible Came to Us: Its Texts and Versions.* New York: Oxford University Press, 1954.

Hill, Christopher. *The English Bible and the Seventeenth-Century Revolution.* London: The Penguin Press, 1993.

Hodge, Archibald, & Benjamin B. Warfield. *Inspiration.* Philadelphia: Presbyterian Board of Publication, 1881.

The Holy Bible: English Standard Version. Wheaton, Illinois: Good News Publishers, 2001.

Hook, Walter Farquhar. *Lives of the Archbishops of Canterbury.* 12 vols. London: Richard Bentley & Son, 1875.

Hotchkiss, Valerie R., & Charles C. Ryrie, eds. *Formatting the Word of God.* Dallas: Bridwell Library, 1998.

Hughes, Philip. *A Popular History of the Reformation.* Garden City, New York: Hanover House, 1957.

Hutchins, Robert Maynard., ed. *John Milton.* 54 vols. Great Books of the Western World. Chicago: Encyclopedia Britannica, Inc., 1952.

Ives, Eric. *The Life and Death of Anne Boleyn.* Oxford: Blackwell Publishing, Ltd., 2004.

Jobes, Karen H. & Moises Silva. *Invitation to the Septuagint.* Grand Rapids: Baker Book House, 2000.

Judson, Edward. *Life of Adoniram Judson.* London: Hodder & Stoughton, 1883.

Keach, Benjamin. *The Baptist Catechism.* Reprinted. Grand Rapids: Baker Book House, 1952.

Kelly, J.N.D. *Jerome: His Life, Writings, and Controversies.* Reprinted. Peabody, Massachusetts: Hendrickson Publishers, 1998.

Kenyon, F.G. & H.F.D. Sparks. "English Versions." *Dictionary of the Bible.* James Hastings, Frederick C. Grant & H.H. Rowley, eds. Rev. ed. New York: Charles Scribners' Sons, 1963.

Kenyon, Sir Frederic. *The Story of the Bible: A Popular Account of How It Came to Us.* Grand Rapids: W.B. Eerdmans Publishing Co., 1967.

_____. *The Text of the Greek Bible: A Student's Handbook.* London: Gerald Duckworth & Co. Ltd., 1953.

Kerr, John Stevens, & Charles Houser, eds. *Ancient Texts Alive Today, The Story of the English Bible.* New York: American Bible Society, 1999.

Kimball, William R. *The Book of Books.* Joplin, Missouri: College Press Publishing Co., 1986.

Ladd, George E. *The New Testament and Criticism.* Grand Rapids: W.B. Eerdmans Publishing Company, 1967.

Lechler, Professor. *John Wycliffe and His English Precursors.* Trans. George Lorimer. London: The Religious Tract Society, 1904.

Lindsay, T.M. *A History of the Reformation.* 2 vols. Edinburgh: T. & T. Clark, 1907.

Lueker, Erwin L. *Lutheran Cyclopedia.* Saint Louis: Concordia Publishing House, 1954.

Lumpkin, W.L., *Baptist Confessions of Faith.* Revised. Valley Forge: Judson Press, 1969.

Lunn, Brian. *Martin Luther.* London: Ivor Nicholson and Watson Ltd., 1934.

MacGregor, Geddes. *The Bible in the Making.* Philadelphia: J.B. Lippincott Company, 1959.

Machen, J. Gresham. *New Testament Greek for Beginners.* Reprinted. Toronto: The Macmillan Company, 1951.

Marius, Richard. *Martin Luther, The Christian Between God and Death.* Cambridge, Massachusetts: The Belknap Press of Harvard University, 1999.

Masters, R.E.L. *Patterns of Incest.* New York: The Julian Press, Inc., 1963.

McAfee, Cleland Boyd. *The Greatest English Classic, A Study of the King James Version of the Bible and Its Influence on Life and Literature.* New York: Harper & Brothers Publishers, 1912.

McClintock, John, & James Strong. *Cyclopaedia of Biblical, Theological, and Ecclesiastical Literature,* 12 vols. [1867–1887]. Reprinted. Grand Rapids: Baker Book House, 1981.

McCrum, Robert. *The Story of English.* New York: Viking Penguin Inc., 1986.

McGrath, Alister E. *In the Beginning.* New York: Doubleday, 2001.

McWhorter, John H. *The Power of Babel.* Reprinted. New York: Harper Collins Publishers, 2003.

Metzger, Bruce M. *The Bible in Translation: Ancient and English Versions.* Grand Rapids: Baker Book House, 2001.

_____. *The Text of the New Testament: Its Transmission, Corruption, and Restoration.* New York & London: Oxford University Press, 1964.

Moynahan, Brian. *The Faith: A History of Christianity.* New York: Doubleday, 2002.

_____. *If God Spare My Life: William Tyndale, the English Bible and Sir Thomas More, A Story of Martyrdom and Betrayal.* London: Little, Brown, 2002.

Mozley, J.F. *William Tyndale.* London: Society for Promoting Christian Knowledge, 1937.

Muir, William. *Our Grand Old Bible: Being the Story of the Authorized Version of the English Bible, Told for the Tercentenary Celebration.* London: Morgan and Scott LD, 1911.

Newman, Barclay M. *Creating and Crafting the Contemporary English Version: A New Approach to Bible Translation.* New York: American Bible Society, 1996.

Norlie, O.M. *The Translated Bible.* Philadelphia: The United Lutheran Publication House, 1934.

Norton, David. *A History of the English Bible As Literature.* Cambridge: University Press, 2000.

Paine, Gustavus S. *The Learned Men.* New York: Thomas Y. Crowell Company, 1959.

Parmelee, A. *A Guidebook to the Bible.* London: Hodder & Stouton, 1963.

Pattison, T. Harwood. *The History of the English Bible.* Philadelphia: American Baptist Publication Society, 1894.

Pelican, Jaroslav. *The Reformation of the Bible: The Bible of the Reformation.* New Haven: Yale University Press, 1996.

Penniman, Josiah H. *A Book About the English Bible.* New York: The Macmillan Company, 1920.

Pollard, Alfred W. *Records of the English Bible: The Documents Relating to the Translation and Publication of the Bible in English,* 1525–1611. London: Oxford University Press, 1911.

Pope, Hugh. *English Versions of the Bible.* St. Louis: B. Herder Book Co., 1952.

Price, Ira M. *The Ancestry of Our English Bible.* New York: Harper and Brothers, 1940.

Ray, D.B. *Baptist Succession.* Cincinnati: G.E. Stevens & Co., 1873.

Reynolds, Samuel Harvey, ed. *The Table Talk of John Selden.* Oxford: The Clarendon Press, 1892.

Rhodes, Erroll F. & Liana Lupas, eds. *The Translators to the Reader: The Original Preface of the King James Version of 1611 Revisited.* New York: American Bible Society, 1997.

Robinson, H. Wheeler, ed. *The Bible in Its Ancient and English Versions.* Oxford: The University Press, 1940.

Ross, Hugh. *An Essay for A New Translation of the Bible.* London: R. Gosling, 1727.

Schaff, David S. *John Huss: His Life, Teachings and Death, After Five Hundred Years.* New York: Charles Scribners Sons, 1915.

Schoeck, R.J. *Erasmus of Europe: The Prince of Humanists 1501–1536.* Edinburgh: Edinburgh University Press, 1993.

Scrivener, F.H.A. *The Authorized Edition of the English Bible (1611): Its Subsequent Reprints and Modern Representations.* Cambridge: The University Press, 1884.

Selden, John. Samuel Harvey Reynolds, ed. *The Table Talk of John Selden.* Oxford: The Clarendon Press, 1892.

Simon, Edith. *Luther Alive: Martin Luther and the Making of the Reformation.* New York: Doubleday & Company, Inc., 1968.

Smyth, J. Paterson. *How We Got Our Bible.* New York: Harper & Row, Publishers, 1912.

Spurgeon, Charles Haddon. From sermon, "The Bible Tried and Proved." *Metropolitan Tabernacle Pulpit.* London: Passmore & Alabaster, 1889.

Stepanek, Sally. *Martin Luther.* New York: Chelsea House, 1986.

Strong, Augustus H. *Systematic Theology.* Reprinted. Valley Forge: Judson Press, 1972.

Tarnes, Richard. *The Passion of the Western Mind.* New York: Ballantine Books, 1993.

Thompson, Bard. *Humanists & Reformers: A History of the Renaissance and Reformation.* Grand Rapids; Cambridge: William B. Eerdmans Publishing Co., 1996.

Torrey, R.A. *Difficulties in the Bible.* Reprinted. Grand Rapids: Baker Book House, 1964.

_____, ed. *The Fundamentals.* Reprinted. Grand Rapids: Kregel Publications, 1990.

Trammel, Mary M., & William G. Dawley. *The Reforming Power of the Scriptures.* Boston: The Christian Science Publishing Society, 1996.

Trevelyan, G. M. *England in the Age of Wycliffe, 1368–1520.* [1899]. New York: Harper & Row, 1963.

Tuchman, Barbara W. *A Distant Mirror: The Calamitous 14th Century.* New York: Alfred A. Knopf, 1978.

Turretin, Frances, George M. Giger, trans., James T. Dennison, Jr., ed. *Institutes of Elenctic Theology.* 2 vols. Reprinted. Phillipsburg, New Jersey: P & R Publishing, 1992.

Tyndale, William. David Daniell, ed. *The Obedience of a Christian Man.* Reprinted, London: Penguin Press, 2000.

Wallis, Charles L. *The Treasure Chest.* New York: Harper & Row Publishers, 1965.

Weekley, Ernest. *The English Language.* New York: Jonathan Cape & Harrison Smith, 1929.

Wescott, Brook Foss, & William Aldis Wright. *A General View of the History of the English Bible.* 3rd rev. ed. London: The Macmillan Company, 1916.

Wild, Laura H. *The Romance of the English Bible: A History of the Translation of the Bible into English from Wycliffe to the Present Day.* Garden City, New York: Doubleday, Doran & Company, Inc., 1929.

Wilson, David Harris, *King James IV and I.* London: Jonathan Cape, 1959.

Wood, Tim. *The Renaissance.* New York: Viking, 1993.

Wordsworth, Christopher. *Ecclesiastical Biography; or Lives of Eminent Men, Connected With the History of Religion in England.* 5 vols. London: F.S. & J. Rivington, 1810.

Zahn, Paul F.M. *Five Women of the English Reformation.* Grand Rapids: William B. Eerdmans Publishing Company, 2001.

Other Sources

"The Bible and the Presidents," February 1992; Grace in Focus, http://www.faithalone.org/news/index.html. (31 March 2003).

"The Black Death: Bubonic Plague," http://www.byu.edu/ipt/projects/middleages/LifeTimes/Plague.html. (21 January 2003).

"The Black Death in England 1338–1340," http://www.britainexpress.com/History/medieval/black-death.html. (21 January 2003).

"The Chicago Statement on Biblical Inerrancy." http://www.Jpusa.org/jpusa/documents/Biblical.htm. (25 July 2003).

"Incredible Growth in Scripture Translation," American Bible Society, http://www.biblesociety.org/index2.htm. (23 July 2002).

Mastrantonis, George. "The Fundamental Teaching of the Eastern Orthodox Church. http://www.goarch.org/en/ourfaith/articles/article7063.asp

"New Scripture Translations Are a Profound Blessing to Remote Peoples of the World," *News from the American Bible Society,* Spring, 2003.

"From Purvey's Prologue to the Wycliffe Bible," http://www.bible-researcher.com/wyclif2.html. (30 March 2003).

Index

M

N

O

P